Dear Reader:

The book you are about to read is the latest bestseller from the St. Martin's True Crime Library, the imprint the *New York Times* calls "the leader in true crime!" Each month, we offer you a fascinating account of the latest, most sensational crime that has captured the national attention. St. Martin's is the publisher of perennial bestselling true crime author Jack Olsen, whose SALT OF THE EARTH is the true story of how one woman fought and triumphed over life-shattering violence; Joseph Wambaugh called it "powerful and absorbing." Fannie Weinstein and Melinda Wilson tell the story of a beautiful honors student who was lured into the dark world of sex for hire in THE COED CALL GIRL MURDER. St. Martin's is also proud to publish two-time Edgar Award-winning author Carlton Stowers, whose TO THE LAST BREATH recounts a two-year-old girl's mysterious death, and the dogged investigation that led loved ones to the most unlikely murderer: her own father. In the book you now hold, DARK DREAMS, legendary FBI profiler Roy Hazelwood teams up with equally legendary true-crime writer Stephen G. Michaud to investigate numerous sexually related crimes—and why they happen.

St. Martin's True Crime Library gives you the stories *behind* the headlines. Our authors take you right to the scene of the crime and into the minds of the most notorious murderers to show you what really makes them tick. St. Martin's True Crime Library paperbacks are better than the most terrifying thriller, because it's all true! The next time you want a crackling good read, make sure it's got the St. Martin's True Crime Library logo on the spine—you'll be up all night!

Charles E. Spicer, Jr.
Executive Editor, St. Martin's True Crime Library

PRAISE FOR

THE EVIL THAT MEN DO

"Take it from me: Roy's insights and experience prove that he is an expert in crime analysis. The story he has to tell is well worth listening to."

— John Douglas, *New York Times* bestselling author

"Nobody knows this territory better than Roy Hazelwood. He was first to explore the world of sexual predators, and charted it with an accuracy and insight that those of us who followed after have used for guidance ever since. In this outstanding book, Hazelwood takes us all with him into the belly of the beast—and more important, into the mind of the beast."

—Linda A. Fairstein, Chief of the Sex Crimes Prosecution Unit, Manhattan District Attorney's Office

"When the world's best true-crime writer teams with the world's best sex-crimes profiler, they produce a book that should have a warning label, 'DO NOT READ ALONE AT NIGHT.' This is a textbook for law enforcement and the forensic–science professional and a compelling description of extremely dangerous people that the lay reader will not be able to put down."

—Dr. Lowell Levine, Director, Medicolegal Investigations Unit, New York State Police

"As an experienced forensic scientist, I knew the material was not new, but as a woman, I locked the doors and drew the drapes. The actions and thought processes of the criminals described in this book will completely unnerve ALL women. It is scarier than any horror fiction, because it is real."

—Cathryn L. Levine, M.S., M.A., Fellow, American Board of Criminalistics, New York State Police

DARK
DREAMS

A LEGENDARY FBI PROFILER

EXAMINES HOMICIDE AND

THE CRIMINAL MIND

**ROY HAZELWOOD with
STEPHEN G. MICHAUD**

St. Martin's Paperbacks

DARK DREAMS

Copyright © 2001 by Roy Hazelwood and Stephen G. Michaud.

Cover photograph by © Koechling/Nonstock.

All rights reserved. No part of this book may be used or reproduced in any manner whatsoever without written permission except in the case of brief quotations embodied in critical articles or reviews. For information address St. Martin's Press, 175 Fifth Avenue, New York, NY 10010.

Library of Congress Catalog Card Number: 2001019268

ISBN: 0-312-98011-6

Printed in the United States of America

St. Martin's Press hardcover edition / July 2001
St. Martin's Paperbacks edition / October 2002

10 9 8 7 6 5 4 3 2 1

FOR OUR CHILDREN:

BOB, KEVIN, KEITH, SHERRY,

STEPHEN, SPENCER, AND ALEXANDRA

CONTENTS

ACKNOWLEDGMENTS

This book would not have been possible without the case contributions from members of city, county, state, and federal law enforcement agencies throughout the United States.

I also want to thank my friends and colleagues in the Academy Group (AGI) in Manassas, Virginia, for their encouragement and many years of friendship. They include Ken Baker, Dick Ault, Pete Smerick, Roger Depue, Steve Mardigian, Mike Napier, Larry McCann, Connie Hassel, Tom Strentz, Marty Rehberg, and Elaine Fox.

There are two officers with whom I served in the military, Tom McGreevy and Charlie Stahl, who became my mentors. A belated public thanks to both of them for helping to shape my thinking.

Many of my former colleagues in the Behavioral Science Unit contributed to my education and experience. My gratitude to my partner of thirteen years, Ken Lanning, and to Art Westveer, Larry Ankrom, John Douglas, Bob Ressler, Steve Etter, Joe Harpold, Bill Hagmaier, Win Norman, Bob Boyd, and Jim Wright, among others.

I am also deeply indebted to the national and international members of the FBI NCAVC Police Fellowship for their guidance and friendship since 1984 and to the mental health professionals whose works have served as guideposts throughout my career. Most have become my good friends.

They include Park Dietz, Janet Warren, Robert Prentky, Ann Burgess, Bob Hare, John Hunter, Gene Abel, Reid Meloy, Chris Hatcher, Robert Freeman-Longo, Ray Knight, Fred Berlin, Peter Collins, Steve Hucker, Judith Becker, Nick Groth, and Kris Mohandie.

Thanks to Jennifer Gerrietts of the *Argus Leader* in Sioux Falls, South Dakota, as well as Ray Flanagan of the Scranton, Pennsylvania, *Times Tribune* and Patti Froning from the South Dakota Attorney General's Office for helping us keep our facts straight. Likewise to prosecutor Mike Pent of the San Diego County (California) District Attorney's Office for his critical review of the Billy Lee Chadd material. Carlton Stowers of Cedar Hill, Texas, cast his expert eye over our pages on Faryion Wardrip.

Michaela Hamilton deserves special thanks for skillfully hammering a sprung manuscript back into shape at the eleventh hour.

Thanks to Charlie Spicer, our editor at St. Martin's Press, for his patience and support in helping to make this book a reality, and to Elizabeth Kaplan, our tireless protectress and advocate.

Finally, I want to acknowledge the unwavering and loving support of my wife, Peggy Driver-Hazelwood. We couldn't have completed the project without her.

DARK
DREAMS

1

INFINITE DARKNESS

A fourteen-year-old girl is kidnapped while hitchhiking with a young male companion. Her abductor immediately kills the youth, then keeps the girl as his captive. He tortures her, binds her with chains, and forces her to pose for photographs in heavy makeup and suggestive clothing. After several days he strangles her with a bailing-wire garrote, then dumps her body in the loft of an abandoned barn.

A twenty-one-year-old woman with no history of arrest or psychiatric problems becomes emotionally attached to a male corpse at the funeral home where she works. After his burial she grieves for the deceased, growing so distraught that coworkers complain of her behavior, and she is forced to resign.

Three years later, while employed at a second funeral home, she again develops a romantic interest in a dead body. Determined this time not to lose the object of her macabre desire, she moves his embalmed remains to an isolated place where she spends three days alone with the body. In a lengthy, handwritten account of the two incidents, she describes touching the second corpse and positioning it so as to simulate cuddling and fondling.

Three male children, ages seven, nine, and ten, take a female playmate to an isolated building where they forcibly

undress her and demand that she perform oral sex on them.
They insert sticks, rocks, and bottles into her vagina and
rectum before releasing the little girl with a threat to kill
her if she tells. The three are later identified and arrested
after assaulting another young female playmate.

Before my retirement on January 1, 1994, I spent sixteen
years examining these shocking crimes, and many others,
as a member of the FBI's Behavioral Science Unit. Most
people associate the BSU with its best-known responsibility, profiling, a discipline that was dramatized in the book
and movie *Silence of the Lambs.* The fictional heroine, Special Agent Clarice Starling, and her nemesis, Dr. Hannibal
Lecter, lent a touch of Hollywood glamour to our often
grim and harrowing investigations.

But besides working the occasional high-profile serial
murder case or testifying at the defendant's trial, our work
also had a less-known side. Since the BSU opened for business in 1972, its personnel have studied aberrant crime,
taught classes, and consulted—out of the spotlight—in
scores of ongoing cases. And all the while, we were learning.

In my research, I chose to focus on previously unex-
plored or poorly understood deviant behaviors. These practices, ranging from dangerous autoeroticism to sexual
sadism, brought me face-to-face with dark instincts I had
never imagined existed.

The most appalling murder I ever encountered was that
of a young girl discovered with her intestines wrapped
around her neck. The child vanished one evening as she
walked a short fifty feet to the next-door neighbors' house.
A few hours later, her body was found several blocks away.
She also had been raped and beaten to death. To my knowledge, the crime was never solved.

In another case, a man hanged himself after leaving
twenty-seven suicide notes around his home, garage, and
car. Perhaps the most surprising incident of my career was
the bleeding death of a woman who nearly amputated her

own arm at the shoulder with a butcher knife.

My casework taught me several essential lessons. The first is that there are no boundaries to what a particular individual might do to other people or to him- or herself. The second lesson is equally wide-ranging: When it comes to sexual behavior, there are no limits to what a person might find erotically stimulating.

Among violent sexual offenders, often the only logic to their crimes is internal. The criminal alone knows why he commits his deviant acts. Although we can find patterns and common elements among them, no two offenders ever commit exactly the same sexual crime. In the world of dark minds, the darkness truly is infinite.

The sexual component of a crime is not always self-evident either. The behavior may be blatant, or it may be so subtle that it escapes detection, even by experts. Then again, some crimes may only seem to be sexually motivated.

I once worked for a public defender whose client was accused of the robbery/murder of an elderly woman. The victim was discovered dead on the floor at the foot of her bed. She had been struck twice in the face with sufficient force (according to the medical examiner) to have stunned her or rendered her unconscious. The cause of death was two stab wounds in the chest. Her pants and panties had been pulled down to just above her knees.

There was no sign of forced entry or of a struggle. All doors and windows were secured. Her purse, containing credit cards, was missing. But more than twenty thousand dollars' worth of jewelry and in excess of forty thousand dollars in negotiable securities were left untouched in her unlocked office safe in an adjacent room.

An ATM security camera caught my public defender's client attempting to guess the victim's cash card number. When he was later arrested, he told the police he'd found the card at a bus stop in a bad neighborhood of town.

I know that's an unlikely sounding story, but I believed him. Here's why:

He'd stupidly allowed himself to be videotaped in front of the ATM, trying to guess the card code. Yet the prosecution contended that this inadequate criminal supposedly was smart and savvy enough to enter a total stranger's house, leaving no physical trace of himself. Then he approached the victim in her bedroom and struck and stabbed her twice before she could raise a hand in her defense.

If this defendant had been capable of such improbable sophistication, I said, then *surely* he also would have searched the open safe to steal her jewels and securities.

I thought this was a staged crime. Someone who knew the victim had killed her then pulled down her clothing to suggest a sexual motive in the case. Further, I said, if I had been that person, I too would have left her credit cards in a rough area, knowing that some punk would try to use them.

I didn't testify in the case. But the public defender presented my logic via her arguments and questioning and persuaded the jury that this defendant lacked the cunning to have committed the crime. The case remains officially unsolved.

Thanks to the vast diversity of human nature, an investigator may expect to encounter a wide range of behaviors. Offenders may be attracted to nonliving objects (fetishism), animals (bestiality), or people. Or they may be drawn to all three.

Some people preferentially act out their desires with prepubescent children (pedophiles), teenagers (hebephiles), or the elderly (gerontophiles). Others select age mates as their victims, and a few will sexually assault victims of any age.

Certain offenders commit exclusively homosexual crimes, others limit themselves to offenses against heterosexuals, and still others are attracted to either gender.

Ted Bundy is an example of a necrophiliac, the term used for one who preferentially assaults the dead. Yet to the vast majority of sexual criminals (as to the rest of us!), such an act is abhorrent.

Some sexual crimes involve only the sense of sight (voyeurism and exhibitionism), only the sense of hearing (telephone scatology), or only the sense of touch (frotteurism). However, most offenders will employ all of the available senses.

Many offenders are aroused by a victim's suffering (sadists), while others are excited by their own pain (masochists). Then there are sadomasochists, who may be aroused in either way—simultaneously or in separate incidents.

Highly ritualistic behavior marks some types of sexual crimes, while others are characterized by impulsiveness. At times, we find strange mixes of both ritualism and spontaneity.

I've encountered sexual offenders who almost always seriously injured or murdered their victims. For others, such injury greatly diminishes or destroys the gratification process.

A victim's torment may be protracted by extended captivity. Conversely, as in cases involving comatose patients, those under anesthesia, or victims who have been given the "date rape" drug Rohypnol, the target might be completely unaware of what is happening.

Some offenders select victims who are total strangers. Others attack those who are well acquainted with them—associates, clients, patients, customers, students, or relatives. In short, you name it—anything is to be expected with sexual criminals.

Sometimes it's hard to draw the line between criminal and noncriminal sexual behavior. After all, many practices that would have shocked previous generations in our country tend to be more common today. The distinction between what is acceptable and what is not may even depend on the jurisdiction where the behavior takes place.

A detective in one of my courses brought to my attention

a case involving a woman and two of her dogs. When she brought some film into her local pharmacy for processing, the employee who developed it saw that the photos depicted the customer having sex with the dogs. The police were called, and an investigator presented the matter to the local prosecutor.

After examining the pictures, the assistant district attorney asked if the dogs belonged to the woman. Why would that matter? the investigator wondered aloud. "Because if they don't belong to her, she can be charged with animal abuse," the prosecutor explained. "But if the dogs are hers, there has been no criminal violation in this state."

Although certain aberrant sexual practices (such as dangerous autoeroticism) are not crimes, society still officially condemns most deviant sexual behavior. This is especially true when children are the victims. Yet ironically, we are increasingly permissive toward the graphic portrayal of sexual violence in practically all forms of the media. Magazines, television, and the Internet are rife with explicit and often violent sexual fare.

In my experience this climate of tolerance is having two important social consequences: First, as deviant behavior becomes more common in the material we read, hear, and see, parallel behaviors quickly appear in sexual crimes, particularly those acted out against strangers. Second, an increasing number of serious injuries and/or deaths are occurring during "rough sex." When criminal charges are filed, defense attorneys try to portray the injurious behavior as "consensual and accidental."

I have been retained by defense lawyers in three murder cases in which the defendant claimed that his partner's death occurred during voluntary "erotic asphyxiation," one form of rough sex. In each case the attorney asked me to review the evidence and advise whether or not I could testify that the death was an accident.

For different reasons I told each of these clients that I

would be unable to assist in the defense because the facts indicated that the manner of death was homicide. Yet in other cases, defense attorneys succeed in presenting a plausible scenario of accidental death. In our "anything goes" society, it can be difficult to convince a judge or jury that any behavior is necessarily involuntary.

Who commits sexual crimes? You may be surprised (as I often am) at the wide range of answers to this question.

Often, when I address audiences and classes, I tell them about the case that opened this chapter—the one in which a fourteen-year-old girl was kidnapped, tortured, and murdered. After dumping her body, the killer anonymously taunted a member of his victim's family by relating truthful, but investigatively useless, details about the location where he left her dead body. He said, for instance, that she would be found in a barn. That was true, but of no help in locating her.

When he was arrested some months later, investigators searched his residence. There they found a trove of telling artifacts—the undeveloped film he had shot of the victim during her captivity, articles of her clothing, bondage paraphernalia, detective magazines, and a variety of weapons.

After presenting the facts of the case, I ask my listeners to guess what the killer looked like. Their responses are as varied as the audience members themselves. However, when I show them two photographs of this criminal, practically everyone gasps in surprise.

The "monster" who committed these heinous crimes was a well-groomed, middle-aged man, six feet tall, and weighing about 185 pounds. In one of the photographs, he is wearing a police uniform; in the other, he is dressed as an airline pilot. Is this the image you expected for a sexual criminal?

My audiences—usually professionals who work within the criminal justice system—often feel uneasy when they see these pictures for the same reason that I do: the sexual killer looks so normal. He looks like us, and that resemblance is very disturbing.

Professionals and laymen alike, we all want sexual offenders to look like perverts so that we can readily identify them in our neighborhoods, schools, and shopping malls. Unfortunately, with the vast majority of sexual offenders, it just doesn't work that way.

In the early 1980s, when authorities in Texas arrested drifter Henry Lee Lucas, hardly a soul expressed any skepticism over Lucas's claim to have murdered as many as six hundred people. Why? Because, according to popular stereotype, Henry Lee Lucas looked like a pervert! He was unshaven, poorly groomed, shabbily dressed. Nearly penniless, he drove a worn-out wreck of a car. Everything about him was uncouth.

His alleged accomplice, Ottis Toole, looked just as bad, if not worse. The appearances of both men fit well within the public's perception of what a serial killer should look like.

We at the BSU cringed when we saw the pictures of Lucas and Toole. We knew that they would reinforce the mistaken notion that sexual offenders typically look different from other people—and thus encourage many innocent victims to overlook dangers that come in more ordinary forms.

In the late 1970s, before Lucas and Toole were captured, we hoped that Ted Bundy had effectively disproved the public's mistaken perceptions. Bundy was handsome, well-spoken, and educated. He did not appear capable of the horrible sexual crimes for which he was accused and later convicted. Bundy's arrest made a lot of people very uncomfortable because it forced them to rethink their previous ideas about sexual criminals. When Bundy stood trial for two murders in Florida, his wholesome appearance complicated the prosecutors' job. Fortunately, both juries heeded the evidence, and Bundy was convicted and sentenced to death.

In contrast, Richard Ramirez, the Los Angeles killer known as "the Night Stalker," fit the public's stereotypical concept of serial killers. In thirteen months Ramirez murdered at least thirteen victims whose ages ranged from six to eighty-four. He sexually assaulted and, in some cases, mutilated the victims after death. Ramirez had dark, penetrating eyes, disheveled black hair, a pentagram on one hand, and poor dental hygiene. He was difficult to control in court, often erupting into verbal and physical obscenities. Richard Ramirez was mentally disturbed, and he looked it!

Sadly, violent crimes committed by the severely disturbed tend to attract a disproportionate amount of attention from the press. In fact, the mentally ill are responsible for less than 3 percent of sexual crimes. Such people usually pose a greater threat to themselves than others. Richard Ramirez was an exception to the rule.

Who is the sexual offender? A few examples demonstrate the wide range of individuals who fit the description.

Jon Barry Simonis was a former star high school athlete with a full-scale IQ of 128 (the average is 90–110). By his own count, Simonis raped and battered as many as seventy-five women across at least twelve states.

The sexual sadist Gerard John Schaefer is believed to have killed more than twenty women—and he was a deputy sheriff. The "Son of Sam," David Berkowitz, was a mailman. John Wayne Gacy was a building contractor active in local politics. Harvey Glatman, the Los Angeles "Lonely Hearts Killer" of the 1950s, was a television repairman. Australian-born spree killer Christopher Wilder, who tortured and murdered women from coast to coast, was a millionaire entrepreneur.

What goes into the creation of a sexual criminal?

During my lectures, I frequently pose this question, "What have you heard are the causes of sexual violence?"

Responses invariably include poverty, childhood sexual abuse and/or emotional abuse and/or physical abuse, violence in the media, pornography, peer pressure, lack of discipline at school or in the home, single parenting, lack of morality in our society, chemical imbalance in the brain, childhood brain damage, genetics, mental illness, inappropriate role models, alcohol and/or drug abuse. All these factors have been proposed by experts as a rationale for seemingly inexplicable behavior. Which are correct?

A wonderful and wise sociology professor once said to me, "Roy, when you have more than one answer to a question, you don't have the answer!"

Any purported explanation for why an individual commits sexual violence is incomplete if it ignores the most important variable, the criminal himself. Each person is a unique product of nature and nurture, genetic destiny, and environmental influences. What has a great impact on one person may have no effect at all on another. So while a number of factors seem to contribute to the genesis of a sexual offender, no single element is the cause of deviant behavior.

Let's take a closer look at a few of the more common theories.

POVERTY

A great number of sexual offenders come from poor families, and a great number of them don't. For every criminal raised in a poverty-stricken environment, we can find countless law-abiding citizens who overcome that disadvantage to lead honest lives.

CHILDHOOD ABUSE

My research on serial rape supports the view that a large number of sexual criminals have been childhood victims of physical, sexual, or psychological abuse. Yet, as is true with poverty, there are many more abused kids who do not become sexually violent as adults.

VIOLENCE IN THE MEDIA

Movies and television often are blamed for glamorizing violence. In 1977, a fifteen-year-old Florida youth named Ronny Zamora claimed in court that he killed an elderly female neighbor because of "television intoxication." Zamora's attorney said his client had become addicted to violence by watching television. Fortunately for society, the jurors didn't buy into that theory.

Books, magazines, and music have also been faulted for promoting violence. Rap music, especially, has been accused of objectifying women and using gender-demeaning terminology in the lyrics. While I might not personally appreciate certain kinds of music or films, behavioral studies do not suggest that men who watch or listen to them are, as a result, driven to commit crimes. Certainly offenders with preexisting fantasies might seek out such stimulation and even attempt to incorporate some of its elements into future crimes. But to say that a cause-and-effect relationship exists is simply not supported by *scientific inquiry*.

PORNOGRAPHY

I dislike pornography for a multitude of reasons, but speaking as a professional, I have to say that I don't believe that it causes sexual violence.

Opponents of pornography often point to Dr. James Dobson's death-row interview with Ted Bundy to support their cause. But they frequently—possibly intentionally—misquote Bundy on the subject. Speaking with the convicted murderer on the eve of his execution, Dobson questioned

Bundy closely about the reasons for his deadly behavior.

Bundy said that pornography had had a tremendous effect on his life, but nowhere in the interview did he say that pornography had made him violent. He did not say pornography caused him to become a serial killer, and there is no reason to believe that was the case.

Nevertheless, my experience, education, and training led me to believe that pornography contributes, both passively and actively, to sexual violence in some individuals.

Humans learn something from every experience, good or bad. What are the lessons that are taught by pornography? First, it treats women and children as objects. By taking away their individual humanity, it supports the mind-set that seeks to use others solely for sexual gratification. Second, it teaches that sex is merely a bodily function, having no special significance. When the essential connectedness of sexual contact is denied, the physical or emotional needs of a partner have no relevance. Third, pornography conveys the message that sex is an expression of instinctive urges, with no need for love or commitment. These are not healthy lessons.

Pornography may play an even more serious role in the process that leads to violent sexual assault by providing offenders with a continuous source of new ideas.

Certain pornographic images validate aberrant tendencies by showing the offender that his behavior is not so unusual within our society after all; in certain circles it is even accepted. Further, pornography reinforces violent sexual fantasies by providing a continuous and never-ending source of richly graphic inspiration.

From my interviews with rapists, sexual killers, child molesters, sexual sadists, and the wives and companions of these sexually violent men, I know that ritualistic sexual offenders not only own pornography but they typically collect it. They pore over it, spending endless hours with a favorite picture or video, all the while reinforcing the aberrant fantasy.

A medical examiner once brought to my attention a rape-homicide case in which the victims, a woman and her prepubescent daughter, were stabbed to death in their home. The mother's body was discovered with her legs bent at the knees and spread apart. It was obvious the killer had intentionally positioned her that way.

The murder weapons were two knives belonging to the victims. Both mother and child had been stabbed multiple times. Shoe prints left at the scene indicated that the killer had been wearing military boots. Before leaving, he took a Polaroid of the crime scene and placed it on top of the victim's television set, where it immediately caught investigators' attention.

When the subject was later arrested, a search of his possessions revealed a detective magazine, inside of which was a picture of a rape-homicide that was practically identical to his own crime. The accompanying article explained that the victim had been stabbed with two of her own knives, her legs had been positioned in the same manner, and the killer, a U.S. soldier, had worn combat boots during the commission of the crime. However, there was no young child in the magazine story. This discrepancy is telling for it suggests that the killer murdered the daughter simply because she was at home when he attacked her mother.

GENETICS

Some years ago, a new theory connected the presence of an extra "Y" chromosome in a male's genetic material to a superabundance of testosterone, which was believed to result in violent behavior. No one has ever developed scientific evidence to support this theory, and it is largely discounted today.

A more recent, and also unsubstantiated, hypothesis holds that individuals can inherit a gene that predisposes them to commit criminal acts. This genetic explanation for criminality poses an interesting dilemma for sociologists, psychologists, criminologists, and penologists.

If such behaviors are determined from birth, professionals could do little to prevent them; and rehabilitation would be a hopeless task. I believe that this theory will prove to be another false lead in the quest to understand violence in our society.

Still another theory, recently advanced by so-called evolutionary psychologists, takes the radical view that rape is a natural biological phenomenon. To paraphrase one adherent, rape is an unfortunate but nonetheless adaptive strategy for passing on one's genes that is seen in a number of animals besides man, including fish, birds, and other primates.

In my view, this reasoning will go the way of the extra Y chromosome theory.

INSANITY

It's all too easy to dismiss sexual offenders as being "sick," "perverted," or "deranged." However, this assumption does not explain the 97 percent of crimes committed by individuals who are not psychotic (insane).

One of the more esoteric explanations for criminal behavior I have heard is brain shrinkage. This theory arose when the executive director of a huge U.S. charity was charged with embezzlement after he stole $250,000 from the organization's funds and took his teenage girlfriend to Las Vegas. The seemingly reputable defendant argued that he should not be held responsible for his acts because his brain had shrunk, thus affecting his ability to discern right from wrong. I didn't buy this defense and neither did the court.

PREMENSTRUAL SYNDROME

A professional woman attacked a state police officer with a heavy, blunt object after he had stopped her for DWI.

Her position at trial was temporary insanity due to PMS, and it was successful.

BLOOD SUGAR IMBALANCE

Even junk food has been blamed for causing violence. In San Francisco in November of 1978, Supvr. Harvey Milk and Mayor George Moscone were gunned down at city hall by Supvr. Dan White. At trial the following May, White's attorney blamed his client's violent behavior in part on the inordinate number of Twinkies that White had consumed. The argument's been known ever since as "the Twinkie defense." White, who was charged with first-degree murder, was convicted of the lesser charge of manslaughter.

Some of these theories and ideas sound implausible, but in the unpredictable arena of human behavior, it doesn't pay to dismiss *any* possible reason, however bizarre it may seem, without examining it closely. Yet I'm confident that no *single* factor of any sort will ever suffice to explain the millions of variations that occur among individuals. No two people are alike, and the factors that combine to cause people to turn to violence—especially sexual violence—will always be unique.

Perhaps the most obvious (and most frightening) explanation of all is that some offenders commit sexual crimes simply because they want to! They like it! And they have no regard for what the rest of society thinks.

This is the dark mind's most disturbing corner of all.

2

IT BEGINS INSIDE THE MIND

In the late 1980s, my BSU colleague, Jim Wright, and I were asked to consult on a series of particularly gruesome murders in California. The case was unusual in that the police didn't learn of the homicides until one of the killers killed himself.

Leonard Lake lived on approximately two and a half acres of woodland property near the town of Wilseyville in Calaveras County, northeast of San Francisco. Lake and his partner, Charles Ng, constructed a building on the property, ostensibly for tool storage. In fact, there was a secret section in the structure designed as a prison cell for captive females.

On June 2, 1985, Lake, then thirty-nine, and Ng, twenty-four, went shopping in a South San Francisco hardware store. A clerk observed Ng shoplift a tool, leave the store, and put the stolen item into the trunk of a car. The police were called and Ng fled, leaving his older partner to explain a series of whys.

Why was the stolen tool in the trunk of a car registered to a missing person? Why were there also unregistered guns in the trunk? Why did the license plate belong on a different car? And why did the driver's license that Leonard Lake produced belong to a missing person named Robin Stapley?

Before the police could begin to unravel these mysteries,

their bearded suspect reached for a cyanide capsule he'd pinned to the inside of his shirt collar and ingested the poison on the spot. Leonard Lake died four days later in the hospital.

Ng subsequently slipped north to Canada, where he successfully fought extradition for many years. In 1999, the Hong Kong–born killer finally was convicted in California for his role in eleven murders committed with Lake and was sentenced to death.

Investigators believe Lake and Ng's actual victim total was much higher. A search of Lake's Calaveras County residences and the surrounding area yielded the remains of several victims, as well as videotapes of Lake and Ng with women who had been reported missing; photographs of these and other missing women in various stages of dress; and Lake's handwritten notes of his daily activities. Jim and I were given copies of all of the material to review.

I was absorbed by a twenty-minute videotape in which Lake ruminates on his motives for committing the crimes. The tape, made prior to the construction of the building, reveals Lake seated calmly and comfortably in his easy chair, his feet extended on the attached footrest. In an even voice, he coolly recounts his desire to construct a bunker featuring a "slave cell" where he intends to keep a female captive as "primarily a sexual slave, but a physical slave as well."

Leonard Lake succeeded in making this dark fantasy come true.

As I listened and watched Lake on the monitor, I was stunned to recognize striking parallels between his observations and those I had recently read as part of my wide-ranging (and belated) attempt to improve my grasp of Western classics.

Seventeen centuries ago, one of the key figures in early Christian philosophy had addressed the same questions that we, as behavioral scientists, were trying to answer in our modern-day work. Strange as it may seem, it was Saint Augustine who helped me recognize the distinct stages that ritualistic sexual offenders pass through on their way from sexual fantasy to aberrant crime.

Augustine wrote that sin is the product of a five-step process. First, he said, the mind conceives of an action. It then considers the action as it relates to the senses—will I gain pleasure from this? Next, the individual considers the possible consequences of the act. If he is willing to risk those outcomes, he decides to act on the thought. Finally, once the act has taken place, his mind rationalizes the behavior.

As I read this passage in *The Confessions,* it occurred to me that if I replaced the word "sin" with the word "crime," Saint Augustine might have been describing many of the sexual criminals I had been studying for more than twenty-five years. Even the language of Lake's videotape echoed Augustine's five-step process.

AUGUSTINE	LEONARD LAKE
1 The mind conceives of an action . . .	"It's something I fantasize about daily"
2 . . . which is referred to the senses.	Lake photographed and videotaped his victims
3 The individual considers the possible consequences	"What I'm talking about is highly illegal and violates human rights, blah, blah, blah."
4 He decides to commit the sin.	"It may not work, but I want to try."
5 Then he rationalizes the act.	"For anyone interested in my rationalization and justification for what I'm about to do . . ."

Just as Saint Augustine recognized that sin begins as an intention, we profilers saw that violent sexual crimes originate in fantasy. Our next challenge was to understand why certain individuals allowed their fantasies to lead them to cross the normal bounds of acceptable behavior. To do that, we had to examine their motivations.

Many people mistakenly believe that rape is a sexually motivated act. In fact, a rapist doesn't commit the crime because he is "horny" or because his wife cheated on him, although he may use those factors as excuses. The rapist uses sex as a tool of aggression. The sexual assault is an assertion of power or an expression of anger, or it may be a combination of the two. In any event, sexual assault primarily serves nonsexual needs.

To illustrate this point, I often tell my students that the oldest rape victim I am aware of was ninety-three years old, and the youngest was two hours old. When I ask how many people believe either of these crimes was committed out of sexual need, not one person has ever raised a hand.

What *did* these two victims have in common? Vulnerability, helplessness, and lack of threat to the attacker. The rapist achieves his gratification, not from the sexual release, but from the thrill of domination, control, and power.

You might define fantasy as *a mental rehearsal of a desired event.* This mental rehearsal plays a central role in the enactment of sexual offenses. It serves as a kind of editing mechanism that allows the offender to focus on the details of the crime that are uniquely arousing to him. To suit his needs, he can rearrange parts and assign them to their appropriate places.

The fantasy also serves as an arena for rehearsal, allowing the offender to practice his crime with no personal risk. Finally, it provides a template or map for the offender to follow while he commits the crime.

The development of a ritualistic offender's fantasy is similar to the production of a stage play. The central figure is the playwright/director—the offender. In his fantasies, he scripts the action, chooses the settings, and selects the props. Of course, he casts himself (who else?) as the star, but he also requires a costar—his victim. Once he has fully developed the criteria for her, he's ready to begin his search for someone to play that role. When the play is ready to open, the crime is about to occur.

Over the years I have recognized two disturbing trends relating to violent sexual fantasies. First, offenders today are conceptualizing their crimes (Saint Augustine's step one) at a much earlier age than their predecessors did. Second, as a result, their fantasies are growing more complex and, in some cases, deadlier over time.

The following example from my case files demonstrates not only this early conceptualization but also what a profiler looks for when he reviews sexual crimes. As you read the case of Robert Leroy Anderson, you will clearly see how this ritualistic offender progressed from the fantasy he scripted in his mind to the horrifying acts he committed in real life.

In 1997, I was contacted by Patty Froning, an assistant state attorney general in South Dakota, who wished to retain me as an expert witness to review two homicides. The murders were committed twenty-three months apart. Froning wanted to know whether I thought they were committed by the same individual.

I later testified under questioning by Larry Long, the chief deputy state attorney general, that I believed this to be the case. In the process of consulting with the prosecution team and investigators, I learned about other aspects of the crimes. The one that struck me most forcibly was the central role that fantasy played in the two murders.

Piper Potts was an attractive young woman from Texas who met her future husband, Vance Streyle, at a Bible college in Oregon. They married in 1988 and three years later moved to a trailer located on forty acres in Canistota, South Dakota, a rural community about twenty miles west of Sioux Falls.

A deeply religious couple, the Streyles realized their dream of having their own part-time ministry, the Prairie View Bible Camp for children. From the road, passing motorists could see the pews they had set up in their yard.

The Streyles had two children, Shaina and Nathan, who were three and two years of age. Little Nathan's second birthday fell on Monday, July 29, 1996, the day they lost their mother.

That morning at about 6:30, Vance Streyle, twenty-nine, drove to his plumbing job as usual. Piper, twenty-eight, ordinarily would have left a short time later to take her children to the baby-sitter on the way to her job at the Southeastern Children's Center in Sioux Falls. In fact, she called the baby-sitter, Mrs. Jordnson, at 9:20 to say they were on their way.

Piper Streyle never arrived at Mrs. Jordnson's house or at her job. Her husband called home at noon and left a message on the answering machine. "Honey, where are you?" Vance asked.

Around three o'clock, Patty Sinclair, who worked with Mrs. Streyle at the day-care facility, called to check on her friend. Shaina answered the phone instead.

"I don't want my mommy to die!" the little girl blurted into the receiver. "I don't want my daddy to die!" Shaina then added, "They're probably killed."

Stunned, Patty Sinclair directed a coworker to call the McCook County Sheriff's Office as she redialed the Streyles' number. Sinclair spoke with Shaina again, but this time she kept the child on the telephone for nearly forty-five minutes until Sheriff Gene Taylor arrived at the trailer.

By now it was after five. Taylor found the children and the family dog, a blond Labrador named Chase, but no sign of Mrs. Streyle. The trailer was in disarray; yet the children had not been harmed physically. Nathan made hardly a sound; Shaina was in tears.

"Mommy's going to die," she told Sheriff Taylor and Jim Stevenson, a South Dakota Division of Criminal Investigation (DCI) agent. Patiently, the two men extracted the three year old's account of what had happened.

"A mean man," as Shaina described him, driving a black vehicle with black wheels, came into the trailer and grabbed their mother. She reported that there was a lot of yelling and that the man shot a gun. Their mother told them to run and hide. Shaina also said that the man had taken Nathan's blue tent, a birthday present he had received the evening before.

As Shaina recounted the fragmented story, her father arrived home. Sobbing in his arms, she blurted out that the man had taken Nathan's tent. Choking back his own tears, Vance Streyle reassured his daughter that it was okay; they had another tent. Shaina was insistent that her mother was going to die, saying, "She's not coming back."

The investigation quickly turned up several witnesses who reported seeing a truck or sport utility vehicle painted a flat, black color in the vicinity of the Streyle residence that day. One couple who lived in the area saw a nervous young man in jeans and a baseball cap walking from the trailer to a black Ford Bronco parked in the driveway.

But authorities had nothing substantive to go on until late on the evening of July 29. That's when Vance Streyle suddenly recalled a visit to the trailer three days earlier by a chubby, balding stranger in his mid-twenties. The man had said his name was Rob Anderson.

Vance notified the police, who returned to the residence to follow up on the new information. Streyle remembered Anderson as an affable guy with a limp handshake. He had driven up in a black Bronco at about 7:30 A.M. the previous Friday, and at first he didn't seem to know what he wanted to say. He seemed surprised that Vance Streyle was home and mumbled something about having driven by the house several times over the past months.

Finally, as Piper Streyle walked to the front door, Anderson inquired about enrolling his children in the Bible camp. Vance told him that the camp was closed for the year, but that they would be glad to add his name to the list for 1997. Mrs. Streyle wrote his name and phone number on a piece of paper, and Anderson left.

By the next morning, investigators had fully identified the Streyles' visitor as Robert Leroy Anderson, twenty-six, a high school dropout and twice-married father of four who lived in Sioux Falls. Anderson worked as a maintenance man on the 11:00 P.M.– 7:30 A.M. shift at John Morrell & Co., a Sioux Falls meat-packing plant.

DCI assistant director Bob Grandpre and other law enforcement officers went to Anderson's house, where they awakened him and said they wanted to speak with him. The suspect pulled on his jeans, a T-shirt, and his baseball hat and voluntarily drove his blue Ford Bronco to the local police station. An investigative team searched the Bronco and his home while Anderson underwent a seven-hour interrogation.

Beneath the carpeting in the Bronco's cargo area, officers found a plywood platform with holes drilled in it, each obviously designed to accommodate wrist or ankle restraints. A toolbox containing chain and wooden dowels also was found in the vehicle, as were traces of black, water-based paint and a partial roll of duct tape. Dog hairs, similar to those of the Streyles' family dog, also were recovered, along with some furniture-moving straps.

Anderson remained calm, denying any knowledge of Piper Streyle's fate or whereabouts, but he did concede that he had visited the Streyles' trailer the previous Friday morning. After some equivocation, he also admitted that he had returned on Monday. He said he had come back because he wanted to use the Streyles' archery range. Anderson claimed that he had knocked on the door, but there was no answer. He said he could hear children playing within and assumed that Mrs. Streyle was taking a nap, so he left.

The conversation touched on topics as diverse as the suspect's boyhood speech impediment, his professed interest in anal sex (which Anderson reported his wife did not share), and the unsolved disappearance of another local woman, Larisa Dumansky. Mrs. Dumansky was a twenty-nine-year-old Morrell employee who had vanished from the meat-packing company's parking lot two years before. Anderson denied any knowledge of her disappearance.

Meanwhile, investigators found a pair of Anderson's blue jeans in the laundry area of his trailer. They were stained inside with both blood and semen. Later tests on the stains would prove inconclusive as to their source. The search also turned up two handcuff keys and a container of black, water-soluble spray paint, such as that discovered in his Bronco.

When the police interviewed one of Anderson's neighbors, Dan Johnson, he recalled seeing Anderson carefully clean the interior of his blue Bronco on the morning of the 29th. Mr. Johnson reported that Anderson then left for a while and returned around 2:00 P.M., when he again cleaned the vehicle's interior.

Confronted with the handcuff keys, Anderson admitted they were his but said he didn't own any handcuffs to go with them. He also denied Dan Johnson's account of the cleaning of the Bronco.

Vance Streyle later picked out Robert Anderson in a lineup as the man who had come to his home on the morning of the 26th. His daughter, Shaina, also identified him as the "mean man" who had forcibly taken her mother away. At 1:30 on the morning of August 2, the Sioux Falls police arrested Robert Anderson at Morrell's and charged him with kidnapping Piper Streyle.

They had identified their suspect quickly—a key to success in any criminal case—but the investigation still was a long way from completion. Piper Streyle was still missing.

Hundreds of officers and volunteers scoured the area around the Streyles' trailer looking for further evidence. They found nothing. However, botanist Gary Larson from South Dakota State University was able to point the investigation in a more useful direction. Larson identified bits of vegetable matter taken from a toolbox in the back of the

Bronco as honewort and black snake root, which are known to grow along certain wooded stretches of the Big Sioux River north of Sioux Falls, near the small town of Baltic. Police realized it was not a coincidence that on July 29, the day of Piper Streyle's abduction, a motorist driving near Baltic had found the torn half of a black-and-white T-shirt that Mrs. Streyle had been wearing when she was last seen.

That's where Anderson had taken her.

A search of the lightly inhabited area turned up the other half of her T-shirt beneath a small tree. Dangling from a branch directly above it were several lengths of duct tape, wadded up together and matted with human hair, that proved to be microscopically indistinguishable from Mrs. Streyle's hair. Nearby were a large dildo and a partially used wax candle. One torn end of the duct tape matched a roll taken from Anderson's Bronco. The vehicle also yielded hair specimens believed to have come from Piper Streyle. Stuck to the blade of a folding knife recovered from the Bronco were bits of cloth fiber that matched her cut shirt.

Anderson was charged with kidnapping Piper Streyle and went on trial the following spring. He was not charged with murder since there wasn't yet sufficient evidence to prosecute him successfully for that crime. The prosecution team, led by South Dakota attorney general Mark Barnett, would show the jury that the defendant had bought the black paint that Monday morning and sprayed it on the Bronco to change the appearance of the vehicle.

The use of water-soluble paint was just one example of how thoroughly Anderson scripted his crime. Applying a coat of easily washed-off, water-based paint is not a spontaneous inspiration. It reflected substantial forethought and cunning.

A reconstruction of events derived from the evidence, witnesses, and informant information established that Anderson drove to the Streyles' trailer on the 29th. He handcuffed Mrs. Streyle, retrieved the note with his name and phone number, carried her out to the Bronco, and then drove to the thinly settled area near Baltic. Securing her to the platform in his vehicle, he gagged Piper Streyle with duct tape. He cut her shirt open with his folding knife, sexually assaulted and killed her, and disposed of the body.

Anderson then returned to the Streyle residence and retrieved a watch he had dropped during the struggle as well as the expended shell casing from the round that Shaina reported he had fired. This second trip to the residence accounts for the Streyles' neighbor seeing him walk from the trailer to the Bronco. Dan Johnson and other witnesses placed him back at home in the Bronco (now blue once more) by 2:00 that afternoon, which means that somewhere along the way he also stopped and washed off the black paint.

On May 8, 1997, Anderson's jury found him guilty of kidnapping Piper Streyle. Two months later state circuit judge Boyd McMurchie sentenced him to life in prison.

No one was satisfied with this outcome. Anderson complained in court that he was an innocent victim of vindictive prosecution. "I hope you rot in hell," he told Barnett just before his sentencing.

"I might," Barnett later said, "but it won't be because I convicted Robert Anderson."

In fact, Barnett was no happier about the punishment Anderson had received than was the defendant, though for a different reason. The attorney general vowed in court that there would be another day of reckoning. "Sooner or later, he'll face a homicide charge," Barnett predicted.

My major conclusion about Robert Leroy Anderson was his clear sexual sadism.

This condition is not well understood. Frequently people mistake cruelty for sadism. Another misperception is that sadists are aroused by the *infliction* of pain. In fact, what excites the sadist is the *suffering* of the victim. It is true that sexual sadists use physical and/or psychological pain to produce suffering, but the suffering is the most important thing to them.

I based my opinion that Anderson was a sexual sadist on four factors: First was his obvious interest in sexual bondage, a hallmark of the sexual sadist. Anderson kept chains, eye bolts, handcuff keys, and furniture-moving straps in his truck, as well as duct tape and a plywood platform with restraint holes. These instruments of bondage were significant because sexual sadists are attracted to, and sexually excited by, the helplessness and vulnerability of a bound victim.

Second, the evidence clearly indicated physical torture. This included, of course, the platform, but Anderson also had wooden dowels and a dildo. He had confessed to an acquaintance his fantasy of forcefully inserting such objects into a woman. The fact that the partially used candle was found near the dildo and shirt suggested that it had also been used to torture Mrs. Streyle.

The T-shirt that had been cut up the middle in the front and back also provided important clues, as did the wadded duct tape with her hair matted in it. I believe that Mrs. Streyle was bound to the platform on her back and that Anderson then cut the front of the T-shirt. The wadded duct tape would have been used to gag her and muffle her screams as he tormented her. Then he turned her on her stomach, cut the shirt up the back, and continued to torture her.

Third, Anderson told the police and several witnesses that he enjoyed anal sex. Our research at the FBI shows that sexual sadists strongly prefer this form of sex. I believe that the discarded dildo and wooden dowels found in Anderson's truck were used to act out this fantasy against Mrs. Streyle.

Finally, sexually sadistic offenders habitually plan their crimes in much greater detail than do other criminals. The evidence showed that Robert Leroy Anderson had an elaborate plan in mind when he called on the Streyles' residence. Piper Streyle obviously was not a random victim of violence. She was chosen well in advance of the abduction, and the area to which Anderson took her was carefully preselected.

Anderson also gathered and/or constructed the materials he needed to act out his aberrant fantasies. He shaped the plywood platform so that it not only fit the contours of his Bronco cargo area but was easily hidden beneath carpeting. His toolbox was essentially a sadist's kit, containing implements of torture. And he had gathered the bondage paraphernalia he needed.

Anderson's ingenious stratagem for temporarily disguising his Bronco reflected meticulous planning. When I speak of this case, someone invariably suggests that Anderson must have gotten the idea from the movie *The Jackal*, in which Bruce Willis also spray paints his car then washes off the camouflage coat in a car wash.

However, Mrs. Streyle was abducted and killed the summer before *The Jackal* was released. This was a case of film imitating life, not the other way around.

Establishing that Robert Anderson is a sexual sadist permitted me to make several other inferences about him. Had he been an unidentified subject (UNSUB)—as is often the case in my consultations—these additional insights might have helped the authorities identify Piper Streyle's killer. As it was, the findings helped flesh out the prosecution's understanding of their suspect.

For example, I could tell the investigators with confidence that Mrs. Streyle's killer probably preferred anal sex, bondage, and foreign-object penetration with his consenting partners.

His movie favorites likely would include features like *Kiss the Girls*, the story of a self-styled Casanova who lives his fantasy by abducting women for his underground harem. Another possibility would be the film version of John Fowles's classic novel, *The Collector*. Fowles's protagonist, chillingly portrayed in the movie by Terence Stamp, also acts on his fantasy, kidnapping and holding as captive the lovely Miranda. It was no coincidence that "Op-

eration Miranda" was Leonard Lake's code name for his
abduction and captivity plan.

Even though the authorities had already identified Anderson as their subject, the insight that he was a sexual
sadist showed them why the other materials were in the
Bronco and at the rural site and why he had invested so
much time in preparing for the crime. For example, when
they later recovered Anderson's murder trophies (jewelry
belonging to his victims), they better understood why he
had kept them.

Sexual sadists almost invariably are psychopaths, but
Anderson's mental anomalies also singled him out as a
narcissist. Narcissism is a personality disorder marked by
self-centeredness and a lack of empathy for others. Such
individuals have grandiose fantasies.

The narcissist's favorite subject is himself, and he frequently exaggerates his accomplishments to impress himself and others. That description certainly fits Robert
Anderson. Fred Devaney, an agent with the South Dakota
Division of Criminal Investigation who played a significant
role in the case, later told me that Anderson compared himself to Albert Einstein in one postconviction interview.

He also revealed an immense amount of damning detail
about himself to others who, in time, came forward with
what they knew.

The first of these witnesses was Jamie Hammer, thirty-
two, Anderson's longtime acquaintance and former roommate. Investigators interviewed Hammer within ten days of
Piper Streyle's disappearance and immediately realized he
was not an ideal witness. He had a police record, a history
of substance abuse, and had sustained a head injury in an
accident, which caused him to suffer partial memory loss.

Jamie Hammer did not inspire confidence, yet authorities
knew that what he had to say, if corroborated, would have
a powerful impact in the capital murder case that Mark
Barnett and his associates hoped to bring against Anderson.

In a series of interviews, and in sworn testimony, Hammer described in detail how his friend, Rob Anderson, al-

ways had been obsessed with murdering women. He said the two of them had discussed the subject hundreds of times, beginning as far back as early high school. The focus of these conversations was how to gain control of a woman, kill her, and then get away with the crime.

For example, said Hammer, Anderson exhaustively considered the subject of body disposal. Once a victim was captured, the ultimate disposal site should be no more than an hour's drive away, he said, and the grave should be predug. They decided that a plastic sheet, placed beneath the victim, was useful for preventing anyone from finding forensic evidence such as blood, semen, hairs, and fibers. Anderson felt that dismembering a victim before burial also was a good practice, although he didn't say why.

They discussed how to build a restraining device, such as Anderson's plywood platform, and the various ways of killing a person. Anderson strongly opposed using a gun. Gunshots were too loud, he said.

Hammer explained that Anderson made tire "poppers," sharp little metal triangles, in the machine shop at Morrell. Anderson spray painted the devices to blend in with the road surface on which they were placed, making it extremely difficult for a driver to see them, particularly at night.

Hammer agreed to try them out.

He told authorities that Anderson would drop him off along a roadway at night with a two-way radio and a supply of the poppers and then drive on to scout for possible victims. When he saw one, he'd radio Hammer with a description of the woman's car. As she approached his position, Hammer would place the tire poppers in the roadway. Anderson would follow the potential victim in his car, pick up Hammer, and then trail their quarry until her tires went flat.

Once such victim was twenty-six-year-old Amy Anderson (no relation).

*   *   *

Late on Thursday night, November 10, 1994, Amy Anderson was driving just west of the little town of Tea with her friend, Stacy Hazen. She noticed a maroon Monte Carlo moving slowly in front of her.

The Chevy pulled over onto the shoulder to let Ms. Anderson pass, then caught up with her, passed her, and slowed again. She backed off the gas as well and kept driving slowly until the Monte Carlo finally pulled away into the distance ahead.

A short while later, she felt her car run over something in the roadway. Continuing on, she dropped Stacy Hazen at home and drove for seven more miles until one of her tires went flat. She carefully pulled over, flipped on her flashers, and walked back to the trunk to retrieve her spare tire and jack. Just as she did, the Monte Carlo drove past again. She watched its brake lights flash before it continued on.

As Amy Anderson opened her trunk and extracted the jack, the Chevy returned once more. This time the driver stopped and turned off his headlights. When he got out of his car, she noticed that the dome light remained unlit. Wordlessly, he approached the young woman and leaned into the trunk as if he was going to help her. Instead, he turned and grabbed her and began to drag her toward a ditch.

They fought briefly before Ms. Anderson broke free. She ran into the road as another vehicle approached. The driver of that car, teenager Christie Craig, and her passenger, Pamela Doud, saw Ms. Anderson running toward them from the ditch, waving her arms in obvious distress. They quickly opened a door for the frightened young woman as they saw two white men get into the Monte Carlo and drive off.

A check of Robert Anderson's employment records showed that he did not go to work at Morrell's that night. Amy Anderson later identified him as her attacker.

Judy Munkvold, who worked with Amy Anderson at a Dean Witter brokerage office, also identified a picture of

Robert Anderson as a walk-in client she had seen there on several occasions.

As I have seen with many other sexual sadists, Anderson bragged compulsively, a narcissistic urge that in the end would prove his undoing. If this careful, intelligent, and patient killer could have kept his mouth shut, he might never have been brought to justice.

This was especially true of the Dumansky case.

Jamie Hammer testified that one day, while he was installing speakers in the trunk of the Monte Carlo that he had purchased from Anderson in 1995, "he [Anderson] said that's where the girl from Morrell's was. He said he stuffed her in the trunk."

Hammer couldn't remember Anderson's exact words, but he knew his pal was referring to the killing of Larisa Dumansky. "What I can remember is she did anything he wanted her to do because she didn't want to be hurt," Hammer added. "He said he didn't have enough time to do what he wanted to."

Attractive young Larisa Dumansky and her husband, Bill, were relative newcomers to America. Native Ukrainian Pentecostals who had been driven from their homeland in 1991 by religious persecution, they settled in Sioux Falls, where both of them found work at Morrell's meat-packing plant. Bill later got a job laying carpet, but Larissa stayed on, usually working the night shift, where she came to know Robert Anderson.

In the summer of 1994, Mrs. Dumansky had been bothered by an inexplicable series of flat tires. Every other day her Dodge Caravan seemed to suffer a puncture. August 26 was no different. Her husband later told me that Larisa was happy that day because the orthodontist had finally removed her braces. "You won't believe how beautiful I am when you see me," she said in their last phone conversation.

Larisa, who believed she was two months' pregnant (her doctor hadn't confirmed it), was already at work on the assembly line at Morrell's when her husband got home. He went to bed as usual, expecting that when Larisa came back after work, she would get into bed and awaken him when his alarm went off the next morning.

But Larisa did not come home that night. The next day, her Caravan was found in its usual place at the Morrell's parking lot. The vehicle was empty, the wheel was turned sharply to the right, and one front tire was flat.

Robert Anderson didn't become a suspect in Mrs. Dumansky's disappearance until the summer of 1996, when authorities interviewed Jamie Hammer in the immediate aftermath of Piper Streyle's abduction. But even then prosecutors understood they needed a lot more than Jamie Hammer's uncorroborated testimony to win a capital murder conviction. Just having a strong suspicion that Anderson had murdered both women was not enough to take before a jury. No body had yet been found in either case.

They didn't have long to wait.

In late May 1997, following Anderson's conviction for kidnapping Piper Streyle, another of his friends came forth with more startling revelations. Glenn Walker, who like Hammer had known Anderson for years, also recalled that his friend's abduction-murder fantasies dated back to high school. "He said he'd really like to try suffocating a woman," Walker recounted, "and then bring her back and then suffocate her and bring her back and just torment her."

Walker had critically important and concrete information as well: the location of Larisa Dumansky's remains—or what was left of them. He took police to a remote roadside location and pointed at a spot beneath a chokecherry tree, saying Anderson had admitted burying his victim there. Walker also recalled what Anderson had confided concerning the details of Larisa Dumansky's final moments.

He said Anderson smirked when he told of putting a knife to her throat in Morrell's parking lot, threatening to kill her instantly if she made a sound. He drove her out to the countryside, according to Walker, and raped her four or five times. She didn't resist at all, but pleaded for her life, telling Anderson she was pregnant. She promised not to tell anyone about the assault if only he'd let her live. Instead, Walker told authorities, Anderson wrapped Dumansky's mouth and nose in duct tape and watched her struggle as she suffocated. Then he buried her beneath the bush. A forensics team recovered scattered fragments of Larisa Dumansky's skeleton at the site, as well as portions of her belt and shoes.

In July 1997, principally on the strength of Jamie Hammer and Glenn Walker's testimony, along with the crucial recovery of Larisa Dumansky's partial remains, Mark Barnett was confident that he had enough evidence to charge Anderson with both the Dumansky and the Streyle slayings. What the attorney general couldn't know was that Anderson was about to stick his own head in the noose.

A month after his sentencing for the kidnapping of Mrs. Streyle, Anderson's cellmate in the administrative segregation section at the South Dakota State Penitentiary secretly contacted authorities with word that Anderson had been talking to him. The man, a small-time drug dealer and thief named Jeremy Brunner, had shared a cell with Anderson for a week, and during that time Anderson apparently had gone into great detail about the murders. He even drew a map showing where he had hidden trophies of his victims, as well as his handcuffs (remember the keys?) and the 9-mm handgun he had carried with him the day he abducted Piper Streyle. What's more, Anderson sought to recruit Brunner in a plot to kill Glenn Walker and to frame another man for the killings.

Brunner, twenty-two, used a fake rap sheet to trick Anderson into believing he had once beaten an attempted murder charge. This proved to be sufficient credentials for Anderson to take him into his confidence. "He asked me how I got away with my murder charge, and that's how the ball started rolling," Brunner later testified.

He said Anderson described himself as a serial murderer "because a serial killer saves something from each of his victims." Brunner's cell mate seemed to relish retelling the crimes. "It was every day, besides when we were sleeping," said Brunner, "and we weren't sleeping too much. It was just like he was reliving it."

Anderson described targeting Larisa Dumansky for murder at least three months before carrying out his crime, Brunner said. He also implicated Glenn Walker in the crime. According to Brunner, Anderson said Walker had assisted in Mrs. Dumansky's abduction but had declined to participate in her rape and murder. Instead, Walker went home, where Anderson later showed up with Larissa Dumansky's body in his trunk. He demanded that Walker bury the victim for him, thereby implicating him even further in the crime.

Brunner said Anderson told him that Walker was also with him on the night he unsuccessfully attempted to abduct Amy Anderson.

Glenn Walker later pled guilty to three criminal counts. One, conspiracy to kidnap Larisa Dumansky; two, the attempted kidnapping of Amy Anderson; and three, being an accessory to commit first-degree murder and kidnapping." He is serving a thirty-year sentence for the three counts.

Anderson bragged about the Streyle murder, too. He told his cell mate that he had been surprised to find Vance Streyle at home on the Friday morning before the successful abduction. On the second visit the following Monday, Anderson brought his 9 mm, intending to shoot Mr. Streyle, if necessary, he told Brunner.

He said he had also revisited Larisa Dumansky's two-year-old grave under the chokecherry bush that weekend because he had come to distrust Glenn Walker's willingness to remain silent. He intended to remove the physical evidence with which Walker might connect him to Dumansky but didn't do a complete job of it. Anderson partially exhumed Dumansky's skeleton, placing parts of it in a bag, and made sure to take away her skull and teeth, which he told Brunner he tossed from his car window as he drove.

In Canistota, once he had subdued Piper Streyle, Anderson remembered to retrieve the slip of paper with his name and address on it before leaving with her. He told Brunner he raped and manually strangled Mrs. Streyle to death in the Bronco, looking straight into her eyes as he did so. "It's the rush right before you do it," Brunner quoted Anderson, "and the rush of having a total stranger do what you want."

Before taking her out to his preselected disposal site by the Big Sioux River near Baltic, Anderson remembered two other items at the trailer that could implicate him. One was his watch, which he'd left behind. The other was little Nathan's new blue tent. During an initial scuffle with Piper Streyle, Anderson's 9 mm had discharged a round that passed through the tent, a shag rug, and the floor under it. (The bullet was recovered from beneath the trailer after Brunner provided this information.)

Anderson put his dead victim on the floorboards, he said, and drove back through town to the trailer to fetch both the watch and the tent. He told Brunner he threw some of Piper Streyle's belongings from the Bronco as he drove. He disposed of her nude body in the river, he said.

Given his criminal background and the fact that his testimony had won him a brief release from prison (Brunner was soon rearrested for possession of methamphetamines and trying to sell bogus LSD and was returned to custody), his sworn evidence as to what Robert Anderson allegedly told him might not have convinced a jury.

But he produced two maps, each in Anderson's hand, and each bearing Anderson's thumbprint.

One guided investigators to Glenn Walker's house in Kansas City, Missouri. Brunner said he was supposed to arrange to kill Walker there. The second one revealed the location of his 9 mm and his handcuffs, tucked away above a doorway in Anderson's mother's basement. Also found in this hiding spot were his victim trophies, rings he had taken from Piper Streyle and the necklace that Larisa Dumansky was wearing the night of her murder.

*   *   *

Robert Leroy Anderson, through his behavior and his conversations with others, provided me with a treasure trove of information about himself. The details Hammer provided show that Anderson was well advanced along the Augustinian five-step continuum as early as fourteen years of age when he was already scripting his play. By the time he committed the Dumansky murder, he had been fantasizing about the crime in explicit detail for at least eight years!

The longer a sexual offender fantasizes prior to committing his crimes, the more specific his desired victim's characteristics will be. Leonard Lake, for instance, said on his video that he preferred his victims to be eighteen to twenty-two years of age, slim, petite, small breasted, with "shoulder length hair if I'm allowed." Anderson also selected his known murder victims according to particular criteria. He told others that he was attracted to Mrs. Streyle because of her legs and to Larisa Dumansky because of her hips.

As mentioned, I didn't believe that Amy Anderson was a random victim either. To suggest that such an organized offender just happened to select Ms. Anderson's car would be too much of a coincidence. After all, he had been in her place of employment several times prior to the abduction attempt. Furthermore, I believe that had Ms. Anderson's tire gone flat before she dropped off Stacy Hazen, Robert Anderson and his accomplice would have attempted to abduct both young women.

Fantasy's role in planning the offense also explains why Anderson modified his car to make night surveillance simpler and easier. He had an acquaintance install a toggle switch to manipulate the front and rear lighting on his vehicle and removed his dome light bulb so that it would not come on when he opened the doors.

I learned this information about vehicular modification with a twinge of recognition. When I was in Binghamton, New York, working on organized crime investigations in the mid-1970s, I often did automobile surveillance at night. I had the Bureau mechanic install switches that darkened either headlight and either or both taillights. This device allowed me to observe a person for long periods at night without being "made." My car became known as "the Batmobile" among my FBI colleagues. How eerie that Anderson had used a similar ploy, not to further justice, but to foil it.

3

INSIDE THE FANTASY

Sexual crimes begin as fantasy, but fortunately only a small minority of fantasies lead to sexual crimes. According to mental health professionals, everyone harbors hidden desires, if only fleetingly. Yet for the vast majority, simply contemplating forbidden acts seems to suffice. Most of us never seriously consider bringing those reveries to reality.

The sexual offender crosses the threshold where others do not. No one knows exactly why an individual graduates from simply imagining his crimes to what the serial killer, Ted Bundy, called "inappropriate acting out." A number of factors probably intersect, but all of them stem from the compulsions to express anger and assert power.

We are fortunate that most sexual offenders do not invest as much time in fantasy as did Robert Leroy Anderson. If they did, law enforcement would have a much harder time identifying and apprehending the sexual criminal.

To help investigators and mental health professionals differentiate between those who have complex and ritualistic fantasies and those who do not, Dr. Janet Warren of the University of Virginia and I developed a typology for sexual offenders.

We divided our subjects into two categories: "impulsive" and "ritualistic," terms for sexual criminals that are comparable to the "organized/disorganized" dichotomy that

John Douglas of the BSU and I had developed earlier for killers. This simple distinction not only helps define an offender's type of fantasy but also helps determine the manner in which he is likely to act it out.

THE IMPULSIVE OFFENDER

This is not an intelligent criminal. He is apt to be dull witted and foolish and is least successful at evading identification and apprehension. As the term *impulsive* suggests, he lacks discipline and self-control. He makes poor decisions and carries out his crimes in an unplanned, unsophisticated manner.

An example of such a criminal (although not a sexual offender) was a thief who was once featured, appropriately enough, on a TV show about the world's most stupid criminals.

On the program a woman reported to passing police officers that her purse had just been snatched, and she provided a very good description of the man who did it. Two blocks away officers arrested him with the handbag still in his possession. They advised him of his rights and then told him that they were going to take him back to the victim for a positive identification.

Upon arrival, and before the woman could say anything, the suspect pointed his finger at her and said, "Yep, that's the woman I took the purse from." Now that's what I call a positive identification! It's also a good example of the impulsive offender.

About the only thing that impulsive and ritualistic offenders share in common is an underlying need for power, feelings of anger, or a combination of the two. At that point all similarity ceases between the two.

The impulsive offender lacks clarity or definition and so do his fantasies. Actually, what goes on in his mind probably doesn't rise to the level of full-scale fantasy. Whereas a ritualistic offender, such as Robert Leroy Anderson, might paint his mental pictures with patience, intelligence, close attention to detail and texture from a richly hued palette, the impulsive offender deals in stick figures. His imaginings are simple and crude, more like fragmented thoughts than well-defined scripts.

The victim appears to him in primitive terms: female-available-vulnerable. She may be a stranger, his wife, a girlfriend, or a street prostitute. He is not a discriminating criminal. Women, to him, serve a single function: They are disposable vessels for gratification. This one-dimensional attitude toward the opposite sex ties in with his view of his role in the crime, a perspective of entitlement: "I want to do it, so I will."

I have interviewed a large number of impulsive offenders over the years, and among them one trait stands out: These men report giving little or no thought to their crimes until they actually encounter their victims. An impulsive offender may decide to commit a crime before leaving home but no further planning takes place until he actually sees the potential victim.

For example, I was called to consult on the case of a serial rapist in Texas who was known to be responsible for at least six assaults. Representative of his modus operandi was a crime he carried out early one Saturday morning.

He had been roaming through a neighborhood, armed with a handgun and intending to burglarize an apartment. He suddenly decided to target a particular second-story apartment, even though it would have been much simpler to enter one on the first floor. He had no idea who or how many people resided inside the apartment or even if anyone was home. He wore no mask, disguise, or gloves. He simply decided that was where he would commit his crime, and he wanted to do it, so he did.

He climbed the patio fence of the occupied downstairs apartment, swung up to the second-floor balcony, and put his shoulder to the locked French doors, tearing them from their hinges as he knocked the door frame loose, creating quite a disturbance.

A woman and her male companion were sleeping together inside. The man got up to check on the noise and was confronted by our impulsive offender, who, until that moment, had thought only of burglarizing the residence. But after discovering the woman, he decided to exploit her availability and vulnerability. Producing his handgun, he ordered the man into a closet with a warning not to interfere or he and the woman would both be killed.

Every phase of the sexual assault was brutal. He forced the woman to perform fellatio and then raped her anally. He was liberally profane, threatening, and demanding as he spoke to her. If the victim was slow to comply, he struck her repeatedly until she did as she was ordered. Before fleeing out the front door, he placed the woman in her bathroom shower and ransacked the apartment.

From beginning to end, his attack showed the recklessness that is so characteristic of the impulsive sex offender. He randomly selected his target with no concern for potential risk and then impulsively seized the chance to sexually assault an available victim, taking no precautions to protect his identity.

THE RITUALISTIC OFFENDER

If the impulsive offender is a glutton, then the ritualistic offender is a connoisseur of his crime.

He is the thinking criminal, a virtuoso of his own aberrant urges. He spends enormous amounts of time in fantasy, carefully working out the details before acting out the mechanics of his ritualized sexual offense. This offender is not as frequently encountered as the impulsive criminal, perhaps because he is more successful in evading detection. The ritualistic offender is cunning, methodical, and usually invisible. He's Ted Bundy, Leonard Lake, Christopher Wilder. Unfortunately, he can also be your neighbor, coworker, or some anonymous employee behind a counter at your local mall. Neither his appearance nor his behavior provides a clue to his dark desires.

Depending on the amount of information available, it is generally a simple task for the trained analyst to determine whether a given criminal is ritualistic or impulsive. Yet even after I establish to my satisfaction that a sexual criminal is indeed ritualistic, I still have a lot of work to do. All ritualistic offenders bring different, individual perspectives to a crime.

By way of analogy, think of a baseball team. All nine players are members of the same club; but they can bring widely differing skills, mental approaches, and levels of experience to the game. A long ball slugger, for example, goes about the game very differently than the spray hitter. Third basemen and pitchers do not see the action on the field in the same way. The same is true with ritualistic offenders; there are many types.

To narrow down the complexities of so many individual offenders, Dr. Warren and I identified five specific components that are common to all ritualistic offenders' fantasies. We call them:

1 RELATIONAL

2 PARAPHILIC

3 SITUATIONAL

4 VICTIM DEMOGRAPHICS

5 SELF-PERCEPTIONAL

RELATIONAL

The relational component is whatever the offender fantasizes the relationship between himself and his victim to be.

Within this category we see a wide range of behaviors. For instance, although these men target strangers as victims, the most common relational fantasy I have encountered among them is boyfriend-girlfriend, husband-wife, or lover. At the opposite end of the relational continuum is the fantasy of "master-slave."

To define a rapist's relational fantasy, I examine his crimes through a three-step process: (1) learning what the offender said to the victim and/or demanded that she say to him; (2) interpreting the amount of physical violence that he used against the victim; and (3) ascertaining the type and sequence of sexual acts involved.

For example, an offender who is acting out a "boyfriend-girlfriend" fantasy is typically not profane and can be even complimentary. He uses little or no physical force, preferring the types of sexual acts I call "criminal foreplay" (i.e., kissing, caressing, and cunnilingus), behavior that reflects his desire to have the victim become (in his mind) an active, willing partner.

On the other hand, a perpetrator acting out a master-slave relational fantasy will degrade his victim verbally with epithets such as "slut," "whore," or "bitch." He demands subservience.

I would expect a high level of physical violence, possibly involving whipping, slapping, or hitting, and the use of painful restraints, such as handcuffs or chains. His sexual acts of choice are intended to degrade and humiliate his victim.

In a sexual homicide, testimony from the victim, of course, is not available; however, investigators can make inferences from other sources.

A few of the methods we use include: (1) accounts given by informants; (2) the nature and extent of injuries sustained by the victim; (3) the materials recovered from the offender; and (4) the theme of his pornography collection.

Robert Leroy Anderson, for example, had a master-slave

relational fantasy. He told Glenn Walker, "It's the rush . . . of having a total stranger do what you want." Anderson repeatedly told Glenn Walker that Larisa Dumansky pleaded with him to do with her what he wanted but not to hurt her. These entreaties, of course, were in vain.

Compare this behavior with that of the offender who fantasizes a husband-wife relationship with his victim. "Tom"* was such a rapist. Responsible for eighteen assaults, he interacted with his victims in a highly individual way. Tom would capture a victim and take her to a river or lake. There he would instruct her to periodically ask the following questions: "Do we have enough money to get the kids' teeth fixed this year?" "What is your bowling average?" "Have you rented the mountain cabin yet?" "When are you going to get the refrigerator fixed?"

Most people would laugh at such nonsense, but to the behavioral scientist, it is critical information. These questions tell me what is in Tom's mind, what fantasy he is trying to bring to reality.

PARAPHILIC

The second component of the ritualistic offender's fantasy world is its paraphilic dimension. *Paraphilia* is the preferred mental health term for sexual deviation. Sexual sadism is a paraphilia, as are voyeurism, masochism, transvestitism, fetishism, telephone scatology, exhibitionism, pedophilia, and necrophilia, to name a few. The ritualistic offender will have a paraphilic fantasy, and he will almost always express this deviance in his crimes.

Robert Leroy Anderson, for example, demonstrated at least two paraphilias: sexual bondage (not officially recognized by the American Psychiatric Association as a paraphilia but generally accepted as one) and sexual sadism.

*Denotes pseudonyms throughout the text.

SITUATIONAL

The third facet of fantasy is the situational component. What circumstance or setting does the offender wish to realize? To help my audiences understand the meaning of the term *situational* I use my lectures as an analogy. They take place in a situation, or setting, of the classroom; and the relationship between myself and the people in the audience is teacher-student.

Anderson's situational fantasy was a torture chamber. He constructed a platform that conformed to his Bronco's cargo space. He had materials to restrain his victim. He also had implements to cause his victim's suffering. In essence, he had created a dungeon within his Bronco.

At the opposite end of the situational continuum, Tom's situational fantasy was domestic, a "home and hearth" setting for his rapes.

VICTIM DEMOGRAPHICS

The fourth component is victim demographics. Recall that the impulsive offender's victim criterion is simply a female who is vulnerable. Not so with the ritualistic criminal. As a result of the great amount of time he spends in fantasizing, this imaginative offender develops highly specific selection standards for his victims. Leonard Lake, as we've noted, always looked for a slim, petite, small-breasted female of eighteen to twenty-two, with shoulder-length blonde hair.

Pedophiles select victims by gender and age but may also have a preference for victims of a particular race, hair color, or even a particular nose shape. Necrophiliacs require a dead victim, of course; beyond that their fantasies are wide-ranging. Whatever the ritualistic offender's demographic profile, it will always be specific to his, or her, fantasy.

SELF-PERCEPTIONAL

The final area of fantasy is the self-perceptional component. How does the offender fantasize his role in the crime? The continuum here ranges from godlike omnipotence to feelings of extreme inadequacy.

Examples of the first type abound. Paul Bernardo, the "Ken" of Toronto's infamous husband-and-wife, "Ken and Barbie," sexual murders forced his victims (including "Barbie," his wife, Karla Homolka) to call him "master." By contrast, San Diego serial rapist Kenneth Bogard, just like Tom, imagined himself the desirable object of his victims' affections.

Never mind that it was necessary to kidnap someone in order to play out their scenarios. Judging from the number of victims the two offenders involved in their fantasies, Bogard and Tom obviously never tired of repeating them.

4

FANTASY MADE REAL

Intelligent and cunning for the most part, ritualistic offenders take a wide variety of routes in pursuit of their hidden desires. With their vivid imaginations, they generate an astonishing array of perversely creative ideas.

They may coerce a wife or girlfriend into helping them realize their fantasies, or they may kidnap, rape, or kill a stranger. But it is important to know that sexual criminals don't always require victims. A ritualistic offender may also enact his fantasy using inanimate objects, paid partners, compliant partners (wives or girlfriends), or even himself.

Also, his behavior may or may not escalate from passive fantasy to outright assault. Any level of behavior may be an end in itself, as is usually true of dangerous autoeroticism. Or the offender may act out in multiple ways at the same time.

For example, he may seek out an aberrant, albeit non-criminal, sexual experience even as he is committing rapes and murders.

INANIMATE OBJECTS

Many sexual criminals who act out against inanimate objects fixate on an article of women's clothing or some other intimate female possession. Others select a surrogate figure, such as a doll or even photographs of an imagined victim from a magazine.

Two cases involving dolls show how disturbing this behavior can be. The first, brought to my attention in the early 1980s, occurred at a university hospital where a curly haired baby doll was discovered in the men's locker room outside the surgical center. The doll was suspended from a white cord, a hangman's noose around its neck.

The toy had been systematically mutilated. Its skin was scorched, and pubic hairs were glued around its groin. An opening had been cut between the doll's legs, and a long pencil had been deeply inserted into it. The doll's wrists were bound behind its back, and a wad of blue tissue paper was jammed into its mouth. Long needles were used to pierce the doll's left eye. On the left side of its chest, approximately where a heart would be, there was an incision, neatly sutured with black thread.

The perpetrator was identified as a premed student working as a surgical scrub assistant. Since he had not committed a crime, no charges were filed against this clearly troubled young man. In truth, he may not have been a physical danger to anyone. Acting out against the doll might have satisfied his fantasy. I wouldn't wager on it though. Luckily, he agreed to seek professional help.

The second case involved behavior sometimes known as pygmalionism, after the mythological sculptor who created an ivory statue of an idealized woman and then fell in love with his own artwork.

A deputy sheriff in a suburban Louisiana community responded at about 4:30 one morning to a burglar alarm at a local discount variety store. The intruder was alerted by the police sirens and slipped out the back door undetected. He left behind a blonde-wigged female mannequin, disassembled at the waist and lying on the floor. The figure's upper body was clothed in a pinafore blouse, and its white-gloved left hand was broken at the wrist.

The UNSUB had removed a light-colored skirt from her

lower body, but the mannequin's hose and panties were undisturbed, as were the dark-colored high heels on its feet. The trespasser's loafers and a black wig rested on the floor near the mannequin's head. An open box of condoms, taken from the store's pharmacy section, rested on the floor nearby.

As in the hospital case, this scene obviously was the work of a disturbed mind. Still, on the evidence available, I can't say what sort of threat, if any, he posed to the community.

Now let's look at still another offender who acted out against inanimate objects. This individual revealed himself as complex, resourceful, and unambiguously a threat to his chosen victim.

Like most law enforcement officers, I tend to title my more intriguing cases. I call this one "the cartoon case," though it was certainly no laughing matter. It remains one of the most interesting and unusual investigations of my career.

The cartoon case began in the early 1980s when Evelyn Smith,* twenty-nine-year-old wife and mother of two small children, living in a midsized New England community, received a call at home from a man claiming to represent a bra manufacturer. The caller told Mrs. Smith that his company had developed a new line of women's undergarments that they were marketing in the region. He invited her to take part in a customer satisfaction survey, offering to send Mrs. Smith six free bras if she would agree to complete a questionnaire assessing their durability, washability, comfort, and fit. She agreed to this proposal and, in an incautious moment she would long regret, revealed her bra size.

The caller unexpectedly said nothing more, so Mrs. Smith hung up and forgot about the conversation. However, about six weeks later the man phoned again to announce that he had her bras and wished to bring them over. Mrs. Smith stalled, telling him that she would have to talk to her husband. She asked him to call back in two days.

When he did, she informed him of her decision not to

participate further in the project. "He asked me what I was afraid of," she later told the police. "Did I think he was going to come over and bite off my tit?"

Shocked, she hung up.

The phone rang again a short time later. "It's a good day for a top down," the familiar voice said. "How about I come over and take yours down?" Again Mrs. Smith hung up the phone.

Two months later she received in the mail four crude cartoons that depicted her likeness in various degrading positions. In one, the female figure was bound and gagged as a masked male figure undressed and raped her. The accompanying text listed her bra size, along with several slang expressions for breasts, and made dark mention of Mrs. Smith's having to earn "her keep" in captivity. Another drawing showed a man holding a knife to her neck as he tore off her bra with his other hand.

Frightened for her safety, Mrs. Smith went to the local police. Fortunately, they took the complaint seriously, and telephone traps were put on her phones. But the police were never able to pinpoint where the calls came from. The victim's attempts at tape recording the calls were not much more successful.

Her anonymous tormentor called once more to say that he knew a brown, unmarked police car had been parked in front of the Smith family residence earlier—which was true. During this call he also delivered an ultimatum. He said he wanted to meet her, and if she didn't cooperate fully, someday he would be waiting for her when she came home. "He stated that he didn't want to hurt me," Mrs. Smith reported, "but his attitude on the phone was threatening."

He told her, "If you don't meet me voluntarily, I'll have to force you; but then it wouldn't be as enjoyable for both of us. I don't want to use force, but I will if I have to."

A few days later a second envelope arrived in the mail. This one contained four more violent cartoons, each explicitly portraying her forced abduction, sexual bondage, and rape. Then five months of silence followed.

When he called again, Mrs. Smith finally got his voice on tape.

"Remember our last conversation?" he asked. "I gave you a choice. You can meet me voluntarily, or I can do it the hard way."

After consulting with detectives, she agreed to meet the man, hoping to lure him into a trap. Three investigators staked out the agreed location, where Mrs. Smith arrived on schedule and waited for forty-five minutes. When the UNSUB failed to make contact, she gave up, conferred briefly with the officers, and then drove home.

Later that afternoon he called again. He said he had watched her in the parking lot, that he had seen her speaking with three men, and that he knew they were police officers. Then he made a new suggestion. He said he would leave her alone on condition that she place two of her bras in a paper bag and drop them into a Salvation Army clothing bin located in a vacant lot across from a fire station.

Again Mrs. Smith notified the police, who once more tried to trap him. She deposited the bras in the bin as directed, and officers kept close watch on it throughout the night and into the next morning. They saw nothing.

Believing the subject had decided not to retrieve the bras, the police went to the bin only to discover they were gone! Unknown to the police, the container had a trapdoor on the back side. Sometime during the night the offender must have crawled through the vacant lot to the bin, opened the trapdoor, and retrieved his prize—Mrs. Smith's two bras.

A month passed. Then one day Mrs. Smith received a package postmarked from a distant state. Inside, she found several more bras, including portions of the two she had left in the bin.

The words, "I want to suck your stiff nipples," were printed on one cup. "I loved stripping you in my mind, next in person!!" appeared on another. Semen stains discolored the fabrics. Also included in the package was the cover of a detective magazine, depicting a man standing behind a woman with a knife to her throat. Her bra is slipping from her breasts. The word "Me" is printed over the male, and over the female was the name "Evelyn."

Another long, ominous silence ensued.

Then came one last menacing note, written on the stationery of a Holiday Inn in a neighboring community.

"You're lucky I didn't go through with my plans for you, Evelyn," it read. "I had everything all set. I had a reservation made in your husband's name, I had tape to tie your hands with, and a Polaroid to take pictures of you tied up and naked. I'm not sure why I let you off this time— maybe next time I won't. My plans were perfect, had I decided to go through with them you would have been completely at my mercy. In fact you still are."

Accompanying the note were Polaroid photographs of a man, presumably the caller himself, nude except for a ski mask.

The police at last had a solid lead. Reasoning that the subject might actually have stayed at the motel, they arranged to examine each of its rooms, comparing the decor with the background in the photograph. Eventually they found an exact match. It was then a simple matter to determine from the motel records who had stayed in that room on the day the letter was mailed.

The suspect proved to be Andrew Johnstone,* a businessman in his early thirties with no known criminal history. Authorities arrested Johnstone at the airport as he returned from a business trip. Inside his briefcase they found a three-ring binder containing approximately one hundred detective magazine covers.

It's pretty clear that the relational component of Johnstone's fantasy was hunter-prey. Not surprisingly, he also exhibited multiple paraphilias, or sexually deviant behaviors. Obviously, he had a fetish for bras. He had demonstrated intense interest in them throughout the case, apparently collected them, and he masturbated onto them. He was also sexually fixated on breasts. Such an aberrant attraction to a body part has been called *partialism,* but that is an old term that has largely fallen out of use.

It was useful to the investigation to be aware of the subject's breast fixation. When Johnstone was identified, detectives knew that he probably collected pictures of breasts, magazines featuring them, or other material relating to them.

Johnstone's fetish meant he also might try to incorporate bras into his sex life, perhaps by asking partners to model them for his voyeuristic pleasure. From both his written and oral communications, it was apparent that this offender had watched Mrs. Smith over time, and he wrote of wanting to see her tied up, a strong indication of voyeurism.

In the profile I prepared for the cartoon case, I wrote that the UNSUB was a bondage practitioner. The cartoons he drew had vividly suggested this theme. When he sent the letter on motel stationery to Mrs. Smith, he wrote about her being tied up and helpless. He specifically mentioned captivity, too. Clearly, the situational component of his fantasy was captivity.

Yet another paraphilia suggested by the evidence was sexual sadism. Consider this fantasy, as he described it to her: "I had a Polaroid to take pictures of you tied up and naked . . . You would have been completely at my mercy. In fact, you still are."

The case information is insufficient to infer Johnstone's ideal type of victim. We don't know, for example, why he chose to telephone Mrs. Smith in the first place. We can assume, however, that she fit his criteria, at least in breast size. Otherwise he would not have devoted so much time to her or put so much effort into learning about her.

The self-perception fantasy was simple to isolate. This offender fantasized himself as being all-knowing and all-powerful—godlike. Note that he phoned to tell her about the brown police car and the undercover officers who were watching her at the meeting place. He also warned that if she didn't cooperate, he would be waiting for her in her home. Finally, he threatened harm. "If you don't meet voluntarily, I'll have to force you," he said.

He wanted her to believe he knew everything that happened, that he could enter her home at will, and that he was prepared to use whatever force necessary to have his way. To reinforce these messages, a short time later he sent her more cartoons depicting forced abduction, sexual bondage, and rape. Thus did he try to put himself in a position of power and reinforce Mrs. Smith's fear.

I was particularly interested that Mrs. Smith heard from her tormentor at unpredictable intervals, from a day or so up to five months apart. In many investigations, overworked investigators too quickly assume that if the UNSUB is not acting out, he has moved, died, been hospitalized, institutionalized, or joined the military. This assumption is usually true, but not always.

The sexual offender is never fully inactive. He may not be acting out against a specific victim, but he will be making plans, selecting new targets, acting out against other victims, or gathering materials. He is never dormant.

Johnstone chose not to act until he was ready. There are theories of criminal behavior based on statistical data, but don't expect the criminals to pay attention to them. Offenders are in charge of their fantasies, and they decide how, when, where, and if they'll act on them. I once consulted on a serial murder case in Florence, Italy, where the killer struck once every seven years! But his behavior was no less dangerous because of its intermittent nature.

In my opinion Johnstone realized that his lack of predictability made him more difficult to catch. Not following a pattern accorded him an enhanced sense of control, thus feeding his all-powerful self-perception. When months passed with no developments in the case, the police naturally turned their attention to more urgent matters. The delays between incidents were also a way for Johnstone to manipulate Mrs. Smith. She would live in dread of the next call or package, but when nothing occurred for several months, she allowed herself to hope the nightmare was over. Then suddenly, according to his whim, he would be back in her life, as though no time had passed at all.

Johnstone was an archetypal ritualistic sexual criminal who put considerable creative thought into his work. Successfully retrieving Mrs. Smith's two bras from the Salvation Army bin not only underscored how deeply he desired to possess them, but also showed the careful planning he devoted to the scheme.

Thinking criminals are keen students of their own crimes, honing their skills with each offense, learning from their mistakes. But they also reach out for enlightenment wherever it may be found. Like many deviant offenders, Johnstone was an avid consumer of detective magazines. At the time of his arrest, a hundred of them were found in his possession.

In the Behavioral Science Unit, we called detective magazines "rape and murder manuals." In fact, it was because detective magazines played such an important role in the cartoon case, that my frequent research partner, the eminent forensic psychiatrist Dr. Park Dietz, and I, together with Bruce Harry, another forensic psychiatrist, decided to make a survey of the genre.

Working with a broad sample of three thousand detective magazines from numerous publishers throughout the United States, we focused on the periodicals' covers, editorial content, and advertisements.

Anyone even vaguely familiar with these pulp publications knows the primary theme of their cover art: partially undressed women with frightened expressions, bound by some sort of ligature, and under menace by a weapon-wielding male. The stories tend to be true-crime tales or articles on investigative techniques, interrogation methods, and the forensic capabilities of law enforcement.

Advertisements almost invariably are directed at the inadequate male. He's told he can learn how to hypnotize women from across the room; how to increase the size of his penis; how to become a private investigator; how to acquire police paraphernalia and identification. This last offer is more ominous than it may at first seem, as in several cases police badges have been used by serial offenders to capture their victims.

Ted Bundy was probably the best-known consumer of detective magazines. He studied abduction and murder stories in them to learn what had worked or hadn't worked for other deviant offenders. In the process he no doubt found material to feed his unique fantasies of possession.

One staple of the pulp genre is the police-stop story, in which an offender poses as a law officer to bring a potential victim under his control. Bundy used the ploy several times himself. Angelo Buono, murder partner with Ken Bianchi in the infamous Hillside Strangler cases, also used a police badge to abduct women. From his extensive records, we know that the counterfeiter and sexual sadist James Mitchell DeBardeleben, known as Mike, a serial offender who traveled throughout the United States, ordered police badges through ads in detective magazines and similarly used them as abduction props.

Returning to the cartoon case, many readers may wonder, if Johnstone was so intelligent, why did he send Mrs. Smith the incriminating pictures that led to his arrest? Why did he use the motel stationery that enabled authorities to identify him?

The answer is narcissism.

Because he had successfully eluded detection for so long and with such apparent ease, Johnstone grew overconfident, believing himself too smart for the police to catch. Consequently, he let his guard down and took unnecessary chances. He must have felt that no matter what he did, he would never be caught.

For many ritualistic offenders, taking risks intensifies the thrill of the crime. Stealing Mrs. Smith's bras off her clothesline might have been a safer, surer way of securing them, but that couldn't compare to the ingenious way in which he extracted them from the donation box while it was under direct police surveillance.

PAID PARTNERS

Ritualistic offenders also act out their deviant fantasies with paid partners. Experienced sexual crimes investigators know that when an offender commits his crimes in a ritualistic manner, they should contact local prostitutes. He likely has attempted to enact with them the same fantasies he plays out with his victims.

In one intriguing California case, an expensive call girl was found dead at a deluxe hotel in a bathtub full of water. The room had been rented under an alias and paid for in advance with cash. The victim was nude. Her hands were bound behind her back, and she had been strangled with a man's tie.

Medical evidence indicated vaginal intercourse occurred perimortem, that is, just at the time of her death. It appeared the perpetrator had bound her and placed her in the tub, where he strangled her as they were having sex.

Investigators wisely sought out other high-priced prostitutes in the vicinity, asking if any of them remembered encountering customers who desired a similar sort of sex. Two of the women reported such a client, a business executive who subsequently was identified, tried, and convicted of the murder.

COMPLIANT VICTIMS

Some ritualistic offenders (most commonly sexual sadists) act out fantasies with compliant victims, usually wives or girlfriends. The compliant victims I have interviewed report that they often were used as props for the deviant fantasies of their mates. Other times, they were rehearsal partners, stand-ins for future victims.

It is not unusual for a sexual sadist to force his victim to sign a "slave contract," a physical representation of the master-slave relational fantasy. One of these women described to me the strict rules she was expected to observe. For example, skirts slit up the sides to her upper thighs were all that she was allowed to wear on her lower body. He permitted no underwear, and she was not allowed to cross her legs in his presence.

This man's deviant interests included fetishism, necrophilia, sadism, and masochism. To help him act out these paraphilias, she sometimes was made to wear fetish items during sex. At other times he directed her to take cold baths and then to lie perfectly still so he could pretend she was dead. On still other occasions, he would demand that she whip him.

Mike DeBardeleben acted out his fantasies against at least four of his five wives. To enhance his pleasure, he even tape-recorded torture sessions with one of them, his fourth wife, Caryn.*

As I listened to the Caryn tapes, I noted his pattern of demanding she call him "Daddy" and beg him to physically abuse her according to a script he forced her to memorize. Then, for comparison, I listened to tapes that DeBardeleben had made with Becky,* one of his stranger-victims. His demands and behavior with both women were virtually identical.

"Do you like the pain?" he asked both partners.

"Yes, I like the pain," both Caryn and Becky answered.

"Do you love the pain?"

"Yes, I love the pain."

"How much do you love the pain?"

"I love it a lot."

Caryn had served as his rehearsal partner for victims such as Becky and countless others.

AUTOEROTICISM

Finally, ritualistic offenders sometimes act out using themselves as props or "costars," if you will. Some years ago, Dr. Park Dietz, Prof. Ann Wolbert Burgess of the University of Pennsylvania, and I researched and wrote the first textbook ever devoted to fatal autoeroticism. We found that such deaths were basically masochistic. That is, most of the 150 victims we studied were acting out masochistic fantasies at the times of their accidental deaths.

Yet masochism wasn't the only feature we detected. A large percentage of the victims also were cross-dressed when they were discovered, a provocative finding that opened a new avenue of speculation. While I still believe the great majority of deaths due to dangerous autoeroticism are grounded in the victims' masochistic fantasies, the males who cross-dress may not be fantasizing only masochistic plots. They may also be acting out sadistic fantasies using themselves as replacements for women who are unsatisfactory, unavailable, or unwilling.

The case of the late Gerard John Schaefer, a Florida deputy sheriff, supports this theory. Shaefer is believed to have kidnapped and killed more than twenty young women, disposing of them in remote swamps. In a photo that he doubtlessly took, Shaefer appears cross-dressed and suspended from a tree in the swamp. From his extensive writings, it is clear that one of his preferred ways of killing his victims was by hanging them exactly this way.

In a similar vein, one of Mike DeBardeleben's abduction-rape victims reported that after he took her to a safe, prearranged location, he changed into a miniskirt and high heels as he bound and photographed her. On a self-recorded audiotape at a different time, DeBardeleben also directly assumed the role of the victim, pleading with an imaginary tormentor in a falsetto voice to "bite my titties."

*   *   *

How does a particular offender choose to act out his dangerous fantasies? At what level of experience, from the imaginary to the actual, will a particular person receive sufficient psychosexual gratification? These are the questions that behavioral scientists continue to explore in the quest to identify and apprehend violent sexual criminals. Unfortunately, the ultimate answers likely will be as varied as the details of the crimes themselves.

5

"AM I GOD?"

The fascinating and complex field of mental health often intersects with the world of criminal justice. If you follow the media coverage of sensational crimes, you have undoubtedly heard about instances when a psychiatrist or psychologist is called into a criminal case to testify as to a defendant's mental condition. Issues of sanity or mental competence to stand trial can have a profound impact on a case's outcome.

Equally important is the contribution that an understanding of criminal psychology can make even before an offender is identified, apprehended, and charged. This is where the behavioral scientist's insights can be most useful.

PERSONALITY DISORDERS

According to the American Psychiatric Association, a personality disorder is any human trait that becomes "inflexible and maladaptive," causing a person "either significant functional impairment or subjective distress." This bland description masks what a twisted, tortured thing "significant functional impairment" can be in a serial sexual offender.

There are many types of personality disorders. Examples include the antisocial personality disorder (APD), the borderline personality disorder (brilliantly portrayed by Glenn Close in the film *Fatal Attraction*), the schizoid personality disorder, and the narcissistic personality disorder.

Personality disorders are common among sexual offenders, but they are by no means confined to criminals. They are diagnosed in men and women of all races and in all cultures and of widely varying degrees of mental health. A personality disorder is not something you welcome, any more than you want to get diabetes or emphysema. But being diagnosed with one does not mean you are clinically, or legally, insane or even noticeably different from many other people.

Nor are personality disorders always obstacles to personal success. Quite the opposite. I have encountered successful people who display all the hallmarks of the antisocial personality disorder, commonly called psychopaths, in disciplines as diverse as law enforcement, medicine, sales, professional sports, and television evangelism.

Some personality disorders that are common in the general population (and not necessarily pathological) take on a much different manifestation among aberrant offenders. Many years ago, Park Dietz remarked to me his belief that narcissism is the most common personality disorder among sexual offenders, more prevalent even than antisocial personality disorder. I have found this to be true, particularly among ritualistic sexual criminals.

THE NARCISSIST

Take, for example, Mr. Johnstone, who victimized Mrs. Smith in the cartoon case. His fantasies were of unlimited success and power. He believed that he was special and could be understood only by other special people. He displayed a strong presumption of entitlement. These are the classic characteristics of a narcissist.

The narcissist demands constant admiration. He does not hesitate to take advantage of others to achieve his goals, and he is indifferent to their feelings and needs. Essentially, he believes that he is the only one whose satisfaction counts in this world. Everyone else is just a prop in his background scenery.

A sexual offender's narcissism can be demonstrated in many ways. Before the crime a narcissistic offender exhibits selfishness, self-centeredness, and an inability to accept criticism, even constructive criticism. During the crime the narcissistic criminal may engage in "high-risk" activity, even though he is otherwise an organized offender.

However, the period following a crime is when his narcissism often is most obvious. One of the classic ways in which such an offender betrays his self-centeredness is by courting the media. After Robert Leroy Anderson's murder convictions, for instance, he granted a press interview. Anderson declined to discuss whether or not he was guilty, but he did speak at length about how similar he was to Albert Einstein. The killer told the reporter he planned to read publications about and by Dr. Einstein in the hope of learning more about *TIME* magazine's Man of the Century.

A SHOW-OFF FOR A CLIENT

Of all the self-defeating actions a narcissist's ego commonly leads him to commit, perhaps the most foolish is a defendant's decision to act as his own lawyer. It's axiomatic that such an attorney has a fool for a client, but it is also a measure of how powerful the narcissistic urge can be that a man must show off for the cameras, even if his performance may cost him his life.

In 1979, Ted Bundy was tried and convicted in front of a television audience for the bludgeon murders the year before of two sleeping coeds at the Chi Omega sorority house at Florida State University in Tallahassee. During the rampage he also assaulted three other young women and left them for dead.

I remember watching Bundy on TV as he defended himself. He pulled off a kind of courtroom triple play during an evidentiary hearing when he appeared as the defendant, his own attorney, and as a witness. In his second homicide trial, for the abduction-murder of a twelve-year-old girl in Lake City, Florida, Bundy even managed to marry his girlfriend as he examined her on the stand! Carol Bundy later became the mother of his child.

Part of the motivation for acting as his own attorney is the narcissistic offender's need to assert that he is special. Connected to that is the excitement of reliving his crime on a public stage. At his Chi Omega trial in Miami, Bundy closely cross-examined a police officer, eliciting gruesome details of the crime scene. The information had no particular bearing on the issue of his guilt or innocence, but it certainly impressed the jury with the gory spectacle— Bundy's handiwork.

Bundy also personally took sworn depositions from a number of the coeds who were in the Chi Omega house that night. He led each of the distressed women through a step-by-step reconstruction of what they saw and when they saw it, right down to the plastic bucket with which paramedics caught one victim's blood and teeth as she coughed them out.

Another highly narcissistic offender, Mike DeBardeleben, also acted as his own defense attorney and is well remembered around the Manassas, Virginia, courthouse for his cross-examination of an assault victim. With Lori Cobert on the stand, DeBardeleben lingered over details of her abduction and assault. Courtroom onlookers sensed his delight in reconstructing the crime and victimizing Cobert once again. "I felt he was really getting into it," prosecutor Lee Millette later said.

His pleasure in reliving his crime led the calculating and highly intelligent Mike DeBardeleben to make an uncharacteristic mistake.

"Now, during the incident, inside this man's car it was dark all the time, wasn't it?" he asked Ms. Cobert.

"I could see," she answered.

"The interior lights were not on, were they?"

"No."

"And there were no overhead interior lights, were there?"

"No."

"The only lights they had there were these little small ones next to the door at the bottom of the door, right?"

"Correct."

How did DeBardeleben know about those "little small" lights next to the door if he wasn't there? No mention of them had come out in any reports or testimony. Prosecutor Millette made sure to remind the jury of DeBardeleben's slip-up in his summation. The panel required just thirty-eight minutes to convict.

GRANDSTANDING ON THE STAND

Another reflection of the ritualistic offender's narcissism after a crime is his insistence on testifying, even when his attorneys advise against it, as they usually do. Wayne Williams, the Atlanta child killer, took the stand and seriously harmed his case by becoming combative with the prosecutor. My colleague in the Behavioral Science Unit, John Douglas, consulted with the prosecution in the Williams case. He correctly predicted the defendant would testify no matter what his lawyers advised.

Williams's highly capable lawyer, Al Binder, created a portrait of his client as an oppressed, innocent "victim of an embarrassed, racially biased system that needed a suspect fast and had found one," as Douglas writes in his book, *Mindhunter*.

To counter that impression, Douglas suggested to prosecutor Jack Mallard that he exploit Williams's mental rigidity, keep circling and circling for hours, and then strike with the question, "Did you panic, Wayne, when you killed these kids?"

The ploy worked. When Mallard reached over to touch

the defendant, then ask his question, Williams replied, "No." Immediately, he realized his mistake and let fly a stream of invective against Douglas and the prosecution team. A very different Wayne Williams suddenly flashed into view, and the jurors took note. "They stared with their mouths open," Douglas writes.

JOURNALS OF DEPRAVITY

The narcissist offender expresses himself most revealingly in the ways he preserves a record of his crimes for later use. He may keep diaries, write manuscripts, logs, or journals. Calendars help him plan and remember dates. He may draw maps, invent codes, take photographs, or record audiotapes and videotapes.

I have read countless pages from offenders' notebooks. I have reviewed thousands of still photographs they've taken of their victims. I have listened to tape-recorded tortures, rapes, and murders, as well as the offenders' narrative descriptions and reconstructions of their offenses. And I've watched videos of them interacting with their captives prior to, during, and after sexual assaults.

This material, together with the crime scene itself, is what I call the ritualistic offender's "work product." It is by far the richest and most reliable source of information, not only about him as a criminal, but about his personality as well. You really can't understand a sexual criminal unless you examine his work.

Statistical data provide useful guidelines, but they tell nothing about an individual. Interviews with sexual criminals may yield helpful subjective information (for instance, how does he select victims?), but I can attest from long experience that hard facts, particularly inculpatory information, are usually in short supply when a ritualistic criminal speaks to the police.

Offenders exaggerate, minimize, project, deny, rationalize, and lie, lie, lie. My rule is to accept nothing a sexual criminal tells me unless I can validate it with reliable witnesses, physical trace and/or evidence, or an analysis of his known behavior. In other words I want to study his work product.

Some self-described experts in aberrant criminal behavior reason from the general to the specific, trying to apply what is known about a class of deviant offenders overall to a particular individual sought in connection with a crime. They might say, for example, that since most sexual criminals are white males of European descent, a particular UNSUB is undoubtedly Caucasian, too.

That was the nearly universal supposition in Seattle a decade ago when three young women, all white, all from white, upper-middle-class communities, were raped, bludgeoned to death, and then left horribly displayed—two in their homes, one in a nightclub parking lot. As the writer Jack Olsen skillfully shows in his excellent book, *Charmer: The True Story of a Ladies' Man and His Victims*, the consensus held that the killer was white, too.

But this was not the case. Had investigators not paid close attention to hard evidence, the black male who actually committed the crimes, George Russell, might have gotten away with murder.

The same was true in the Wayne Williams case. When the FBI dispatched me to Atlanta to consult in the child murders, the newspaper stories quoted alleged experts to the effect that a white man was killing Atlanta's black children, and therefore the crimes were racially motivated.

I was certain, from the outset, that a black man was the killer. Why? Because I visited the overwhelmingly black neighborhoods where the youths had disappeared. Any white man attempting to abduct a child would have been noticed and reported at once.

Many law enforcement officials have learned the hard way that it is a mistake to uncritically accept what an offender tells you. Probably the most egregious example of this error was the wild story related by drifter Henry Lee Lucas, who claimed to have killed six hundred or more people with his partner, Ottis Toole. A lot of open murder cases were closed because of Lucas's "confessions," only to be reopened after he was proved to be a liar.

The practice I find most troubling is the deliberate refusal to consider a criminal's work product. One psychiatric expert witness once told me that he would not look at crime-scene photographs when evaluating a murder defendant for trial. Reason: He was afraid the photographs would bias his judgment! I should hope they would.

FOND MEMORIES

The crime scene is a central feature of a sexual criminal's work product, his canvas, if you will. For many offenders, the work is so valuable that they devise elaborate and occasionally ingenious ways to preserve it for later delectation.

Why does the offender keep records when the practice raises his odds of being caught and dramatically increases the possibility of conviction? Isn't this stupid? Does he want to be apprehended? What's so important about these materials that he'll risk so much to maintain them?

When I ask offenders this question, they most frequently reply, "So I could relive the crime." Based on my experience, I believe that's an honest answer. Here's how serial killer Billy Lee Chadd put it:

"I just filed it [a murder] away in the corner of my mind where I was beginning to compile quite a few dark secrets," wrote Chadd. "A corner from which I could summon out the memories to look at them again and again. To relive my crimes and revel in the horror of my victim."

The records themselves, along with the information contained in them, can have deep importance to the sexual criminal. It is well established that certain ritualistic offenders take personal belongings (such as a driver's license, photographs, or items of clothing) from their victims to help them later reenact their crimes in their imagination.

Some of these men acknowledge that they do something similar when making a record of their crimes. They are creating trophies or souvenirs, tangible artifacts of the experience.

I think another, more subtle, motive may lie behind this practice, too—particularly among those who record their crimes in text, photos, or tapes. Mike DeBardeleben is an illustrative example.

COUNTERFEITER AND KILLER

DeBardeleben was brought to justice in May of 1983 by U.S. Secret Service agents, who pursued him across the United States as a counterfeiter. He was one of the most successful, and artful, lone wolf forgers that the U.S. government has ever encountered. Only after his apprehension was it discovered that DeBardeleben was also a kidnapper, rapist, bank robber, murderer, and a dozen other types of felon.

Because so many of his crimes were sexually aberrant, the Secret Service asked me to consult on the case. In that capacity I reviewed DeBardeleben's work product— to my knowledge, the most detailed and extensive self-documentation by any sexual sadist since the Marquis de Sade. From bloody underwear to audio tapes to sheaves and sheaves of notes, DeBardeleben saved it all.

As I reviewed the photos he had taken of his victims, I noticed one series showing a young female being forced to fellate him while on her knees. Seen in the photos was yet another set of pictures scattered around DeBardeleben's feet. These shots depicted an earlier victim being forced to perform the same act on him in exactly the same position.

I was mystified, unable to figure out DeBardeleben's intent or what significance the photos on the floor held for him. I considered that he might have used those pictures to batter his victim psychologically or perhaps as a visual example of what he wanted her to do.

Both theories were reasonable. From listening to his audio tapes of other crimes, I knew that he gave precise verbal instructions to his victims, and that he enjoyed verbally battering them.

Still, these answers weren't entirely satisfying.

I turned the question over in my mind for quite some time until one day at home, while I was writing out my monthly checks, the answer suddenly struck me. DeBardeleben was using the pictures to critique his criminal interaction with the victim! A compulsive perfectionist, he was looking for possible ways to improve on his attempts to bring his fantasies to reality. Just as a SWAT team always meets after an exercise to critique its performance, or a football team reviews game films, DeBardeleben was conducting a comparative analysis of his sexual assaults!

Yet reality can never fulfill fantasy's expectations. Why? Because fantasy is always perfect. Mike DeBardeleben surely recognized this but was not deterred. He was determined to make the criminal act conform as closely to his deviant fantasy as possible.

"THEY'LL NEVER CATCH ME!"

Another reason why ritualistic sexual offenders like to keep records is what you might call "the bulletproof syndrome." As a narcissist, the serial sexual offender simply doesn't believe the authorities will ever apprehend him, so he doesn't fear capture or discovery of his records. Johnstone, the cartoon case criminal, was an example of this attitude.

When I have the opportunity to interview one of these men, I always ask if the death penalty would have deterred him from his crime. Without exception, he'll say no. I asked one rapist why, and he responded by asking me a series of questions.

Had I ever skipped school?

Yes.

Did I know in advance that I would be punished if caught?

Yes.

Then why did I do it?

Because I didn't think I would be caught, I said.

There you go, he said.

Extreme narcissism leads the criminal to the belief that he is superior to everyone in general, and to law enforcement in particular. He considers himself invulnerable to identification and arrest. Even if he did consider the possibility of arrest, the offender typically becomes so focused on acting out his fantasies that the question of detection becomes immaterial. Billy Lee Chadd, whom you'll soon get to know, became so emotionally involved in one of his crimes that he could easily have been overpowered by the victim.

Law enforcement should be deeply grateful for the narcissistic personality disorder; it is the serial sexual offender's Achilles' heel. You can almost take for granted that after a while the bulletproof syndrome will set in, and he will begin to take unnecessary risks. Boredom will push him in search of the bigger jolt he gets from pushing the envelope, risking more.

Don't confuse such outrageous behavior with a hidden wish to be caught. Ted Bundy, for example, was arrested three times during his killing career. On each occasion he was drunk or high and was driving erratically late at night in an unfamiliar neighborhood. You might expect that someone as intelligent as Bundy would make a mistake like that only once, at most.

In my view Bundy wasn't inviting capture, either subconsciously or consciously. He meant to stay free, he wanted to keep killing, but his narcissistic ego prevented him from correctly perceiving the peril of his behavior.

The authorities who arrested him in Florida had no idea that Bundy (already infamous throughout the West) had murdered the sleeping coeds in Tallahassee and the twelve-year-old child in Lake City. He was headed from Florida to Houston and could have easily reached his destination had he not been drinking and driving erratically on the streets of Pensacola. This behavior led to his recapture. If not for this classic narcissist's misstep, Bundy would have gone on to kill again.

I don't believe any aberrant offender ever wants to be caught, even subconsciously. I do believe that some honestly are appalled at their behavior and sincerely would like to stop what they are doing. Some offenders have told me that they were scared by their violent fantasies and behavior, but I have never met an offender who said that he wanted to be caught.

One sadistic serial rapist, Jon Simonis in Louisiana, did tell me he was glad he was caught before he committed murder, which he feared he would soon do because "rape was becoming boring." He wasn't bothered by the crimes he had committed so far, and he certainly did not want to be locked up or punished for them. He just didn't want to kill.

PSYCHOPATHS

Perhaps the most frightening personality disorder is that of the psychopath. Professionally, the condition is known as *antisocial personality disorder (APD)*. This term has replaced *psychopath* in the modern psychiatric lexicon, just as psychopath once replaced *sociopath*. In earlier times, people in this category were called "morally insane" or simply "evil."

Psychopaths do not feel remorse or shame, guilt or appropriate fear. They do not learn from punishment. They are easily bored. They like excitement. They find it difficult to delay gratification, no matter where their self-interest may lie.

In a classic (though not scientifically validated) test of

psychopathy, the subject is told he can have a quarter now or a five-dollar bill tomorrow. The psychopath always takes the quick two-bits.

Psychopaths are chronic liars, even when they have no need or reason to lie. They have no understanding of, or concern for, the harm they cause others.

I once asked a psychopath what he thought about love.

"Intellectually I understand the concept," he said, "but I have never experienced it."

This man had raped and tortured more than fifty women across twelve states. Two of his victims, devout Christians, visited him in prison, hoping to bring their attacker to Jesus. I asked him if he felt it was healthy for the women to continue calling on him.

"Probably not," he answered, "but it sure is good for my ego." Typically, his own gratification was his only concern.

"A NORMAL, EASY-GOING GUY"

Sexual serial killers, for all their depredations, remain rare among criminals. Rarer still is the opportunity to review their most private records, which are their most prized possessions and are usually well hidden.

In the course of my work as a behavioral investigator, I've been given access to the innermost thoughts and fantasies of a wide number of these criminals. One example stands out because the offender, Billy Lee Chadd, wrote an extremely detailed account of his crimes and fantasies after he was captured.

Chadd, who originally meant the manuscript to be published—he hoped to make money with it—appears to have embellished his accounts in places, according to Mike Pent, the California deputy district attorney who prosecuted him. Nevertheless, Chadd has provided us an intimate window on his mind. Without such documents, we would know far less than we do about these bizarre and extremely dangerous men.

Billy Lee Chadd, a native San Diegan, husband and father, described himself as a "normal, easy-going guy." Eventually, he claimed to have killed scores of people. In his manuscript the number is just four. Mike Pent says his office was able to confirm three.

Chadd's first confirmed homicide, committed at age twenty, was the 1974 rape-murder of a thirty-year-old San Diego woman. She was found lying in bed on her stomach. Her hands and feet were bound with window sash cord, and she had been blindfolded with a towel. The young woman had been violently raped vaginally, anally, and orally. Chadd also strangled her and used a steak knife to stab her repeatedly in the neck.

In his clinical, emotionless confession, Chadd said he went to the first murder victim's residence intending only to burglarize it. Inside, however, he confronted her as she emerged from her tub, naked and wet, and became aroused.

From his confession it might appear that Billy Lee Chadd was an *opportunistic rapist,* a term I use to describe a man who arrives intent on committing one crime, usually robbery, but seizes the opportunity to commit another— rape.

But Chadd was also a sexual sadist who left nothing to chance. He took the woman to the bedroom and raped her. Afterward, realizing that she could identify him, he decided to kill her. That is the essence of his confession.

As an investigator, I would have been happy to obtain such a straightforward admission of guilt. It meant that the case was closed and Billy Lee Chadd would be taken off the streets for a long, long time.

But then came a twist. In jail Chadd handwrote a manuscript that he titled "Dark Secrets." Its contents certainly merit the title.

When "Dark Secrets" came into my possession, I prevailed upon my wife-to-be, Peggy Driver, to type the manuscript. She presented me with fifty-seven pages of appalling typescript, double spaced. The fact that she later married me, despite the assignment I had pressed on her, attests to Peggy's selfless nature.

SELF-PORTRAIT OF A KILLER

"Dark Secrets" is Chadd's intimate reflection on his crimes and why he committed them. Portions of the text are graphic. Throughout the document, Chadd casts himself in the most positive light possible. His intelligence is evident, as is his belief that he is essentially normal. In both regards, he is an archetypal ritualistic offender.

He says he led "a double life," a husband and father who nevertheless had this little problem—a violent streak toward women. He rationalizes his behavior by noting that he came from a broken home. Both his mother and stepfather were alcoholics. From the time he was eight, Chadd writes, he can remember very few times his mother was out of bed before noon. Friends taught him how to steal at an early age. He boasts that by age eleven he could drive a car, and that he stole them "quite frequently," without suffering any serious legal consequences.

At age fifteen Chadd fell in love with his future wife, with whom he says he "began having sex when I was sixteen . . . We made love almost daily until July of my 16th year. Then all hell broke loose in my life."

Chadd describes his first real trouble with the law, a rape case, as a miscarriage of justice. This is the aberrant offender's familiar pattern of blame projection. It's always someone else's fault.

One midnight, he writes, a visiting friend, drunk and also high on drugs, announced that he wanted to go across the street to rob a house. Chadd claims he stayed in his friend's truck, only to be awakened some hours later by flashlights and voices. It was the police, and he was under arrest. According to Chadd, he could not have committed the crime because of his unspecified physical abnormality, which the victim could not help but notice had he been her attacker.

Yet she made no mention of it in her testimony. Chadd's attorney apparently refused to pursue the matter. "I even told him to ask these questions. I wasted my breath. I was found guilty on her testimony and a partial footprint found in her driveway. . . . I was sentenced to two years."

Chadd escaped from the California Youth Authority (CYA) on two occasions. The second time, he writes, he "really did" rape someone.

A subsequent sexual assault begins with a random knock on a door. "Bad luck for the poor lady that she was home. I told her our car had broken down and I asked if she would let me use her phone. If she would have said no and closed the door, nothing may have ever happened to her. She did say no, but she then explained that her husband was at work and she never let strangers in when she was alone. ALONE."

Chadd returns to the house, breaks through the front door with a brick, and discovers the woman in her bathroom. He grabs her by her hair. She begins to scream. He puts a knife to her throat as he drags her back to a bedroom and tells her to shut up or he'll kill her. "When we got to the bedroom, I just shoved her down on the bed and threw up her housecoat. I tried to cut her panties off but my knife wasn't sharp enough . . . I pulled her panties off and pulled down my Levi's and got on her . . . she just laid there. So I told her to start moving or I'd hurt her. . . .

"Up till that night, I had balled quite a bit but I had never experienced such sexual pleasure. I was completely overcome with passion. I dropped my knife . . . I even lost my vision for a few seconds. I collapsed on her and I was so spent I couldn't even move. Had she only known my condition, she could have picked up the knife and stabbed me and I couldn't have done anything to stop her . . .

"I told her to stay on the bed and I left the house . . . Later that night, I thought about the rape and I decided it wasn't bad at all. And I knew I would do it again."

* * *

Chadd blames the criminal justice system for making him into a sexual predator, but the passage above amply demonstrates the power of his aberrant urge: "I never had experienced such sexual pleasure."

Still, at this stage, he was a young and relatively inexperienced offender. This is obvious from the minimal amount of time he invests in victim selection, the crude method of entry (throwing a brick through the door), the lack of any attempt to protect his identity, and the failure to control (bind and gag) the victim after his departure. Even without benefit of Chadd's written reconstruction, an experienced investigator could look at these telltale signs at the crime scene and conclude that the rapist was fairly new to his chosen crime.

When Chadd reflects on his excitement during the rape, we begin to observe his tendencies toward sexual sadism. This deviance will emerge in a much more pronounced fashion in his descriptions of his murders. Chadd unwittingly tells us a crucially important fact about his narcissism when he writes of revisiting the rape in his mind. He decides, "It wasn't bad at all." Moments before he'd called it the best sexual experience of his life, even saying that he had collapsed and nearly was blind for a few moments.

Chadd needs to project the idea that nothing means very much to him, especially anything to do with a victim. She's his to use and discard. He is in total control. He dominates and is not dominated. Of course, he then admits the opposite—that he was not in control, that his urges, not his will, directed his actions. "I knew," he writes, "I would do it again."

At seventeen, Chadd was transferred to CYA's Youth Training School. There he attempted suicide by hanging. "If I would have been successful," he writes, "four people would be alive today."

He was then sent to Atascadero State Hospital (ASH) where, Chadd claims, he had his first homosexual encounter. "It wasn't exactly my cup of tea, but it was sex."

He writes of first using drugs and of trading homosexual acts for drugs at Atascadero. He also claims that following his transfer back to CYA, he blackmailed a teacher into giving him good grades by threatening to tell the authorities about the teacher having sex with a staff member. Whether true or imagined, such an episode served to reassure Chadd of his power, even over those in authority.

According to his manuscript, upon release Chadd committed his first and only nonsexual murder. As he describes this killing, which San Diego authorities cannot confirm, it occurred on the roadway bridge while he was hitchhiking.

Chadd recalls seeing a young man and his dog sitting by the road on the other side of the bridge. He crossed over to them and sat down as well, although the stranger clearly had already staked out the spot. Words were exchanged.

The other hitchhiker was both big and tough looking, Chadd writes, but he was certain he could take the stranger. So without warning Chadd kicked up at the other man's groin, and a fist fight began. Chadd was knocked down then picked up a big rock as the stranger moved in to punch him again. As he did so, Chadd smashed the stone into the man's forehead, dropping him to the ground. Suddenly, Chadd explains, he realized the stranger was utterly in his power. He felt godlike, able to grant life or take it away, although he does not appear to have considered his options for long. Chadd smashed the unconscious man's head open, killing him at once.

He says he was surprised at how easy murder is and how much he enjoyed it, particularly the feeling of supremacy. Chadd pitched the man's body, as well as his travel bag and dog, over the bridge and into the river below, discovering as he did so that he felt little fear of discovery for his crime.

"Later that night I thought about what I had done. I asked myself why I did it. But no answer came to me. I wasn't sorry or anything. And I admitted to myself that I enjoyed it. And I wondered if all murderers felt as I did." He explains that though he wished to share how he felt with someone, he realized the smarter move was to keep it to himself. "I just filed it away in the corner of my mind, where I was beginning to compile quite a few dark secrets. A corner from which I could summon out the memories to look at them again and again. To relive my crimes and revel in the horror of my victim . . ."

In his matter-of-fact account of the hitchhiker's murder, the primary issue expressed is power. Chadd is beginning to perceive his need for it. During the rape he drew psychosexual pleasure from exercising power and control and wrote about it. In the young man's murder, his narcissism blossoms: ". . . it was easy and I was enjoying the feeling of supremacy. A supremacy like I had never known before."

Chadd also is maturing as a criminal. This time he takes action to protect his identity. He throws the victim, along with his belongings and dog, into the river. "No witnesses, no body or weapon. I was pretty confident," Chadd writes.

The lack of fear is, in itself, abnormal. Chadd has crossed a critical barrier. Not only has he killed, but he recognizes that it was easy and believes he won't get caught. He likes it and he's getting good at it. He is learning through experience. He is about to become a serial killer.

One of the most striking aspects of Billy Lee Chadd's writings is his complete lack of self-knowledge. Like many serial killers, he can't articulate why he doesn't feel normal guilt or fear. "I asked myself why I did it," he writes. "But no answer came to me. I knew what I had done was wrong. But where was [sic] the feelings of guilt that were supposed to accompany such a deed? What was it that caused me to feel such elation? What was it that allowed me to take another human's life with no feeling of remorse?"

This lack of remorse is a classic symptom of the psychopath's personality. It becomes even more apparent as

Chadd's memoir continues. He remembers going home to his pregnant wife, whom he brutalized when she refused him sex. "I started to choke her. I could see fear in her eyes. . . . My wife was cowering in a corner with tears in her eyes. The fear she showed would fire me even more. I couldn't see her face, just those eyes, afraid and pleading. I felt myself slipping into the strange feeling of supremacy again. I wanted to kill.

"Then I suddenly realized who I was choking. I thought, 'My God, what am I doing?' I let her go, but the drive to destroy was still there. I don't know how but I shifted my anger from her to inanimate objects. I started breaking anything that would break . . . I kept shouting 'DIE! DIE!' Not anyone in particular, just 'DIE!' "

Chadd writes that he then left the family trailer. "Without her fear to feed upon," he recalls, "I slowly started to calm down." His actions were being driven by his sexual sadism and his desire to destroy. The description in "Dark Secrets" of his second killing, but first known sexual murder, stresses both themes. Here is his account of the 1974 rape-murder of a San Diego woman.

"My body was giving me massive spurts of adrenaline," he writes. "My heart was going like a trip hammer as I reached for the door knob . . . The excitement and fear poured back over me again. . . .

He discovered her standing in her bathtub, naked, and forced her at gunpoint into her bedroom, where the assault took place.

"She was writhing in pain, and I loved it. I was now combining my sexual high of rape and my power high of fear to make a total sum that is beyond explaining. I can't begin to describe the feeling. It is one that must be experienced to know how it feels. I was completely beyond all contact with reality. I was alive for the sole purpose of causing pain and receiving sexual gratification. I have never experienced a high like this from any drug."

He remembers laughing on the way home in his car. Neither afraid nor sorry for committing the brutal act, he says he'd never felt more satisfied in his life, like a "supreme ruler." He even relived the rape-murder in a wet dream that night.

Chadd did not restrict himself in "Dark Secrets" to actual crimes. When his three-year-old son died at the hospital, he turned his deviant wrath on the female doctor who treated the boy. "I would lay awake at night and fantasize about what I would do before I killed her. The ways of torture that I called to mind would have done justice to the Marquis de Sade. Oh, he had nothing on me . . ."

Chadd explained his fantasy was to kidnap the doctor and take her up into the mountains to slowly dismember her, enjoying her screams as he did so. When only her head and torso were left, he intended to paralyze her, cut out her tongue, blind her, and puncture her eardrums. Then he would leave the doctor for the police to find, knowing that the hospital would keep her alive, creating a "living hell" for her.

A year after he committed the murder in San Diego, Chadd was working in Las Vegas, where he met Delmar Bright, twenty-nine, a hotel porter. According to Chadd, Bright offered him twenty dollars and a six-pack of beer if he would pose in the nude. Chadd agreed. Then, still according to Chadd, Bright made a homosexual advance and, producing some extension cords, asked that Chadd tie him up. Chadd agreed, told Bright to lie on his stomach and to put his hands behind his back.

"He did and I tied him up . . . I took my knife and laid it next to the bed. I took another cord and put it around his neck in a slip noose. I said, 'Give me one good reason why I shouldn't kill you.' He obviously thought I was just playing around. He started to tell me that he had my pictures, and I had left fingerprints all over the house. Damn! he was right! I mentally thanked him for reminding me. I said, I'm going to kill you faggot!

"My high was beginning to take over again . . . I started breathing hard and my palms got all sweaty . . . I felt the now familiar exuberance sweep over me again. I was going to kill."

Bright began to laugh. "It was all a big joke to him . . . But it was all too real for me. I wanted to kill, but there was something missing. FEAR! He wasn't afraid. I got my knife and showed it to him . . . This is for real. I saw a twinge of uncertainty in his eyes now. It was working, he was beginning to get scared. I put the knife to his throat and cut him. Not deep. Just enough to draw blood.

"Here it was. I could see it now. Terror. He knew I was serious. He opened his mouth to scream, but I yanked on the cord and the scream came out as a strangled gurgle."

Chadd commits yet another bloody murder and masturbates in the midst of it. Then after describing how he "sanitized" the apartment of possible forensic evidence, Chadd recalls, "I started to giggle as I walked away from the place. By the time I got to the corner, I was laughing hysterically. I calmed myself and still smiling, hailed a cab."

Like Robert Leroy Anderson and many other ritualistic offenders, Chadd was finally undone by the narcissistic need to share details of his murder. He tells his wife, who is so frightened by the admission that Chadd backs off, saying it was just a joke. From my experience with this type of killer, I believe that had Chadd thought his wife would countenance such behavior, eventually he would have involved her in his sexual murder fantasy and possibly in the crimes themselves.

Chadd describes how he and his family hitchhiked throughout the United States and his eventual enlistment in the marines. He reports that he enjoyed his military service and became proficient in martial arts.

Eventually, he chanced upon his fourth murder victim.

She was a young woman who, with her eighteen-month-old son, asked Chadd where a particular bus stop was. Chadd showed her the location, and they caught the bus to her house. When he learned that she rode the bus home from work each day, Chadd offered to give her a lift once his car was repaired.

She let him inside, where he began kissing her. She was responsive until Chadd tried to undress her. She told him that her other children were due home soon, and he pushed her onto the bed and began to undress her forcefully. She reacted violently and stood up.

"I was no longer in control," Chadd writes. "My monster decided I couldn't handle it. So with a roar of rage, he got up off the bed and grabbed her by the throat and started choking her. All I could do was watch. I tried to stop what was happening, but I could not. It wasn't me anymore . . ." In the end, "I wanted her to know I was going to kill her. I needed the fear that knowledge would bring . . . I'm the Hillside Strangler. I'm going to kill you, bitch . . . Oh, the luscious terror she showed. It was the best yet. Looking at me coming closer with the cord, knowing I was going to kill her, had her paralyzed with fear . . . I started strangling her and I was laughing as I watched her eyes . . . Yes this was it . . . The joy I felt couldn't compare with anything I could try to imagine. The ultimate high." He stabbed her in the back, shouting, "Die, you bitch!" The victim's cause of death was a slashed throat.

Once again, Chadd cannot resist the urge to share what he had done. This time, he tells his brother. Like so many serial killers, he has begun to unravel. Chadd might have gone on killing for years had he been able to keep himself together psychologically. But the same combination of rage and aberrant urges that turned him into a killer eventually combined to overwhelm and consume him.

His last entries tell of becoming drunk and trying to run his wife down with his car. Apparently, he was arrested in connection with this incident. The end of his criminal career came shortly thereafter when he was working at the Naval Medical Center San Diego near Balboa Park. He noticed a dying officer's wife and daughter as they came to visit each day. Chadd consulted the hospital records, determined where they lived, then abducted and raped both women. He was arrested in Louisiana for these assaults.

Fingerprints subsequently connected him to all three of his known homicides. When confronted with this evidence, Chadd confessed to the three murders plus the fourth homicide of the hitchhiker, which the police were unable to confirm.

Horrifying though Chadd's account is, its value to society lies in its ability to educate us about the nature of a sexual offender with a number of personality disorders. Chadd was narcissistic, seeking only his own gratification. He was sociopathic, with no regard for the welfare of others. And he exhibits an appetite for sexual sadism that grows as it seeks satisfaction. He's serving a sentence of life with no possibility of parole in the California state prison system.

6

SEXUAL SADISTS

The most resourceful, destructive, and elusive of all deviant offenders is the ritualistic sexual sadist. Just as the great white shark is the renowned predator of the oceans, the sexual sadist is the most dangerous and cunning of all aberrant criminals. He also presents the greatest challenge to law enforcement.

The sexual sadist is a meticulous planner, spending inordinate amounts of time inside his own head. He may devote months or even years imagining his intended crime, turning it over in his mind, playing with it, as one might examine a prism in a sunbeam, studying all the different ways it refracts the light.

He hates surprises and any kind of spontaneity. If possible, he will rehearse every step of his crime repeatedly and do everything imaginable to reduce his chances of failure. As a result the first crime of a sexual sadist may easily be confused with another aberrant criminal's thirtieth offense. Such was the case with Robert Leroy Anderson's homicides. They reflected such meticulous care in their commission that had I not known he was the perpetrator I would have assumed a much older and more experienced criminal had committed them.

This talent for planning is an important reason why po-

lice agencies try to learn whether a sexual sadist is responsible for any crime under investigation.

The sexual sadist is also stunningly brutal. As we saw
with Billy Lee Chadd, the fantasies he wishes to enact with
a victim are horrendous. His sexual pleasure is derived from
her suffering.

Mike DeBardeleben once wrote what amounts to the
sexual sadist's credo:

> **Sadism:** The wish to inflict pain on others is not the
> essence of sadism. The central impulse is to have com-
> plete mastery over another person, to make him/her a
> helpless object of our will, to become the absolute ruler
> over her, to become her god, to do with her as one
> pleases are means to this end. And the most radical aim
> is to make her suffer. Since there is no greater power
> over another person than that of inflicting pain on her.
> To force her to undergo suffering without her being able
> to defend herself. The pleasure in the complete domi-
> nation over another person is the very essence of the
> sadistic drive.

In the late 1980s, Park Dietz, Janet Warren, and I decided
to study these rare and deadly offenders. We originally set
out to conduct face-to-face interviews with the men. But
after unproductive sessions with five of them, we realized
we were wasting our time. Not one cared to discuss himself
except to deny or rationalize his behavior or to project the
blame for his situation onto someone else.

Consequently, we chose to conduct a descriptive study
of the men, relying on other sources (i.e., police reports,
mental health evaluations, court transcripts, the offender's
records) for our information.

STUDYING THE SEXUAL SADIST

Out of sixty-five candidates, we chose thirty men for our
study. It was not a simple task to isolate this group. To

qualify for inclusion each must have committed an offense in which he inflicted suffering in order to sexually arouse himself. The *infliction* of pain, we knew, was not what aroused them. It was the *suffering*. This is not a trivial distinction.

Billy Lee Chadd, for instance, found "something missing" in his assault on Delmar Bright until it hit him: "Fear! He wasn't afraid." So what did Chadd do? "I got my knife and showed it to him." Once Bright exhibited that fear, Chadd regained his erection. That is a quintessential moment of sexual sadism.

Bright's sexual orientation probably was immaterial to Chadd. Sexual sadists are sexually voracious, indiscriminate, capable in many instances of coupling with humans of either sex or any age, as well as animals and inanimate objects as the opportunity presents itself. It was Bright's fear, not his gender or sexual orientation, that excited Chadd.

One way to understand sexual sadists is to review what they aren't. Dietz, Warren, and I identified seven behaviors that commonly are confused with sexual sadism:

1 NONSEXUAL SADISM

2 CRUELTY DURING A CRIME

3 PATHOLOGICAL GROUP BEHAVIOR

4 STATE-SANCTIONED CRUELTY

5 REVENGE-MOTIVATED CRUELTY

6 INTERROGATIVE CRUELTY

7 POSTMORTEM MUTILATION

A nonsexual sadist gains pleasure from causing others pain or discomfort, usually in a social or work environment and most often to subordinates or perceived inferiors. The source of this enjoyment is the sense of power he gains from frightening, humiliating, and demeaning others. He may even inflict physical or emotional abuse. However, he is not a sexual sadist unless he is sexually excited by his victim's suffering.

I was in the army many years ago, and once worked for a sadistic officer. At one point he counseled me to put my house up for sale because I was about to be transferred. I did so and quickly found a buyer.

When I told the officer of the sale and asked when I would be transferred, he smiled and said that he had not made up his mind, adding that I should have checked with him before disposing of my residence.

I knew this game. He enjoyed tormenting. people to prove his power over them. So I didn't plead with him, as he hoped I would. I did not point out that I now faced enormous financial, not to mention personal, difficulties. Instead, I returned his smile and said I was content either way because my wife and I had intended to sell since we wanted a larger home. His smile disappeared. The next day I was notified that my transfer orders were on the way.

Cruelty is a common feature of sexual crimes, which by their very nature are hurtful and demeaning. However, that cruelty rarely is *sexually* sadistic. Brutal, yes. But fortunately, true sexual sadism is unusual, even among sexual criminals. In my opinion, fewer than one in ten sexual assaults are committed by sexual sadists.

I was once retained as an expert in a civil case involving a male intruder and his two victims, a man and his wife. After robbing the couple at gunpoint in their hotel room, the thief forced them to disrobe, almost as an afterthought.

He then pulled up a chair, ordered the couple onto their bed, and directed the man to perform cunnilingus on his wife. The robber watched for about thirty minutes as this went on. At one point he leaned forward and attempted to fondle the woman's breasts, but he desisted after her husband threatened him with violence. The offender left a short time later.

No one would deny that this offender treated the couple in an intentionally cruel and degrading manner. But beyond the strong suggestion that he was a voyeur, there is no behavioral evidence that he was sexually aroused by his victims' fear and suffering.

Pathological group behavior occurs when three or more individuals engage in a single crime, typically a gang rape. Let's look at an example.

The victim was a nurse. As she arrived at the hospital for the midnight shift, she was accosted by a youth with a shotgun. He forced her into the rear seat of her car and, with three of his friends, drove her to a deserted warehouse.

Over the next few hours, the four teenagers raped her vaginally, anally, and orally. They penetrated her with foreign objects and urinated and defecated upon her. The nurse has never recovered from the psychological trauma of this extremely vicious assault.

Yet however brutal and cruel the youths were, they acted as they did to impress one another with their power, ferocity, and utter lack of concern for the victim. They acted in concert, as a pack, not as individuals. Of course, any one of them might have been a sexual sadist, aroused by the victim's extreme suffering and humiliation. But the focus of the gang rape, in and of itself, was not sexually sadistic.

State-sanctioned cruelty, whether Nazi genocide or the torture chambers of the South African apartheid regime, is frequently confused with sexual sadism. Surely sexual sadists are drawn to such work. But while a deliberate governmental policy of heinous cruelty toward perceived enemies is certainly a reprehensible policy option, it is not a program designed to accommodate those who are sexually stimulated by the suffering of those being tortured.

Recently in the former Yugoslavia, the Serbian-led army systematically enslaved the Muslim women of Bosnia. They were placed in camps where Serbian soldiers made use of them as physical and sexual slaves. Girls as young as fourteen were traded for cash or appliances, such as television sets. Older females were gang-raped by as many as fifteen or twenty men at a time. Some of the women suffered such assaults intermittently for months.

Similarly, Human Rights Watch estimates that in Sierre Leone rebels of the Revolutionary United Front Party systematically raped, maimed, and mutilated thousands of women and children over the course of that country's bloody eight years of civil war.

Doubtlessly some of these rapists were sexual sadists, too. But even though the assaults apparently were state sanctioned in Yugoslavia and part of an organized wave of terror in Sierra Leone, there was no evidence in either country that a *policy of sexual sadism* had been put in place.

Revenge-motivated cruelty is, as the term clearly indicates, an act of retribution. The Mafia, for example, has a history of torturing and killing informants, or snitches. Sometimes, as a warning to others, the unlucky victim is given a "Sicilian necktie"; he's found dead with his tongue protruding through a slit in his throat just below his chin.

When I served with the army in Vietnam, I occasionally encountered dead Vietcong soldiers with their amputated penises in their mouths. This was the work of South Vietnamese soldiers who believed humans meet their god in whatever form they were in when they died. Of course, the Vietcong believed the same thing and performed the same amputations on slain South Vietnamese.

As appalling as the behavior is, such acts are done for a specific reason and sexual sadism is not it.

World headlines alert us to notorious cases of interrogative cruelty. One well-known victim of the deplorable practice was DEA agent Enrique (Kiki) Camarena, who was kidnapped, tortured for four days, and then murdered by Mexican drug traffickers in Guadalajara in 1985. Another was William F. Buckley, the CIA station chief in Beirut, who was abducted, tortured intermittently for six months, and then killed in 1984 by the Islamic jihad. Their deaths were economic and political crimes; in both instances the victim was tortured in an effort to extract information about the workings of his agency. Sexual sadism, if it was present, was incidental not the primary motivation.

Finally, *postmortem mutilation* is another horrific act frequently confused with sexual sadism. It shouldn't be. If a sexual sadist is aroused by a victim's suffering, a dead victim, by definition, is of no sexual interest to him.

In a 1980 article, John Douglas and I dusted off an old term, *lust murderer*, for the postmortem mutilator. This killer typically focuses on his dead victim's breasts, abdomen, rectum, or genitals to express his anger and frustration. Although the victim may be either a male or female, the crime is most often heterosexual, and both the offender and the victim are usually of the same race.

Jack the Ripper, for instance, was a lust murderer not a sexual sadist. Another member of this fearsome fraternity was James Lawson, who teamed with James Odom when both were inmates in a California mental institution to abduct and murder a female convenience store clerk in South Carolina.

Odom and Lawson took her to an isolated area, where Odom raped the woman and turned her over to Lawson, who quickly killed her by cutting her throat. Then Lawson amputated both her breasts and her reproductive organs. He might also have consumed a portion of her body.

The two men were arrested the next day and both were later convicted. "I wanted to cut her body so she would not look like a person and destroy her so she would not exist," Lawson later told officers.

GREAT WHITE SHARKS

Sexual sadists sort themselves along a behavioral continuum. At one end we have fantasy and nothing more. Then
innocuous solo sex. Then the behavior intensifies. The sexual sadist acts out with consenting or paid partners. Finally,
there is full-blown, criminal sexual sadism that results in
severe injury or death. Sadists at this extreme of the spectrum, a group whom I call "the great white sharks," form
a distinct minority even among sexual sadists.

Of least concern to law enforcement is the sexual sadist
who is content merely to fantasize a victim's suffering. He
is aroused and masturbates but never attempts to act out
the fantasy. Such behavior is certainly strange, but just as
surely, it is not criminal. Society cannot punish people for
what goes on inside their heads. Nor is it criminal to graduate to the next level, practicing sexual sadism with a compliant or paid partner.

Further along we encounter "muted" sexual sadism. This
term was coined by Dr. Robert Prentky, a noted forensic
psychologist. He defines muted sexual sadism as a crime
with the elements one would expect to observe in overt
sexual sadism (bondage, captivity, demeaning photography
of the victim) minus the physically injurious violence
(whipping, burning, painful insertion of foreign objects).

The sexual sadists of interest to Dietz, Warren, and my-
self were the great white sharks, those at the extreme end
of the continuum. Twenty-two of these men had killed 187
victims, and seventeen of them were serial killers. Probably
best known among them were John Wayne Gacy and the
Hillside Stranglers, Angelo Buono and his cousin Kenneth
Bianchi. Others in the study were equally violent: Mike
DeBardeleben, Gerard John Schaefer, Billy Lee Chadd, and
Harvey Glatman. This last, known as Southern California's
"Lonely Hearts Killer" of the 1950s, is of special signifi-

cance to me because his reign of terror introduced me to
what became my life's work.

IT'S CULTURE, NOT RACE

If you were to look at photos of the thirty sexual sadists in
our study, you would be struck by two things: The first is
the sheer ordinariness of these men's appearances. You
couldn't, by looking at them, imagine the horrors they inflicted on their victims.

Equally striking is their skin color. The vast majority of
sexual sadists in our study—twenty-nine out of thirty—
were whites of European descent. The question has interested me over the years: Why are so few ritualistic sexual
killers black or Hispanic?

In fact, blacks and Hispanics are statistically underre-
presented, not only among sexual sadists, but among most
classes of ritualistic serial criminals. Bob Ressler and John
Douglas, in their serial killer survey, interviewed thirty-six
murderers responsible for 118 deaths. Of these, thirty-three
were white males. When Ann Burgess and I studied
forty-one serial rapists (responsible for 837 rapes and more
than 400 attempted rapes), our group comprised thirty-six
whites and five blacks. In my study of twenty compliant
wives and girlfriends of sexual sadists, seventeen were
white, two were Hispanic, and only one was black.

A similar disproportion occurs among people who in-
dulge in dangerous autoeroticism. While not criminal, this
practice is certainly a form of ritualistic sexual behavior. In
our study of 150 fatalities that resulted from it, 139 of the
victims were white and only 7 were black.

The lone black offender in our study of thirty sexual
sadists expressed his sexual sadism in a highly individual
way. He would capture victims and keep them in his residence for up to six weeks. During that time he conditioned
their behavior using poisonous snakes. The women were
kept nude from the waist up most of the time and totally

nude on occasion. He gave them meticulous instructions on how to please him and even had them memorize a set of "ten commandments" he had composed for them to obey.

To my knowledge, this man never killed anyone. Unlike other sexual sadists, he released his victims when he grew bored with them. However, the women were instructed that they must return to him if he so demanded. If they didn't, or if they reported him to the police, he warned them they very likely would find a snake in their shower, under their bedcovers, in their car, or in their mailbox. It was a very effective form of psychological coercion. The women did as they were told, without exception.

A FLAWED THEORY

The question of black versus white behavior among deviant offenders arose in the early 1990s at a program for top law enforcement executives at the FBI Academy. After I had spoken, Ira McKenna, the highly respected black chief of police in Detroit, Michigan, asked me a question.

What differences, if any, he inquired, had I noticed in the ways black and white rapists committed their crimes? I answered, in part, that black rapists cross the racial line much more frequently than do white rapists, and that black rapists tend to assault elderly women much more often.

On the way back to my office I thought further about the question. Surely it was worth deeper exploration. So I decided to compile a list of behaviors I had commonly seen in ritualistic sexual assaults and then assess each from both a black and a white perspective. Based on my experience, I listed the race of the offender more closely associated with a particular behavior. The following is a partial listing of my original chart.

BEHAVIOR	WHITE	BLACK
Cross-racial rape		x
Assault of the elderly		x
Brings a rape kit	x	
Physical torture of victim	x	
Captivity for twenty-four or more hours	x	
Records the crime	x	
Takes a trophy or souvenir	x	
Sexual bondage	x	
Behavioral scripting of victim	x	
Verbal scripting of victim	x	
Costumes victim	x	
Modifies vehicle / space for crime	x	

As I looked at this analysis, I felt I was close to a possible major breakthrough for law enforcement. I could think of several rape cases in which the victim was unable to identify the race of her attacker. If an investigator could determine that any or all of the above features were present, I reasoned, then couldn't the race of the unidentified rapist be surmised? It seemed like a promising project.

Then, over time, my wonderful theory came crashing down. I began noting cases in which several of the behavioral features I had associated with white offenders were present, yet the attacker turned out to be black.

The case of Malcolm Malone* was one of several that made me rethink my hypothesis.

Larry Ankrom of the BSU and I once interviewed an incarcerated black sexual sadist who had raped more than forty white women. Malcolm Malone was a well-educated and intelligent professional. His rapes were highly sophisticated. He had left no fingerprints and protected his identity so well that half of his victims thought he was white and the other half believed he was black.

The key to his success was patient and obsessive planning. In some cases he invested up to two years in preparation before carrying out an assault. Besides maintaining a secret 3×5 card catalog of his victims, on which he recorded a name, address, and age for each, he also kept track of the amount of fuel his car consumed and the number of miles he traveled in the course of each lengthy surveillance.

His modus operandi was to enter a victim's home when she was away and conduct a careful study of her private life. He read her magazines, looked in the medicine cabinet to check her prescriptions, thumbed through her checkbook, noted her taste in alcohol, examined her phone bills, and read her mail.

In the process he came familiar with the layout of the residence. In some instances he broke into the victim's home on the night before the intended attack to hide the "rape kit" (i.e., rope, gloves) he liked to employ in his assaults.

The idea behind all of his meticulous planning and investment of time was to emotionally traumatize his victim even as he physically brutalized her. Characteristically, he would reveal the intimate knowledge he had gained by questioning the frightened woman.

"Why are you taking (such and such) medication?"

"Congratulations on paying off your car last month."

"Why don't you call your mother in Tampa more often? The last time you called her was March 14."

"Why did you cancel your subscription to *TIME*? You took it for two years."

"You need to write your brother Billy more often. He has written you three letters without a reply."

Very quickly, Malone would convince a victim that he knew everything about her. She had no secrets, nothing that was hers alone. This is a vivid example of the master-slave relational fantasy. The sadist perceives himself to be a god, her god, and he can prove his godlike omniscience to her by flaunting the information he possesses.

He'd tell the woman her boyfriend's name, and often he knew when they last had sex together. Then he would demand that she describe the encounter in detail, telling her that if she left anything out, she would die. One of his victims was a mental health professional. As he raped her, he forced her to explain his motive.

Malone finally was caught inside an intended victim's empty house after a neighbor saw the lights go on and called the police. He answered the officers' knock at the door and calmly explained that he was alone in the residence because he lived there. However, when an astute policeman asked him the telephone number, he didn't know it and was arrested.

Under my working hypothesis, Malone's behavior would have suggested to investigators that he was white. Yet he clearly was black. He had been raised in a middle-class home by his black mother, who was employed as a professional. During the interview, Malone told Larry and me that he dated only white women. He was married to a white woman at the time of his crimes.

I credit my experience with his case for leading me to a fuller and more practical understanding of the factors governing offender behavior. As similar cases involving black ritualistic sexual criminals came to my attention, I noted that these offenders also tended to come from middle-class or higher families. I realized that it isn't race but socioeconomic and cultural influences that determine these behaviors.

As a corollary, I believe that as more blacks and Hispanics move into the middle class, they will begin to display more of the ritualistic behaviors currently associated with white offenders.

COMPULSIVE DRIVERS, POLICE BUFFS, TRY-SEXUALS, AND FAMILY MEN

Our study of the thirty sexual sadists yielded many surprising and provocative results. Seventeen of them had no arrest record prior to the crimes for which they were imprisoned. The fact that some of the most heinous offenders operating in North America had no arrest history is a strong testament to their planning and intelligence.

Twelve of them were compulsive drivers. This is a behavior found often in the more physically violent sexual offenders. Ted Bundy (who was not a sexual sadist) drove enormous distances in search of victims. Jon Simonis, a serial rapist and sexual sadist included in our study, drove eighty thousand miles in just ten months.

Simonis told me that driving gave him a sense of freedom from responsibility. A student of mine, with strong credentials as a psychologist, suggested that driving provides the offender with constantly changing visual stimulation requiring no effort on his part. He can simply sit in his seat and watch the scenery change.

Nine of the thirty men were police buffs. They collected police paraphernalia, drove vehicles that resembled police cruisers, maintained scanners, and might even have taken courses in police work or applied to become officers.

Mike DeBardeleben, who may hold the record for long-distance driving among sexual offenders, operated a Thunderbird that he had modified to resemble an unmarked police car. He also installed red lights and a siren beneath the Ford's grille. Inside he kept both a police scanner and a two-way radio.

One method he used to gain access to victims was to "patrol" lightly traveled roadways late at night and early in the morning, searching for women drivers who were alone.

When he spotted a likely victim, he would pull her over with grille lights flashing. He would show her a badge (purchased out of a detective magazine) and advise the woman that she looked very much like a female robber being sought by the police. Therefore, he claimed, he had to take her to the station for an elimination lineup.

We know from survivors of these encounters that DeBardeleben would handcuff them, place them in his car, wrap duct tape around their heads, and then drive them to preselected locations where he raped and tortured them, sometimes for days. DeBardeleben is believed to be a murderer as well as a rapist, but authorities have not been able to establish how many, if any, of his police-stop victims he killed.

Gerard John Schaefer was working as a deputy sheriff when he arrested two young women and took them to his "dumping ground." Schaefer was a very intelligent sexual sadist who spent almost every waking hour thinking and writing about sexually violent acts toward women and drawing pictures of them, too. I wanted to interview Schaefer, and through his girlfriend, Sondra London, he sent me a letter.

Schaefer began by acknowledging his guilt for two murders, that of Mary Alice Briscolina in October of 1972, as well as "her pal, Elsie." He continued, "It's an open-and-shut situation except why they had to die. How they did in fact die. The sadism part. How one has to watch while the other dies; knowing she'll be next. That's what you want to hear, right? . . . Naturally there needs to be a spirit of cooperation here, so I'll take the first step toward that end. I'll give you Briscolina on the house."

Schaefer's interest in law enforcement remained strong over the years. The sadists in our study believed in the old axiom, "Know thy Enemy." He wrote me that he tried to keep up with everything on homicide investigation. In the same letter he mentioned my book on autoerotic fatalities in connection with an argument he'd had over whether women engage in autoerotic bondage and orgasmic asphyxia. Apparently, he used me as an authority.

In a second letter his narcissism was unmistakable. "Not because I'm a practitioner myself, but because of my being somewhat of a recognized authority on sexual ritualism . . . I can see why you need my help. You really don't have much actual knowledge about the rituals you investigate, do you? Plenty of speculations, to be sure, but nothing concrete . . . My speciality, as you may know . . . is 'Death Strap Bondage.' "

Schaefer was familiar with the article I coauthored on detective magazines. "In your work: Detective Magazines; Porn (sic) for the Sexual Sadist, page 202, Case 1. That's certainly Harvey Glatman. The gal he tied up and strangled was Ruth Mercado. The cop who worked the case was Pierce Brooks, who's now with some serial killer unit [Pierce Brooks, now deceased, was the first unit chief of the FBI's Violent Crime Apprehension Program, known as VICAP]. Why the reluctance to say so in the story? Glatman was gassed in 1958. He can't sue anyone."

Thirteen of the group were married and fifteen were fathers. Nine of them committed incest with their children. One of the men in the survey, Gerald Gallego, is believed responsible for ten murders. In addition to his crimes against strangers, Gallego reportedly forced himself on his daughter from her childhood well into her teens. On one occasion he allegedly assaulted her anally as a birthday present! Another time he is said to have sexually assaulted both his daughter and a female friend who was visiting.

We could document that fifteen of these men had at least one consenting homosexual encounter as an adult. Six had cross-dressed, and six had a history of voyeurism, obscene phone calls, or exhibitionism.

Taken together, the reported incest, homosexual acts, cross-dressing, and assorted paraphilias produce a group portrait of what my old friend and BSU partner, Ken Lanning, called "try-sexuals" because they'll try anything sexual.

Dr. Gene Abel, an Atlanta-based mental health expert who is internationally recognized for his work with sexual offenders, has found that aberrant offenders rarely exhibit just a single deviation. If you know an individual is a voyeur, for example, you can expect to find that he is engaging in at least one additional paraphilia, such as fetishism.

Documenting such behavior, of course, is another question. Peeping, obscene calls, and indecent exposure typically are treated as nuisance offenses, troublesome but not serious. Yet before disregarding such offenses, investigators should try to ascertain just what the caller said over the phone or what an exhibitionist said as he exposed himself. "You are lovely, and I would like to make love to you" is very different from, "I want to stab you till my arm falls off."

The caller in all likelihood is masturbating to this fantasy as he speaks. The idea is what arouses him. A person with such violent fantasies should be identified and evaluated for treatment, if possible, because he poses a potentially grave danger to society.

PREFERENCES AND PASSIONS

We found considerable uniformity in our sample group when it came to their preferred sexual acts with victims. Seventy-three percent of the sadists preferred anal rape; 70 percent preferred fellatio; 58 percent vaginal intercourse; and 40 percent foreign object penetration.

Why such a strong preference for anal sex? It is tempting to surmise a connection to their adult homosexual experiences. But I don't think the answer is that simple. Remember, anger and the will to power are the sexual sadist's primary motivations; in addition, he is aroused by suffering. That's why I believe his preference for anal rape is tied to the pain and degradation such an act exacts upon the victim.

This would also explain the common preference for fellatio. While not nearly as physically injurious, fellatio can be highly traumatic emotionally. It requires not only that a victim participate against her will, but that she perform an undeniably intimate act in a demeaning way with a total stranger.

Similarly, penetration by a foreign object is degrading. In my opinion, it is the ultimate objectification of a woman. It was a favorite of DeBardeleben, Anderson, and Malone, all of whom tortured victims by inserting oversized dildos into their rectums.

DEAD ON THE OUTSIDE

A major surprise for me in the survey was how unemotional and detached most of the men seemed with their victims. Prior to reviewing the tapes and videos they kept of their crimes, I expected they would be hyperventilating from the excitement, the way Billy Lee Chadd described his own ecstatic moments. My assumption was wrong. Chadd was the exception.

One of Mike DeBardeleben's victims told police, "He was like a boring schoolteacher," repeatedly instructing her on what she was to say and how she was to act. On the several torture tapes he recorded, the only emotion DeBardeleben shows is occasional anger when a victim fails to accurately repeat the words of a script he's given her, or she doesn't perform sexually in the manner he demands. The more frenzied his victims become, the more detached DeBardeleben becomes. The same was true of Leonard Lake.

The great white sharks are into power and control. To them emotions, especially fear, indicate a weakness that they associate only with victims. In fact, for sexual sadists, the victim must by definition show fear. He, on the other hand, must exhibit power and control over others *and* over himself.

"You have two choices," Leonard Lake says on one videotape in a flat voice, "you can either cook, clean, and fuck for us; or we will take you in the back, tie you to the bed, rape you, take you out in the woods, shoot you in the head, and bury you. What is your decision?"

Not only was Lake reinforcing his narcissistic self-image of godlike power; but he was also conveying to his victim, who fully realized her helplessness, that he was her opposite, the omnipotent controller of her destiny.

TERRIFIED ON THE INSIDE

Such posturing masks a very different inner reality for most sexual sadists. Fear, in the form of paranoia, is one of their constant companions. Indeed, after narcissistic and antisocial personality disorders, I noted a wide prevalence of paranoid personality disorder (PPD) among our thirty subjects.

Persons with PPD are suspicious, mistrustful, hypervigilant, and constantly concerned with being betrayed. The paranoiac harbors illogical doubts about the loyalty of others and reads hidden meanings into innocent remarks or events.

Mike DeBardeleben's reading ran to titles such as *You're Under Surveillance* and *How to Tell If Your Phone's Been Tapped*. At his various trials for counterfeiting, kidnap, and rape, he repeatedly alleged a federal conspiracy against him, spearheaded by Mike Stephens, Greg Mertz, and Dennis Foos, the three Secret Service agents who investigated DeBardeleben after his capture. More than once he accused Foos of Nazism, a bizarre allegation that he never explained.

"I was framed," he railed at one of his trials, "framed in a sinister, evil, and insidious machination, a conspiracy, if you will!"

He even denounced one of his ex-wives for her imagined role in the plot against him, even though this emotionally broken woman never testified and still sobs at the mere mention of his name.

STRANGE BEDFELLOWS

I'm sure many readers will be surprised to learn that in my experience the two types of sexual offenders with the most characteristics in common are sexual sadists and pedophiles.

This seems counterintuitive, I know. Most pedophiles are not physically violent, while the sexual sadist is very likely to be so. However, when you look at these two more closely, certain striking similarities emerge.

First, a clarification of terms. Pedophile and child molester often are used interchangeably, but they are quite different. *Pedophile,* in psychiatric usage, describes an individual who is preferentially attracted sexually to a prepubescent child (generally thirteen years of age or less). However, a pedophile does not become a criminal until he molests a child. It is entirely possible for a pedophile to act out his sexual preferences only in his mind or with a consenting adult or paid partner who plays the role of a child. That is not criminal behavior.

Child molester is a legal term used to describe any person who sexually molests a child, which most definitely is criminal behavior. All child molesters are criminals, and a pedophile who acts out against a child consequently is a child molester. The adult male criminal pedodile deliberately preys on children.

Here is how he and the sexual sadist are alike:

- Both are ritualistic sexual criminals. They have highly developed fantasy lives and carry out their crimes according to a script.
- Both are highly motivated (their crimes give them deep satisfaction) and they invest great amounts of time, money, and energy to their criminal behavior.

- Neither experiences remorse or guilt. The sexual sadist believes that his victims deserve to suffer. The pedophile doesn't believe he's caused harm to the child.
- Both are highly practiced at rationalizing their behavior and consequently are poorly motivated to change.
- Both recognize that society abominates them, and they take steps to study their deviant desires and behaviors to better understand them and to evade arrest.
- Both collect theme-oriented pornography and/or erotica that serves to complement their preexisting fantasies.
- They possess average or better intelligence and social skills. They mesh well in society. Friends and associates are surprised and supportive of them when they are identified.
- Both are likely to commit incest with their natural children and will molest stepchildren or other minor relatives.
- They record their criminal sexual acts. This provides them with a means of reliving and improving on their criminal acts.
- Their rate of recidivism is much greater than for other sexual offenders. They tend to be model prisoners and consequently are released more quickly and, having learned nothing from their punishment, quickly begin practicing sexual deviance again.
- Both are highly narcissistic.
- Both have a low threshold for sexual boredom and involve their victims in progressively offensive and demeaning behaviors.
- Most sexual criminals slow down with age. There is no known burn-out age for these two offenders. Unless stopped, such men will offend well into their sixties or seventies.
- They have greater numbers of victims than other sexual offenders. Once these men begin to act out criminally, they will assault until they are caught.

- They are predominantly middle-class offenders. This is another reason why other people are surprised when they are identified.

Criminal sexual sadists pose one of law enforcement's greatest challenges. Though rare, they are intelligent men who invest great amounts of time in planning their crimes, and they easily blend into society because they "look like us."

Above all, they are determined.

As Jon Simonis told Ken Lanning and me: "There are a lot of steps you can take to help eliminate the average criminal, who is just spontaneous and reckless and careless. But if somebody wants somebody bad enough, it's nearly impossible to prevent. They could have the best security in the world. They could have guards and dogs and everything else. But if you have the time and the patience, the opportunity is going to arise when you can hit someone."

7

SEXUAL SLAVERY

In 1990, I attended a case presentation in San Francisco given by Christine McGuire, then an assistant district attorney in Santa Cruz, and Chris Hatcher, a well-known forensic psychologist, since deceased, with whom I had consulted on a number of cases.

McGuire and Hatcher spoke before a professional audience about an astonishing case that Christine had prosecuted (and in which Chris had testified as an expert witness)—the kidnapping and seven-year sexual enslavement of college student Colleen Stan. The story, which Christine has recounted with writer Carla Norton in their book, *Perfect Victim,* began when Stan, twenty, started hitchhiking south from Eugene, Oregon, through Red Bluff, California, on May 19, 1977. Colleen was on her way to a friend's birthday party in the Northern California hamlet of Westwood, about one hundred miles south of Red Bluff.

As she stood beside the road with her thumb out, a blue Dodge Colt drew to a stop. Inside she saw a young couple, Cameron and Janice Hooker, with their baby daughter. The Hookers told Colleen that they were headed in her direction. She gratefully got into the backseat.

Colleen could remember no particular reason why this mild-mannered couple seemed to become more and more sinister to her as they drove along, but they did. At a rest stop, the young woman had to argue herself out of bolting their company at once.

Then it was too late. Out in the middle of nowhere, as the Hookers drove to what they said was a brief side excursion to explore some ice caves, Cameron Hooker stopped the car, pulled a knife, and told Colleen to do exactly as he said. Thus began seven years of hell during which Colleen was confined in a box kept beneath the Hookers' bed. She was sexually abused and degraded, and brainwashed into believing that she deserved the life of suffering to which they subjected her. On several occasions she might have succeeded in escaping but did not attempt it.

Perfect Victim provides a full account of this horrendous tale, and I recommend it to the reader. It would be an understatement to say that Christine and Chris kept their audience spellbound that day in San Francisco.

Following their presentation, several people approached me with the same question: "Wouldn't you love to interview Colleen Stan?" To their surprise, I said I was more interested in interviewing Janice Hooker. She was married to Cameron Hooker for thirteen years. I wanted to know what their courtship was like. What kind of father and provider he was? What did he read or watch on television? What type of sexual partner was he? What were his childhood and adolescence like? Did he collect things? If so, what? Did he have political views? Why did she cooperate in Colleen Stan's abduction?

So many questions occurred to me. Then I got a great idea.

I had already interviewed a great many people with strange and violent stories to tell: serial rapists, sexual sadists, child abductors, killers of all sorts, and relatives of their victims. My colleagues in the BSU had also interviewed a wide range of aberrant offenders: serial killers, assassins, traitors, child abductors, and serial arsonists. But to my knowledge, no one ever had systematically interviewed the wives and girlfriends of sexual sadists.

A STUDY IN SERVITUDE

I brought my idea to John Campbell, unit chief at the BSU. He approved the research project, which I undertook in collaboration with my old research partners, Park Dietz and Janet Warren. Together, we developed an interview protocol, or questionnaire, that covered more than five hundred separate facts.

This was by far the most interesting and emotionally challenging series of interviews I ever conducted. Identifying the women wasn't difficult; I had extensive personal knowledge about many sexual sadists, plus I enjoyed wonderful support and cooperation from FBI agents, police officers, mental health professionals, and prosecutors throughout the country.

Eventually, we interviewed twenty "compliant victims." I refer to them as compliant, not to excuse any criminal behavior, but rather to make clear that they, too, were victims of physical, sexual, and emotional abuse at the hands of sexual sadists.

In contrast to the sexual sadists' stranger victims, however, the wives and girlfriends acquiesced in their treatment.

COMPLIANT VICTIMS

One of the most surprising facts to emerge was how quiet and conventional these women's lives were before they met the sadistic male. All were of average or better intelligence, and they had completed from between eleven and sixteen years of formal education. Only two were unemployed at the time they began their relationship with the sexual sadist.

Eight of the women worked at unskilled jobs, six in skilled positions (i.e., secretary, salesperson), and four were professionals (i.e., teacher, business owner). Five members of the study group were in school (four in high school and one in college) at the time they met the man. Only two had used drugs before becoming the sadist's partner. Almost all eventually would abuse illegal drugs.

They had no criminal histories to speak of—fewer than five arrests among them. One had shoplifted a tube of lipstick at age fourteen. Another had tried to steal a typewriter. A third was arrested at eighteen for stealing a check.

The main thing they shared was intimacy with a type of sexual offender who views all women as evil. He thinks of them as bitches, whores, sluts, and worse. The sexual sadist's agenda is to prove himself right in this opinion. Consequently, he doesn't select a prostitute or drug addict as his wife or girlfriend. Instead, he chooses a woman from a nice middle-class family and gradually transforms her into a sexual slave willing to join him in any act, no matter how degrading or depraved, to prove her love or to keep him from leaving.

Although each woman had a unique story to tell, the men they were involved with used the same techniques to bring them under their control. The process was amazingly consistent from offender to offender, and it comprised five identifiable steps.

THE ROAD TO A LIVING HELL

First, the sexual sadist identifies a likely partner/victim. A variety of traits make a woman vulnerable to such men. Youthfulness, low self-esteem, inexperience, naïveté, difficulty making decisions, or recent emotional trauma, such as the breakup of a relationship—any of these factors can make a person more easy to manipulate.

I also noticed in my interviews that many of the women tended to be dependent. In fact, I believe some of them would be professionally diagnosed with dependent personality disorder (DPD), described in *Diagnostic and Statistical Manual,* 4th edition (DSM IV) as "a pattern of submissive and clinging behavior relating to an excessive need to be taken care of." Sexual sadists have a deadly radar for such women.

The second step is seduction. The sexual sadist's goal is to have the targeted woman fall in love with him. He is complimentary, uncritical, full of nice surprises, such as gifts and flowers. He generally works hard at making her happy. Eventually, she falls in love with him, and her love becomes a very effective weapon that he uses against her.

You can move a lot of garbage across the bridge of love: alcoholism, infidelity, addiction, abuse. The compliant victim loves almost unconditionally; she'll endure remarkable amounts of abuse, pain, and heartache once she's fallen in love. And she'll acquiesce in loathsome acts of which she once was utterly incapable.

Janice Hooker, for example, apparently wanted a second child by her husband, Cameron. He instinctively exacted a price. As Colleen Stan later told a TV reporter, "I was basically a trade-off. 'You can have another child if I can have a slave.' . . . So I was a trade-off."

In step three, the sexual sadist reshapes his compliant partner's sexual norms using some basic behavior modification techniques. When, for example, she accedes to a sexual request beyond her level of experience, she is rewarded with feigned kindness, affection, and attention. If she refuses him, he pouts, ignores her, and generally tries to make her feel guilty. Eventually, he manipulates her into performing sexual acts that not only are beyond her experience but also her previous moral threshold.

This, of course, further reduces her self-esteem. Over time he no longer finds it necessary to reward her sexual acquiescence; he simply demands it. If compliance is not forthcoming, he physically and verbally abuses her.

The fourth step, often carried out in concert with step three, is to socially isolate the woman from her family, friends, and associates. He can't afford to have his partner confide in others about what is taking place in the home so he gradually reduces her contacts outside their relationship.

The stratagems he employs are roundabout and often cunning. One of the women owned a clothing boutique. As she explained to me, she and her employees would go to lunch together and pay via what she called a "New York split": the bill was divided equally among those present, regardless of what each one had to eat. She always had a wonderful time at these meals, as her employees were also good friends of long-standing.

Then she married a sexual sadist. He convinced her that even with the New York split she was spending too much money on lunches. He proposed that they both limit lunch spending to $1.50 a day and suggested that they put the amount they saved toward the purchase of new furniture she wanted. She found it difficult to disagree and consequently no longer went to lunch with her employees. He had successfully separated her from her friends and coworkers without betraying his true motivation.

Another woman had regularly telephoned her mother long-distance until her sexually sadistic husband made saving money the excuse for cutting back the calls to once a month, and then for no more than ten minutes at a time.

A third young woman and her sexually sadistic new husband moved into a beautiful lakefront house 150 miles from her nearest friends and family. He had insisted that they move to that location. Three days later he began to abuse her physically and sexually. Isolated as she was, she had no one to turn to for help or advice.

The fifth and final step is punishment. Once the relationship has reached this point, all pretense of love and caring disappears. The woman is isolated from family and friends, and she is wholly dependent on the only person left in her life—the sexual sadist.

By now he has thoroughly conditioned her to comply with his perverted sexual demands; and because she does so, he is able to affirm his belief that all women are evil. He reasons that no decent woman would participate in such disgusting behavior. Because she does participate, she justifies the hatred he has secretly had for her from the beginning. In his twisted logic, she deserves to be punished.

Among my case files, one woman's story stands out as a telling example of this evil transformation.

ANN'S STORY

Ann* came to my attention several years ago when Tamia Hope, an assistant prosecutor in the Los Angeles County District Attorney's Office, asked me to be a witness in connection with physical and sexual abuse charges she was bringing against Lyle,* a Los Angeles businessman.

Ann was a married, thirty-six-year-old insurance broker at the time she met Lyle. I would describe her as a naive and trusting person. Ann informed me that although she had been sexually active in her marriage, she had never engaged in any type of sadomasochistic sex, nor had she ever engaged in oral or anal sex before meeting Lyle.

They met when he walked into her office to inquire about a sizable life insurance policy. He was about forty years old, moderately handsome, and very well dressed. Ann said she was impressed by how attentive he was during their initial conversation. Although his purpose ostensibly was business, she remembered that they touched on many personal topics that day, including their respective marriages and expectations in life.

Six months later Lyle called to say that he was interested in another, much larger policy. They met for lunch at an expensive marina restaurant. At the time Ann was having marital problems, and she was depressed. Lyle's compliments and the undivided attention he lavished on her during their meal were more than welcome. She was in need of a sympathetic listener.

He was intelligent, articulate, and also very funny. Their lunch lasted for several hours, and then they went for a drive. Eventually, they checked into a motel, where Lyle proved to be a considerate sexual partner.

Over the next month he sent flowers and other gifts and

called often, becoming a confidante with whom Ann was comfortable sharing any problem. Their sex life intensified, too. To demonstrate her love, Ann agreed to Lyle's request that she perform oral sex. He seemed extremely appreciative, which pleased her a great deal.

He encouraged Ann to leave her husband, and she did so for a month. Even after a marital reconciliation, Ann continued to meet and to have a sexual relationship with Lyle. Not surprisingly, her marriage eventually failed.

She moved into an apartment and gave herself even more fully to Lyle. Ann told me she had fallen so deeply in love with him that she believed he could never do anything to harm her.

Then their relationship began to change. Gradually, he induced her into smoking crack cocaine, and this habit became a repeated feature of their relationship. She would go to his house, and he would insist that she smoke crack before any other activities took place. One evening, while Ann was under the influence of the drug, he had anal intercourse with her. For the remaining year of their relationship, he never had vaginal sex with her again.

Step by step, with infinite patience, Lyle seduced her into a world of perversity and pain. Certain now of her emotional dependence on him, he told her that he preferred women with large buttocks. To please him, she agreed to consume large quantities of calorie-laden liquids. As Ann's buttocks grew larger, Lyle periodically would measure and photograph them. Of course, this increased weight further lowered Ann's self-esteem and dependency. Who else, she reasoned, would love her but Lyle?

Increasing her use of cocaine, he also began inserting foreign objects into her, including large flashlights, an ironing table leg, and a large cylindrical wooden club that he called "the donkey dick." He recorded these and other acts with photographs as well as with charts and notes that were seized during the subsequent criminal investigation.

As is true with almost all sexual sadists, Lyle was aroused by bondage. Using ropes, belts, and handcuffs, he bound Ann in a variety of ways and postures, all designed to cause her pain and humiliation. He would fasten her wrists and ankles together. He would place her facedown with her wrists tied to her knees and with her buttocks raised to facilitate anal intercourse. Lyle routinely beat her so hard with a whip that she bled. Soon the whip end became frayed and had to be replaced.

Another favorite fantasy prop among sexual sadists is the slave contract. Lyle drafted and forced Ann to sign one that read: "I, Ann, do hereby bequeath to Lyle total ownership of my person and possessions. This entitles him to do whatever he pleases to me. He has the right to expect total obedience and the right to impose punishment as he deems necessary. I release Lyle from all liability, both personal and financial. I will be responsible for all of my own bills. I have willingly entered into this contract." (Signed)

"I became convinced I was his slave," Ann later told me, "and he could do anything he wanted to me, even kill me. I didn't enjoy what he was doing, and I didn't want him to do these things to me. But when I refused to cooperate, he would hurt me so bad that I was afraid not to do as he ordered. If I did what he wanted, he would be nice and not hurt me so much. Because of this I wanted to be the best slave possible, and I worked hard at it."

Among the humiliations Lyle forced on Ann was anal sex with at least two other men. On each occasion he forced her to get high by smoking cocaine, bound her, beat her, and placed her in a closet on her knees. He then led the other man into the closet and told him to penetrate her anally. Ann recalled that on one occasion Lyle instructed the other man to "fuck her so hard her head hits the wall."

Interestingly, he would not permit the man to ejaculate.

Lyle isolated Ann from family and friends, but he could not completely mask the horrors he inflicted. Ann's productivity dropped at work. On several occasions she had no choice but to wear clothing inappropriate to the season in order to cover her bruises. With nowhere to turn, she continued to accept the horrendous abuse.

Then Lyle demanded that Ann quit her job and devote her entire life to being his slave. She told me that her job was her final link to sanity, and she realized that if she complied with his demand to quit, she would not survive physically or emotionally.

One day, after he had gone out, she somehow found the courage to make a break. She gathered together the Polaroids he'd taken of her buttocks, plus the frayed whip, the written scripts she'd been forced to follow as he assaulted her, her bloody clothing, and fled.

ANN'S QUEST FOR JUSTICE

Ann's first step was to enter a substance-abuse program to kick the cocaine habit that Lyle had induced. Upon completion of the lengthy program, she went to the police to file rape, assault and battery, and false imprisonment charges against him.

The two Los Angeles police detectives who were assigned Ann's case realized the difficulty of making such charges stick in court. How were they to prove that she wasn't a masochist who had gone along voluntarily? Still, the two men were convinced of Lyle's criminal behavior, and they vigorously investigated the case.

After reviewing the detectives' findings, a male assistant prosecutor also thought the case too difficult to prove and declined to take the matter to court. A year later, however, he was replaced by Tamia Hope. She wanted justice for Ann. "I'll try the son of a bitch," Tamia reportedly said after hearing the details of Ann's ordeal.

One potential obstacle was Ann herself, who feared confronting Lyle in court. She was unsure of her ability to stop him from regaining control over her. She asked that she be allowed to hold a stuffed animal during her testimony, as that might give her the strength to get through it. Tamia was supportive, and the judge approved the unusual request.

It worked. After effectively recounting her grim story at a preliminary hearing with Lyle sitting nearby, she told us, with some pride and relief in her voice, "He's not as big as he used to be." I thought to myself, What a wonderfully telling statement.

Tamia Hope proved herself a resourceful prosecutor, and I admired her strategy. Aware that Lyle would probably claim Ann was a consenting partner in everything that took place, she charged him with several crimes for which Ann's consent or lack of consent were less of an issue or no issue at all. For example, she filed multiple counts of illegal possession of cocaine.

Hope also charged Lyle with false imprisonment, assault and battery, and accessory to rape. The accessory count became possible after the police had identified one of the men whom Lyle had invited to have anal sex with Ann in the closet. As part of a plea bargain, that man agreed to testify against Lyle.

Drug possession wasn't going to be difficult to prove, since cocaine was seized during a search of Lyle's residence. The charges of false imprisonment and assault would depend upon whether the judge believed that Ann was truly a victim and not a willing participant.

Tamia Hope was more than equal to the task. First, she had me explain under oath what sexual sadism is and how these men characteristically act out their aberrant fantasies against consenting and nonconsenting partners.

There wasn't much that Lyle's attorney could do to refute my testimony because at no time did I say that his client was a sexual sadist. I simply explained the beast, but didn't give him a name.

Then the two detectives testified effectively about their interview of Ann and what they had learned in their subsequent investigation.

Then Ann testified. Unsurprisingly, she was subjected to a brutal cross-examination. Lyle's attorney tried to demonstrate what he called her "willing participation" and attempted to document his argument with established facts.

One was the undisputed fact that Ann had, for months, driven to Lyle's home on Friday evenings and returned to work on Monday mornings. She had also purchased some of Lyle's sadistic paraphernalia for him, including the dog collar and the dildo.

The attorney's intent was to characterize Ann as a masochist who didn't just endure Lyle's sadism but was aroused by it. She was shaken by the accusations and innuendo but clutched her stuffed animal and firmly rebutted the lawyer, explaining that what he called "willing participation" was really just fear of what Lyle would do if she didn't comply.

Afterward, we all agreed that the single most important prosecution witness at the hearing was a psychiatrist. He testified that after examining Ann for several hours, he believed she suffered from post-traumatic stress disorder (PTSD) and was therefore incapable of giving informed consent to her own abuse. The defense naturally attacked that opinion, but the psychiatrist was magnificent on the stand: calm, firm, professional, and highly credible.

The defense lawyer resorted to a familiar tactic: If you can't attack the evidence, attack the collector of the evidence. He asked the psychiatrist how much the state of California was paying him. But the defense attorney had forgotten the first rule of a lawyer in court: Never ask a question to which you don't know the answer.

In a clear voice the doctor said he had waived his fee. Because he had never seen or heard of such a horrendous crime, he had examined Ann at no cost and agreed to testify without compensation. He had also volunteered to treat her at no cost until he believed she had recovered from PTSD.

The defense had no further questions.

Rather than risk the impact such testimony might have on Lyle's jury, the defense agreed to a plea bargain. Plea bargains are not unusual in such cases. Once the issue of consent has been overcome, the defense is confronted with dealing with a jury of citizens who tend to focus, not on the complicated nuances of the law, but rather on the horrors that one human being can inflict on another.

I believe it likely that many of the battered spouses seen by mental health professionals and victim advocates may also be compliant victims of sexual sadists. These men may go unidentified because of the battering's masking effect—the treater focuses *only* on the battering and not the rest of his behavior—or because the professional does not have the experience to recognize the sexual sadism in the relationship.

When I teach a course that includes discussion of compliant victims, it is not unusual for psychologists in the class to begin questioning their female patients, probing to see if they, too, are in a sadistic relationship. Judging by the phone calls and letters I receive from these professionals, many of the women are.

Tragically, many cases of sexual sadism remain hidden from society because, by their very nature, the compliant victims are unable to reach out for help.

8

PROFILING

"Discovery," the chemist Albert Szent-Györgyi once said, "consists of seeing what everyone has seen and thinking what nobody else has thought."

In Szent-Györgyi's case, the discovery was vitamin C. The Hungarian Nobelist's insight applies equally well though to the study of aberrant minds, particularly to profiling them. When done correctly, a profile is a detailed analysis that reveals and interprets significant features of a crime that previously had escaped notice or understanding. Profiling is thinking about a case in a way no one else has.

Let's try it out.

At 2:00 A.M. on a summer Thursday not too long ago, a state trooper stopped for a cup of coffee at a convenience store located on a heavily traveled four-lane road. He found the store's front doors open and all the lights on, but the clerk, eighteen-year-old Kathy,* was nowhere to be seen.

Her car was parked outside. On the counter by the register were a quart of chocolate milk, which had begun to sweat, and a package of powdered-sugar miniature donuts. Kathy's purse was in its usual place on a shelf behind the counter. Nothing seemed to be missing from it.

The store lacked both an alarm system and surveillance cameras. There were no signs of a struggle, and an appropriate amount of money was in the cash register, suggesting that no theft had occurred. The rear door was locked and chained.

The officer found a telephone beneath the counter. According to phone company records, Kathy had made no calls that evening. Her last known customer was a young man who had purchased some gas and milk at 1:10 A.M. He was cleared of any involvement in the disappearance.

Nothing was known of Kathy's fate until nine months later when two rabbit hunters came upon her skeletal remains twenty-seven miles away. The men had been hunting in a remote area accessible only via an unpaved road that ended on an undeveloped parcel of land about two miles square, bounded by farms and pastures. Its owner resided in another state and had no contact with the property other than to pay taxes on it.

The hunters were walking about 500 yards from the road when they came across some lingerie, pornographic magazines, and an inflatable doll. They ignored this material and continued to hunt. About 250 yards deeper into the woods, they began to follow a path cut through the heavy scrub-tree overgrowth.

Approximately 125 feet farther on, they encountered a circular clearing about twelve feet in diameter. In the center of the clearing was a wooden rack shaped like a large upright X. Across the top of the rack was a wooden pole with rope suspended from it. Three leather straps were attached to each of the two wooden cross pieces. The hunters noticed a woman's slip, obviously weather-worn, hanging from the center of the rack.

They immediately called the police.

A CHILLING DISCOVERY

One of the first items that officers noted at the scene was a continuous length of colored, plastic-coated wire that led into and away from the clearing. In one direction it led back down the route the hunters had taken along the cleared path, past the doll, lingerie, and pornography, to the dead-end road. The wire also led in the opposite direction from the rack. Investigators followed it for fifty feet until they found scattered bones and tattered clothes: Kathy's remains.

The clothing appeared to have been cut from her body. Around her neck were the remnants of her brassiere, together with two circular lengths of twisted coat hanger wire. One piece was five inches in diameter and the other three inches. The victim's hair was entwined in each.

None of her bones were broken or fractured. The medical examiner determined that Kathy had been strangled to death with the smaller piece of wire.

ENTER THE PROFILER

My role in this case was unusual. The police had developed a suspect but requested my assistance in approaching his ex-wife as a potential witness. Before I could do that, I needed to know something about her relationship with him, which in turn meant I needed an unbiased idea of what he was like.

The best source of information about an aberrant offender is his work product. Accordingly, I asked to examine the crime-scene materials in order to build a profile of the killer. My interpretation would inform me about the suspect, and these inferences, in turn, would guide me to make suggestions about interviewing the ex-wife.

After reviewing case materials, my first questions are always focused on the victim—what type of person was murdered? This is critical information. To understand what happened to Kathy, I needed to know who she was: her personality traits, habits, occupation, lifestyle, and sexual behavior.

Kathy was an unusual type of victim for such a crime. She was working at the convenience store to earn money for college. Kathy didn't abuse alcohol and had nothing to do with drugs. She had a steady boyfriend and no interests or habits that would have brought her in contact with criminals. The one important risk factor was her working the late shift at the convenience store (law enforcement officers call them "stop and robs").

Those who knew her reported that Kathy would have fought an attacker unless the odds were dramatically against her. Since there was no sign of a struggle at the store, this information suggested several possible scenarios. She could have been abducted by someone she knew. Or her kidnapper might have conned her into leaving the store. For example, he could have told her that someone had broken a window in her car. Or he might have had a gun. Or maybe several abductors were involved. Such a variety of possible explanations is typical when assessing behavioral clues. The important thing is to maintain an open mind, not to lock in on only one possibility.

Kathy was taken from a well-lighted place of business on a busy road. It was a location that the criminal could not control because someone could walk in at any moment. In my opinion the offender took a high risk of being observed, interrupted, or identified when he committed the crime.

I next considered the abduction site. The still photos I was given showed that the donuts were shelved in one corner of the store and the milk in an opposite corner. Setting aside the possibility that individuals unconnected to the crime left these items on the counter, I believed they pointed toward an MO and the likelihood that a single individual was responsible. A plausible reconstruction suggested itself: The UNSUB calmly walked around inside the store, ostensibly in search of what he needed, but in fact on the lookout for other people and for the presence of surveillance cameras.

This scenario indicated that he was a deliberate, cautious offender, interested in reducing his risks as much as possible. He could casually bring the donuts to the counter, and then the milk, without arousing Kathy's suspicion. In the process he discovered what he wanted to know about the location.

Since nothing appeared to be missing from either the cash register or Kathy's purse, I determined that she was his objective not the money. No fingerprints were found on either the donut package or the milk carton. This suggested that he either wore gloves or had wiped the items clean. Since the crime occurred in June, when gloves would have been out of place, wiping was a logical assumption.

The next question was: Were we dealing with an organized or disorganized killer? The evidence so far suggested to me that an organized offender had kidnapped and murdered Kathy.

The distinction between organized and disorganized offenders gives investigators a shorthand way to assess from crime scene evidence whether the perpetrator is deliberate and experienced or in a rush, careless and sloppy. The organized offender usually brings with him his preferred weapon and whatever else he needs to commit his crime. He leaves as little evidence as possible of himself and what he has done. The disorganized offender, on the other hand, has not thought ahead. He acts impulsively, using any available weapon, and may leave both his victim and ample evidence of his own identity (i.e., fingerprints or blood) where they can be readily discovered.

The fact that Kathy's car was not taken was further evidence that this UNSUB was organized. He had driven to and from the store in his own vehicle. Had hers been missing, we would have had to conclude that he probably arrived on foot or at least did not have access to transportation, which is a sign of disorganization.

THE CRIME SCENE

The next issue to consider was the location he chose to take Kathy. It appeared that he had prepared the site in advance, a further suggestion of his high degree of organization. The choice also showed he was familiar with the outdoors and comfortable there, too. The plastic-coated wire strengthened that impression. I guessed that he had laid the wire on the ground to guide him as he navigated the heavily overgrown acreage at night without the use of a flashlight.

A similar practice was once used in the military. Prior to wireless communications, soldiers installed the communications wire that ran from headquarters to forward areas. Those returning to headquarters were told to "follow the commo wire." I reflected, This man is a thinker.

The bra around Kathy's neck, I surmised, originally had been used as a gag and had slid downward as her body decomposed. The two pieces of wire also served specific functions. In my opinion, the five-inch twisted loop was placed around Kathy's neck as a collar, to which her abductor attached a lead to guide her as he followed the "commo" wire in the dark. Obviously, her wrists would have been bound, too. I also concurred with the medical examiner that the three-inch loop was the actual weapon of death. He would have used it to slowly strangle Kathy after acting out his aberrant fantasies.

As for the lingerie, magazines, and inflatable doll, I felt these were not connected to the crime. For one thing, the magazines were dated both prior to and after Kathy's abduction, and they fell into the category of "soft" porn. This meant that whoever had brought them was a regular visitor to the remote site, where he could masturbate undisturbed. The lingerie was mostly weather worn, but there were also relatively new items of all different sizes and types.

Experience told me that a man with an autoerotic interest in such articles was far more passive than the killer we sought. The man who captured Kathy, bound her to the rack, and killed her in such a slow, agonizing manner would not have an unprotected collection of soft pornography. Kathy's killer was a sexual sadist. He would have a well cared for collection of pornography dealing with bondage, anal sex, and captivity. He would prize his collection too much to allow it to be exposed to the elements or theft.

My audiences always are curious about the plastic-coated wire. Was it just a coincidence that it ran past the magazines, doll, and assorted lingerie on its way to the rack in the clearing and then Kathy's remains?

In short, yes. I can't completely account for this fact, except to point out that the very seclusion that attracts a sexual killer to a remote site can also make the place attractive for other sorts of sexual purposes.

For example, Ted Bundy abducted and killed two women in one afternoon at Lake Sammamish State Park near Seattle. The subsequent search of the surrounding woodlands turned up twenty-six pairs of women's underpants, none belonging to either of Bundy's victims.

Sexual crime investigations also routinely reveal sexual deviants who live nearby or knew the victim or had access to the crime site but had nothing to do with the crime in question.

Another key source of information was the rack. This sadist had built it with the finest lumber and coated it with spar varnish, commonly used on quality watercraft. The rack had deep importance to him, undoubtedly connected to his aberrant fantasy.

No nails or screws were used in its construction. Instead, it was fastened with wooden dowels and glue. The leather straps were positioned to be used as wrist, thigh, and ankle restraints. They were not simply tacked to the crosspieces, but were attached through the wood itself. Here was a clear indication of his interest in sexual bondage.

Kathy's clothes were cut from her body, suggesting that she was dressed when she was bound to the rack. Her bra was used as a gag in her mouth. In such a position, she would also have been vulnerable to torture and sexual assault.

The location of the crime scene and the obvious amount of preparation underscores how comfortable the killer was in the outdoors. As the profile took form, I noted that he probably had outdoor hobbies, such as hunting and fishing.

It turned out that he loved to camp.

Connecting this inference with the bulkiness of his rack, I guessed that his vehicle of choice was large and rugged. Since he also clearly was meticulous, I said the vehicle would be well cared for.

He drove an immaculate four-wheel-drive pickup truck with a camper top.

Because I felt he was a sexual sadist who practiced bondage, my profile suggested he would have collections of bondage paraphernalia.

Not only did he save bondage magazines, he also owned a pair of handcuffs and practiced bondage on his wife.

The overwhelming majority of sexual sadists are white males, and this man seemed to be no exception. His demonstrated organization and caution suggested that he wasn't a young person. I placed his age from the late-twenties to mid-thirties.

He was a white male, thirty-six years of age.

The skilled construction of his rack suggested to me that he made a living by working with his hands.

He was a mechanic.

From the police I learned the suspect had been married, and from my studies of sexual sadists I knew he had probably dominated the former wife through sexual and possibly physical abuse.

At the time of the offense he was married. His wife, however, had left him in the months since then because he broke her arm as he forced her to participate in anal sex.

If he was a military veteran, I said, he would have served in the ground forces. The more aggressive sexual offenders who serve in the military perceive the army or marines as the most macho branches of service and therefore more compatible with their self-image.

The killer had served in the army.

The complexity and multiple components of his crime, plus the clear evidence of detailed advance planning, told me that this offender was of high-average or better intelligence, but I didn't think he was educated beyond high school.

He was of high-average intelligence, and he had completed a high school GED while in the army.

My research shows that these men typically appear friendly and outgoing, so I described him as an extrovert with a good sense of humor.

"Life of the party" was how his friends described him.

In order to reduce their risk of capture, organized killers most often select total strangers as victims. I therefore believed this killer probably was a stranger to Kathy.

He was.

Organized killers tend to hunt outside their neighborhoods. I surmised that this one resided a good distance from both the abduction and disposal sites.

He did not live or work within forty miles of either.

THE ART OF THE PROFILE

This sketch of Kathy's killer did not require higher psychic powers: no ESP, second sight, intuition, or voodoo. It was a purely deductive exercise based on the facts of the crime and my experience with such crimes and offenders.

When I joined the BSU in 1978, profiling was a little-known and spare-time service some of us unofficially provided to local law enforcement officers if they specifically requested us to do so. Usually we were called in when police officers who had been selected to attend the FBI National Academy brought their files on strange and unsolved crimes with them to Quantico. We would review the records and then provide our best opinion of the UNSUB's characteristics and traits.

At first we called our work "psychological profiling." Mental health professionals immediately complained that this was misleading, and they were right. We were not licensed psychologists. So we began to call the process "criminal personality profiling." Once again, we ruffled sensibilities. After all, what did a bunch of FBI agents know about the human personality?

We again changed the title, this time to "criminal investigative analysis," and when no one objected, the term stuck. Eventually criminal investigative analysis (CIA) came to describe not just profiling but all of the various operational tasks performed within the BSU.

Our informal franchise quickly evolved. Officers began calling to request a profile even if they had a suspect identified or in custody. What they actually wanted was our input on any number of matters where the outcome might hinge on personality and behavior, both the suspect's and theirs. Sometimes investigators asked us to suggest interview strategies. Other times an officer would want to know what type of materials should be included in search warrant lists.

Could we suggest how a certain individual may have committed a murder, or how he disposed of the body? What type of investigative strategy might be most successful against a particular UNSUB? Or what type of trial strategy did we recommend for a particular type of case and defendant?

In response to this broad range of requests, one of the techniques we developed was IPA, or indirect personality assessment. In an IPA you collect as much detailed information as you can about a particular individual in order to identify his strengths and weaknesses. Then, joining that information with your knowledge of criminal behavior, you develop strategies for law enforcement.

You might advise a proactive investigative technique to draw out a particular type of offender. Then you might suggest when and how to interview him. Some types of offenders respond well to a patient, sympathetic approach. For others, a simple hand on the shoulder, from behind, can have a galvanizing effect.

Later, you might give advice to the prosecutor on the content of his opening remarks, his cross-examination strategies, or even his order of witnesses. Prosecution strategies used in the trial of Atlanta child killer Wayne Williams are a good example.

Another of our services was linkage analysis. Here, we examine behavior in a series of crimes in an attempt to assess the likelihood that one person was responsible for all, or some, of them.

Equivocal death analysis (EDA) also emerged as a BSU subspeciality. An EDA weighs the available evidence to determine if a homicide, suicide, or accident most likely occurred. The process is similar to profiling except that you deal with a lot more variables.

Profile is among the most overworked terms in the law enforcement lexicon. There are drug courier profiles, child molester profiles, terrorist profiles, and even racial profiling. The usage has spread into society as a whole, so that today we often hear of medical profiles, mental health profiles, and even frequent flyer profiles.

In the BSU sense of the word, a profile is a listing of the characteristics and traits of an unidentified person. It is not meant to put a name and address on an UNSUB. But if done properly, the profile identifies the offender's personality type in a way that helps police narrow the focus of their investigation.

Profiling is subjective rather than objective; more art than science; an investigative tool rather than a magical solution to crime. I would never testify that a particular person must have committed a crime because he or she fit my profile. Likewise, I don't believe profiles should be part of an affidavit filed in support of an arrest or search warrant. The evidence that an investigator has compiled from experience or research (her own or that of others) is a far more valid basis for search warrants.

I also strongly urge anyone interested in entering this field as a career to be extremely cautious. There are a growing number of frauds out there who claim they can teach profiling, for a price. Some even claim that they will also find the student a position once he or she is trained. Proceed with caution!

While these sellers of magical elixirs may be superficially conversant in the lore and terminology of profiling, they're selling fairy tales, not facts. One woman told me that she'd paid a thousand dollars for "expert" training plus a guarantee of employment. But when it came time to place her, she was told that unfortunately all profiling positions were filled at the time.

In my experience the *only* legitimate profiling courses have been programs within the FBI National Center for the Analysis of Violent Crime (NCAVC) at Quantico, which includes the one-year police fellowship program begun at the Behavioral Science Unit (BSU) in the mid-1980s and the subsequent police understudy program taught by NCAVC-trained police fellows.

SETTING LIMITS

When we first started to define what profiles could and could not accomplish, we established three criteria for a crime to be considered for behavioral analysis.

1. It must be a violent or potentially violent crime.

2. It must be unsolved.

3. All major leads must be exhausted.

While profiling unquestionably could have been adapted to nonviolent crimes, we wanted to restrict the types of cases we would examine in order to contain the volume of work.

A particularly upsetting example of why we restricted profiling to unsolved offenses came early in my career at the BSU. Two students of mine, both detectives, asked if I could spare some time to examine a homicide they were working. I agreed to do so after class. For several hours I studied the crime-scene photographs and the accompanying materials and asked the two men questions.

Finally, I presented an oral profile of the type of person I believed had committed the murder. After I finished, one of them said, "You are absolutely correct. That's what he was like."

I asked what he meant by that. They explained that the case was solved and the person responsible was awaiting execution. They just wanted to see if I knew what I was talking about! From that point on, the criterion of "must be unsolved" was added.

Another rule we established is that we would accept cases only from the agency responsible for the investigation or prosecution of the crime. This precluded the possibility of one jurisdiction requesting a profile in the hopes of proving a point or embarrassing another. It also ensured the cooperation of the agency with the necessary information.

Because the crux of profiling is behavior, certain crimes may simply not yield enough information to infer what the unknown criminal is like. Among the most difficult cases to profile are those in which there is (1) no known cause of death, (2) an unidentified victim, or (3) lack of behavior to study and analyze.

If I am brought into a case in which the only evidence is a skeleton, with no forensic information to indicate how the victim was killed, how can I arrive at opinions as to the type of person who committed the murder? I can't.

An unidentified victim presents another set of obstacles. As in Kathy's case, a profile often starts with what we know about the victim. If a female, was she a housewife, student, drug abuser, hitchhiker, alcoholic, prostitute, sexually promiscuous, or a saint? Each possibility would take the process in a different direction. How would she have reacted to a violent attack? Would she have gone home with a total stranger? If we don't know the answers to such questions, we are only guessing and not analyzing.

I can hypothesize a case in which a rapist says nothing, commits no physical violence, and engages in no sexual behavior other than vaginal rape. This situation would provide insufficient behavior for me to study, and without that, I would have nothing to analyze. The same would be true of a homicide in which the only behavior is a single-shot murder. Profilers need something concrete. We don't use crystal balls.

THE RIGHT STUFF

Clearly, profiling is not suitable work for everyone. Based on our experience at the BSU, here are some of the attributes we know are needed to be successful.

John Douglas, Bob Ressler, and I used to interview FBI agent applicants for positions within the profiling section of the BSU. Every one of them had excellent investigative records and came to us with the highest recommendation from his or her respective FBI field office. But that did not necessarily make the candidates suitable for the training or the work. We established criteria that are used to this day.

To begin with we looked for *life experience*. We wanted someone who was mature, had been successful in life before coming to the Bureau, and had at least five years investigative experience with the FBI. Consequently, almost every person we selected was between thirty and forty-five years of age.

Open-mindedness was our second criterion. A profiler must be willing to consider different possibilities as well as the differing opinions of others. Too often an investigator locks in on one idea or explanation and refuses to budge. His self-worth seems to hinge on being correct. Such a person will not be able to profile successfully.

A critical attribute is *common sense*, which to us meant practical intelligence. Common sense isn't all that common. For example, intelligent, educated people sometimes allow what they've been taught to get in the way of their common sense.

When I was stationed at the army's Fort Rucker in Alabama, our family dog, Happy, developed mange and began losing hair in patches. I took the him to the vet, who gave Happy two injections. He also gave me salve to apply daily and a prescription for pills that the dog was to be given three times a day.

After a week of medication, Happy's condition showed no change. My neighbor, a helicopter pilot from Tennessee, suggested applying "burnt lube oil" (that is, used motor oil) to the infected areas. He said that's how his family had always treated mange at home on the farm.

Willing to try anything to help the long-suffering Happy, I purchased a quart of used motor oil and applied it. Bingo, the infection cleared up within a matter of days. When I later told Happy's vet about the burnt lube oil, he said, "Oh, that's what we used to do on the farm in North Dakota."

"Why didn't you tell me that earlier?" I asked, thinking of the expense and trouble of the ineffective pills.

"Roy," he said candidly, "I have too much education to prescribe burnt lube oil!"

Another important criterion is *intuition*. Webster's calls intuition, "The direct knowing of something without the conscious use of reasoning; the ability to perceive or know things without conscious reasoning; keen and quick insight." Every criminal investigator will tell you about some legendary detective he or she knew who possessed uncanny intuition. Somehow this person just sensed the truth of a matter where no one else could. I've seen this faculty at work, and it is a critical asset to the profiler. I just don't believe there's such a thing as intuition.

I prefer to think of the human mind as an immense hard drive, a massive collection of data from which nothing of potential value to its owner is ever deleted. This information may not be dancing around in your forebrain, but it is ready when you need it.

I believe that what we call intuition is simply stored and forgotten experiences that the conscious mind somehow can instantaneously retrieve, combine, and process in a way that, superficially at least, seems miraculous or preternatural.

Next, the prospective profiler must be able to *isolate personal feelings about the crime, the criminal, and the victim*. Deviant sexual crimes often are horrible. The analyst must isolate himself from that horror or else run the risk of becoming a vicarious victim. One of my close friends in state law enforcement, a trained profiler, eventually was overwhelmed by the continuous stream of grotesque rapes and murders and finally retired in order to regain his peace of mind.

One way to keep the crime and criminal at a distance is to avoid using inflammatory language. As much as you naturally loathe the behavior you are analyzing, the use of slang pejoratives such as "weirdo" or "wacko" only threaten the dispassionate analysis necessary for accurate and thorough analysis.

Often the greatest emotional challenge is to isolate oneself emotionally from the victim. Sympathy can hinder clear thinking. Antipathy can affect objectivity.

Here's a case in point. In Alaska, a fifteen-year-old Eskimo prostitute, also known to police as an alcohol and drug abuser, reported that a customer had flown her in his private airplane out into the Alaska wilderness. There the man had forced her to undress. Then he told the young woman he would give her twenty minutes to run and hide before he began to stalk and shoot her.

She refused to take any part in this game, so he flew her back to the airport and released her. The victim reported her experience but was not believed, partly because the man she had accused was a respected member of the community and partly because of her own unsavory history. Yet two years later, the man in question was arrested for the murder of seventeen women!

Strong analytical logic and *patience* are necessary. Call it systematic reasoning, the ability to see how B logically follows A. Add to that a willingness not to hurry or leap to conclusions (intuitively or otherwise). A profiler must study the crime in detail, systematically capture behaviors as he or she detects them, and reason through the facts with meticulous care to a synthesis of the available information, the profile.

In my classes I constantly remind students to proceed one step at a time. "But I know the answer," they'll say. So then I ask them to write down what they believe to be the answer and to continue to work on the problem. Invariably, when they're done and I ask in private about their original answer, they'll say something like, "Oh, I threw that away."

Finally, a profiler must be able to view the crime from the offender's perspective; he must *think like the criminal.* To do so requires a special mind-set, since an aberrant crime probably will make sense only to the criminal, not to the victim, and certainly not from society's perspective.

You must enter the offender's sphere of reality, take on the criminal's point of view. People say, "Oh, I could never do that." But with training, it becomes easier than you might think.

For example, let's say that a criminal buries his victim six feet deep in the middle of a forest. Why?

Thinking like that criminal, I'd have to say that first of all, I didn't want the body found, and second, I don't mind (may even enjoy) the necessary physical exertion, and I obviously feel at ease outdoors. This line of reasoning would become a piece of the profile.

Life experience, open-mindedness, common sense, intuition, ability to isolate personal feelings, analytical logic, and the ability to think like the criminal. What attribute is missing here that you would expect to be included for such cerebral work? You're probably thinking, what about education?

To the consternation of our colleagues in the European mental health professions and academia, we established no preset educational requirements for becoming a profiler. Continental professors and doctors tend to assume that only the intellectually elite could possibly be qualified to profile or conduct the necessary research. We believe that if a person possessing the necessary attributes could also adequately express himself verbally, both orally and in writing, then an advanced degree was nonessential. Over time we've been proven correct.

HOW PROFILING WORKS

How do you create a profile? The answer depends on who you ask. To me, the process involves four steps. Two individuals whom I respect and admire, John Douglas and Park Dietz, believe there are more. I often joke that four are all I can remember, but humor aside, simplicity has distinct advantages. The fewer steps involved, the fewer missteps you're likely to make. Keep it simple is a useful slogan.

The four steps taught in the Roy Hazelwood school of profiling are:

1. Identify what significant behaviors occurred.

2. Form an opinion as to why they occurred.

3. Reconstruct the sequence of events.

4. Determine what type of person would have committed this crime in this way for these reasons.

To put it another way: what, why, how, and who. It is at this point that my students begin to realize why we chose analytical logic as one of a profiler's fundamental qualities.

Following is a hypothetical case presented strictly for the edification of the reader. Assume that an eighteen-year-old Caucasian woman was murdered in her apartment and left on the living room floor. The first step in the profiling process is to write out a list of what happened or did not happen (e.g., no theft) during the crime.

This woman was reported to be a very aggressive person who would have fought an attacker. She did not date cross-racially. There was no forced entry, and nothing was known to be missing from the apartment. The disorder in the kitchen, bathroom, bedroom, and living room suggested a struggle; the victim had defensive wounds on her hands and forearms, and she had been struck on the head with a wooden lamp from the living room. She was stabbed several times with a paring knife and once in the heart with a butcher knife; both knives were from the victim's kitchen. She had not been sexually assaulted, but her clothing had been displaced to reveal her breasts and vagina.

Next, the profiler would ask the why questions and then supply possible answers. Why was there no forced entry? One possibility would be that she knew her attacker and admitted him. Why was nothing taken from the scene? The purpose of the attacker's presence was not theft. Why were there signs of a struggle in every room of the apartment? The victim must have fought the attacker, and the offender didn't control her. Why did she have defensive wounds? She was conscious and not bound. Why had she been struck with a wooden lamp? The subject hadn't brought a weapon, and the lamp was immediately available. Why was she stabbed multiple times with a paring knife? The attack continued throughout the apartment with the paring knife. Why was she stabbed once in the heart with a butcher knife? The killer simply wanted to ensure she was dead. Why was her clothing displaced to expose her, but no sexual assault occurred? Perhaps the offender staged the crime to mislead police.

Step three occurs simultaneously with step two. As we move through the why, we begin to observe factors that suggest the sequence of events. The offender knocked on the door and was admitted by the victim. An argument began in the living room, and he used the wooden lamp to strike her. She fought him and the fight continued into the kitchen, where the victim picked up a paring knife. The subject took it away from her and stabbed her. She retreated into the bathroom, then the bedroom, raising her arms to fend off the attack, and finally back to the living room, where she lost consciousness from loss of blood. The subject grabbed the butcher knife from the kitchen and drove it into her heart to ensure her death. He then attempted to stage the crime as a sexual offense by exposing her breasts and vagina.

Step four, what are the characteristics and traits of someone who would commit this crime in this manner for the reasons set forth? In an actual case, a profile would not offer an opinion based on so little information. But for the sake of continuing our hypothetical exercise, we can take our profiling efforts a few steps further.

Most crimes of this nature are committed by men; and because this victim did not date cross-racially, the offender was most likely a white male. If she admitted him, the subject was probably an acquaintance. The victim was a healthy eighteen year old who put up a great struggle that did not cause her attacker to cease. Therefore it could be assumed that he was in his early to mid-twenties, in good physical condition, and was equally as aggressive as the victim. The impulsiveness, extreme violence, and persistence of the attack indicate that the killer had an explosive temper.

We'll stop the exercise at this point. In its basic outline, this hypothetical crime serves to take some of the mystery out of profiling. Of course, much more analysis would have been accomplished in an actual case, and many more characteristics and traits would be provided. The point is the facts of a crime can be interpreted to create a portrait of an offender.

9

A SERIAL RAPIST

The dark imaginings of a ritualistic sexual criminal are never static. He is always considering new assault scenarios, new victims, new props and gear. This chapter will detail a case in which a seemingly power-motivated serial rapist evolved into one who committed his crimes primarily out of anger.

Power-motivated rapists are the most common type of ritualistic, stranger-to-stranger rapists. Anger-motivated rapists, while less common, are more apt to physically brutalize their victims. They also tend to increase the frequency of their attacks as time passes.

Since I retired from the Bureau, the bulk of my profiling assignments have been from law enforcement organizations. Rarely do I take on a private citizen as a client. When Mark Burget* first contacted me, identifying himself as the father of a victim of a so-far unidentified serial rapist, I hesitated to get involved. I explained that it was a strict condition of mine that the local police approve of my involvement and that they provide their reports for my review. He said that would be no problem. In fact one of the detectives working his daughter's case had recommended me to him.

I also warned Burget not to expect miracles. Profiling

does not magically identify criminals. He said that had been explained to him. I added that I would require full and complete descriptions of all the offender's sexual assaults, including the one against his daughter. Again, Burget assured me he understood. Curiosity prompted me to ask why he was involving himself this way.

He said his daughter, Frankie, was highly intelligent and mature, and she had dealt with the horrible crime so capably that both he and his wife looked to her as a model. As he spoke, I realized how sincere he was. He was brimming with the pride of being the father of this young woman.

"Roy," he said, "my daughter is my hero."

I took the case.

This serial rapist preyed on the student district of a southern university town. All of his victims were single, white, female college students.

The first known victim was Margaret Jones,* twenty-six, who lived alone in a ground-level apartment. On Saturday evening, March 18, 1995, Margaret went jogging, came home, watched some television, and took a shower. Later she couldn't recall if she locked the front door, which in any event could be easily opened with a credit card or laminated driver's license.

As Margaret emerged from the shower about 9:30, a white male grabbed her by the neck from behind and pulled her into her bedroom.

Although he had tied one of her green kitchen towels over his face, the lights were on and Margaret could see that he was a white male in his mid-to-late twenties.

She struggled. He choked and hit her, leaving bruises on Margaret's right thigh and knee, plus scratches around her collarbone and lower knee. Her lower lip was severely swollen. The victim reported that she dissuaded him from vaginal rape. Instead, he placed a pillow on her face as he performed cunnilingus, then rubbed his penis over her until he ejaculated.

As he wiped the semen from her body with the green towel, he said that he had been watching her, and he apologized for the assault. Nothing was stolen. On his way out he told Margaret to stay on the bed and not to call the police.

The next assault occurred the following month. Frankie Burget,* twenty-four, lived in a ground-floor apartment similar to Margaret Jones's. On Saturday night, April 22, the third-year pharmacy student attended a party, from which she returned at about 1:30 A.M.

Frankie shared her apartment with a male law student who spent most of his time at his girlfriend's. He was gone that night as she telephoned her boyfriend, undressing in her bedroom as she spoke. The window had no shade and was open as usual. After saying good night, Frankie read until 3:30, when she turned out the light and went to sleep.

Approximately forty-five minutes later, the young woman was awakened in her bed by a man's voice. He put his hand over her mouth. "Don't scream or I'll kill you," he said. "Just do what I say."

From his breath, she could tell he had been drinking. Later, an empty beer bottle was found on her kitchen counter.

The police learned that the intruder had already menaced at least two other young women in the same neighborhood that night. The first was twenty-two-year-old Lory Taylor,* who lived in a ground-floor unit in the same apartment complex. About 10:15 Lory's cat began acting strangely. The animal jumped from its perch on the bathroom windowsill and scampered behind the refrigerator. She shut and locked all her windows, turned the lights out, and went to bed.

At approximately 10:40 she heard a noise and saw a flashlight beam through her window. Turning off her air conditioner, Lory could hear someone attempting to remove the wood-frame screen from her bathroom window. She turned on her apartment lights, peeked out the front door, called a friend in the complex, and then ran to the friend's apartment. From there she telephoned the police.

The responding officer accompanied Lory back to her apartment, where he noted that the screen had been removed from the bathroom window. Lory spent the night at her friend's place. The next morning she returned to her apartment and found that her bedroom had been ransacked. The bathroom window screen had been slashed several times in the center.

Nearby lived twenty-two-year-old Beth Freedman.* From what investigators were able to piece together, sometime after 11:00 that Saturday night, the intruder tried to get through a window of her apartment. He slashed the screen, removed it, and broke out the pane. However, her front door was locked, and there was no evidence that the offender had gotten into the apartment.

The police surmised that after the attempts against Lory Taylor and Beth Freedman, the intruder remained on the complex grounds, still searching for a victim. When Frankie Burget arrived home, she must have caught his attention.

He apparently entered Frankie's apartment through an unlocked living room window. When he awakened her, she screamed. He struck and choked her, telling her, "Just go limp and I won't hurt you."

He had brought with him a filthy, ragged towel, with which he tried to mask the bottom of his face, but it kept slipping. When it did, Frankie could see he was a white male, in his late-twenties or early thirties, and that he wore his hair in a crew cut.

He began to fondle her and to compliment her on her "gorgeous" body. He said he knew that the only way he could ever have her was to "fuck" her. "Do you know you look like a goddess?" he asked. "You look so beautiful. As soon as I saw you through the window, I knew I had to have you." He also said that he had tried to speak to her on two occasions, and she had ignored him.

Frankie Burget struggled again, and he reacted by hitting

her and choking her until she couldn't breathe. When she went limp, he tore up a pillowcase to make ligatures. She ran for the window and tried to scream for help. He grabbed her again, managed to dodge a kick from her knee, closed the window, and pulled her back to the bed.

"I won't hurt you if you just stay still," he said again. "I'm going to have to tie you up because you aren't co-operating."

He ripped the pillowcase and ordered Frankie to lie down on her stomach with her arms behind her. When she asked to have her wrists tied in front so that she could breathe more easily, he refused.

He raped her anally. As he did so, one of her hands came loose. As Frankie brushed back hair from her face, he hit her again and tightened the knot.

In all, Frankie Burget suffered scratches and bruises to her hands, right arm, and lower neck. Her right eye was severely swollen and bloodshot, and her lower lip and jaw were bruised. She also suffered the physical and psychological traumas that usually accompany a rape.

When he finished with the anal rape, she thought he was about to leave. Instead, as the intruder sat on the edge of the bed looking down at her, he changed his mind. "You know," he said, "I was only seeing you from the back. You look so good from the front I just can't leave yet."

The victim later reported that he now had trouble maintaining an erection. He pushed her onto her back and raped Frankie vaginally even as he lost rigidity. "You feel great," he said.

Frankie told him he was hurting her and asked him to stop. He responded by saying, "Okay, okay, I'm sorry. I'm sorry." But he didn't stop.

When she asked again, he answered, "Just shut up! You try anything, I'll kill you."

When he finished for the second time, he said he planned to stay all night to prevent her from calling the police. She told him that if he intended to avoid detection, leaving while it was still dark was a smarter idea.

He saw the logic in what she said. Before departing, however, he made a strange request. "I want you to do something for me. I don't want you to hate me. Hate will just eat you up inside. So don't hate me." He apologized for the assault and then added something even odder. "I know this is going to sound stupid. I feel like we have been friends for years. You know, like we're old friends and we're just sitting here."

She noted that he hadn't brought a weapon or worn gloves. But Frankie did see him wipe the doorknob with his shirt on his way out.

The next known assault took place nearly four and a half months later, on Friday, September 8, 1995. Peggy White,* twenty-three, had just graduated from college and was spending her last night in the apartment she had occupied with another young woman during the previous nine months. This evening her roommate was out of town.

Peggy spent most of Friday packing and hauling trash to a Dumpster located a hundred feet from her apartment. She was in and out so often throughout the day that she saw no need to lock the door.

That evening, a male friend visited her from 5:30 until 10:30. Afterward, Peggy continued packing for another forty-five minutes or so before carrying out one last load of trash. She left her apartment door open while she was outside then closed it and went upstairs to watch television.

Moments later, a white male she would later describe as being in his early forties jumped out from a closet and ordered her into her roommate's bedroom. There he produced a pocket knife.

"Get undressed," he demanded.

As she began to do so, he asked if she had a roommate. Peggy said the woman was away in Augusta, Georgia. She took off her outer clothing and then stopped. He touched her with the knife, and she removed her undergarments.

She tried to cover herself, but he told her to move her

Robert Leroy Anderson. Like many sexually sadistic killers, his homicidal fantasies dated back to his early teens. *South Dakota Attorney General's Office.*

Glenn Walker. He led authorities to Larisa Dumansky's remains. Robert Anderson later plotted to have Walker killed. *South Dakota Attorney General's Office.*

One of Anderson's tire spikes. He fashioned them in his employer's machine shop. *South Dakota Attorney General's Office.*

The Blue Ford Bronco. Anderson painted it black with water soluble paint the day he abducted and murdered Piper Streyle, then washed it off. A plywood platform in the rear was fitted with wrist and ankle restraints. *South Dakota Attorney General's Office.*

Piper Streyle's torn shirt (ABOVE LEFT) and a photo taken inside Anderson's mother's house (ABOVE RIGHT). Searchers found a crevice between the wall and the ceiling in the basement. Using a hand-held mirror to see inside it, they found one victim's necklace, another victim's ring (PICTURED), and a gun. *Both photos: South Dakota Attorney General's Office.*

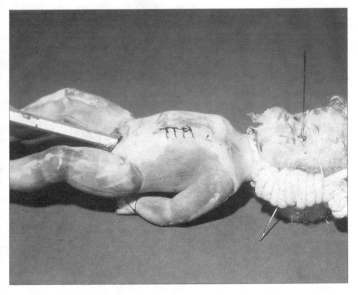

The mutilated doll and mannequin. Acting out against inanimate objects is normally not a crime. However, it may be the first evidence of a violent fantasy. *Both photos: Collection of Roy Hazelwood.*

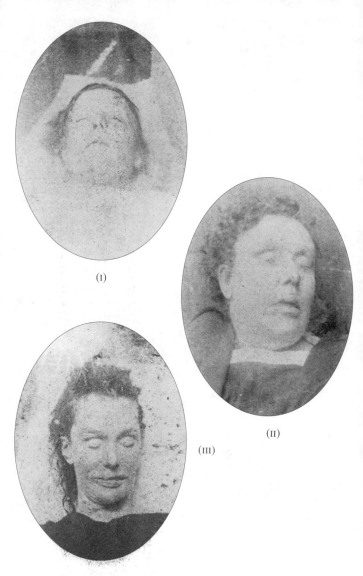

Polly Nichols (I), Annie Chapman (II), and Elizabeth Stride (III). Three prostitutes who were victims of Jack the Ripper. *Collection of Roy Hazelwood.*

Faryion Edward Wardrip. At the time of his arrest, the Texas serial killer was telling friends that he planned to become a minister. *Wichita County District Attorney's Office.*

U. S. Secret Service
115-CO-1-33,756-2

James Mitchell DeBardeleben

James Mitchell DeBardeleben. Counterfeiter, rapist, kidnapper, and sadistic killer. He kept detailed records of his crimes and his fantasies. *United States Secret Service.*

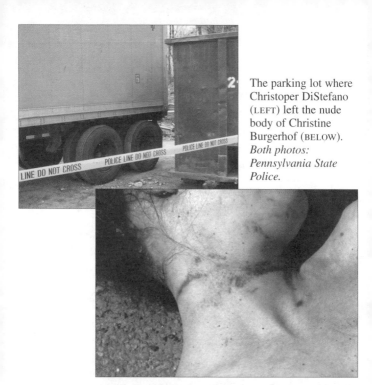

The parking lot where Christoper DiStefano (LEFT) left the nude body of Christine Burgerhof (BELOW). *Both photos: Pennsylvania State Police.*

The undisturbed desk of Ms. Burgerhof at the store front massage parlor. *Pennsylvania State Police.*

The closet from which the safe was removed. Note the hammer that was used to loosen the safe from the shelving. *Pennsylvania State Police.*

A massage bed with wood fragments, coat hanger, and two screwdrivers used to remove the safe from the closet shelving. *Pennsylvania State Police.*

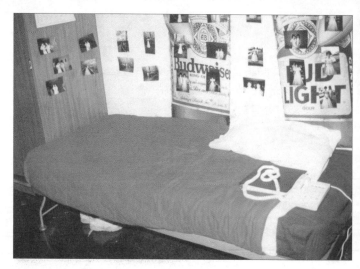

DiStefano's bedroom wall reflects his "shrine" to Christine Burgerhof. *Pennsylvania State Police.*

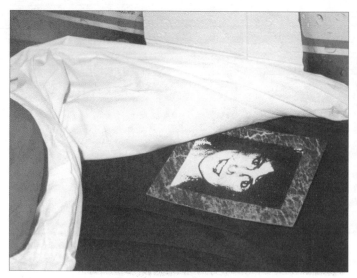

Ms. Burgerhof's picture was found beneath the covers of DiStefano's bed. *Pennsylvania State Police.*

arms so he could see her breasts. When she sat on the bed, he removed her only remaining garments—her socks.

White asked that he not rape her anally, as it would be too painful. He seemed agreeable to the request, telling her that if she performed oral sex he would leave. But after she began to do so, he pulled away. "You're not doing a good job," he said. "Stop."

Then he told her to lie on her stomach as he applied lotion to her anus and penetrated her with his finger. She pleaded again that it was painful, so he rolled her over, lubricated her some more, and raped White vaginally.

As he did so, he asked if she had a douche. He didn't want her to become pregnant.

"That wouldn't help," she said.

"It would a little bit," he answered.

"Why don't you just pull out?" White asked.

He said he had already ejaculated.

She asked him to leave.

"I want to do it some more," he said, and vaginally raped her again.

"You're sexy," he said. "You have a really nice butt."

When he stopped, he told her that he was going to leave. "I'm sorry I hurt you. I'm sorry I had to do this to you."

But he didn't leave. When Peggy asked if she could dress, he said, "No, I want to watch you lie there naked."

After allowing her to use the bathroom, he raped her a third time. Finally he dressed and prepared to go. When he tried and failed to unplug her telephone, White helped him in order to keep him from breaking it.

Before leaving, he used a towel to wipe her vaginal area, the lotion bottle, and the doorknob.

More than six months passed before he struck again. On Sunday, March 17, 1996, Marti Joseph,* twenty-one, went out for a bottle of milk about seven in the evening then came home and cooked dinner. Around 8:15 she slipped into the shower. As Marti washed, she heard footsteps in the hallway and assumed that her male roommate had returned home.

After the shower she wrapped a towel around her and walked into her bedroom, closing the door behind her. Just then a white male, somewhere in his thirties, "sort of wrinkled and scary-looking" with "saggy," bloodshot eyes, came up behind her wielding a butcher knife from the kitchen.

Marti immediately asked him not to kill her. He said that he wouldn't as long as she did as she was told. He asked her age.

"Drop the towel," he demanded. Marti did so. He placed the knife tip on her navel, and with his other hand he touched her breast.

"Stand right there and turn around," he told her. "Stand right here in front of me." He then fondled her vagina from behind.

"Turn around and get down on your knees."

As Marti did so, her roommate suddenly knocked on her door. He had come home from school and wanted to know if she was on the telephone. She called out that she was.

The intruder instantly headed for the closest window, which was painted shut. Marti helped him open a second window located above her dresser, which he crawled through with an assist from the victim.

The butcher knife and a towel from the house were later recovered outside.

The final assault occurred three hours later. Mary Gilbert,* age twenty-two, spent the early evening painting the front bedroom of the duplex apartment she shared with another young woman. At nine o'clock Mary, her roommate, and her roommate's boyfriend shared a pizza. The couple then left.

At ten, a friend dropped by for coffee. She suggested that Mary prop open a window to air out the place. The friend departed for home about eleven, and Mary headed for the shower.

Ten minutes into the shower, the curtain was pulled open and there stood the rapist, threatening her with a long, bread knife from her kitchen. She thought that he was in his mid-thirties. She described him as tanned and weathered, with rough hands and hair the length of an outgrown crew cut.

He had come in through the window she had propped open for ventilation. He was using a pair of her pants to try to conceal the lower part of his face.

Mary grabbed the curtain rod and tried to jab him with it. He tore the rod from her hands, threw it to the bathroom floor, and then forced her into her roommate's bedroom, where he told her to lie on the floor. She screamed and tried to resist.

"Shut up!" he said, covering her mouth with his hand.

He struck her head against the floor, punched her, then picked up a nearby flashlight and beat Mary in the face and abdomen with it before choking her to the point of breathlessness.

"Either be fucked or killed," he repeatedly said.

Mary kicked him and made a dash for the door. He grabbed her again, forced her to the floor, inserted his fingers into her vagina, then raped her. He also inserted his fingers into her anus.

She told him, "My roommate and her boyfriend are going to be home any minute."

He said he would kill them both and then hit her again in the stomach and abdomen with the flashlight and pushed her up onto the bed. She kicked him in the groin, and he hit her several times in the stomach. Then he raped her vaginally once again.

"It won't take long," he said.

This time he quickly withdrew. "I'm not going to come," he said. "I'm going to leave."

The rapist arose, dressed, and left the room, then returned. "Roll over, I want to fuck you in the ass," he demanded.

But when Mary didn't respond, he said, "Well, I better be going before your roommate gets back." Then he grabbed both her breasts, saying, "Ya got nice titties," and walked out of the room. He smashed her telephone and cut the lines on his way to the front door.

*   *   *

There was no doubt that a single perpetrator had committed the rapes; all the DNA specimens matched.

From an investigative point of view, the fact that he was growing progressively more violent made it all the more urgent that he be stopped. In the Margaret Jones case, he choked her and hit her with his fists. But he didn't rape her when she asked him not to. One year and five victims later, he severely beat Mary Gilbert with his fists and a weapon and raped her twice.

I began my profile by noting that age is always the most difficult of all offender characteristics to determine. The victims varied widely in their estimates. I surmised that chronologically he was between twenty-six and thirty-three, but sexually and emotionally, he was immature. His initial actions were to look at and touch his victims. In his later assaults, when he encountered resistance, he immediately resorted to threats and violence.

I advised that the perpetrator's wife or girlfriend would report similar behavior, a tendency to look at and play with her, and a habit of pouting or getting angry and leaving the room if he didn't get his way.

His behavior also suggested that he had low self-esteem and was intimidated by his victims. That may sound like an odd thing to say about a rapist, but recall that he told Frankie Burget that he had tried to talk to her and how he knew that raping her was the only way he could ever have her.

He told Mary Gilbert as he raped her, "This won't take long," as though he was trying to assure her that he would be leaving quickly. I felt this lack of self-esteem would be perceived by others as a lack of confidence and that he would exhibit a lack of pride in his appearance. He would be poorly groomed, just as the victims themselves reported.

I believed that he drove a pickup or sedan, that it would be in poor condition and improperly maintained, would have high mileage, and would be at least five years old.

His lack of personal pride would extend even to the care of his vehicle.

I also doubted that he had taken part in any team sports. It was far more likely that he had engaged in solo pastimes.

Sexual offenders are usually experiencing stress at the time of their attacks, and I said such would be the case with this offender. The stress might be relational, medical, financial, sexual, or caused by substance abuse. The rapist had discovered that the assaults momentarily relieved the stress and restored to him, at least for a while, his personal sense of power and control.

I felt that this would explain the reason why he was so determined to find a victim on the night of April 22–23, 1995. Having been unsuccessful at Lory Taylor's and Beth Freedman's apartments before midnight, his stress increased and he remained at the complex until 1:30, searching for a victim. When he spotted Frankie Burget, she became his target. We see the same persistence with this offender several months later. Scared off early in the evening by Marti Joseph's male roommate, he acted out three hours later against Mary Gilbert.

What he failed to understand was that the temporary relief he experienced after each rape was illusory. In reality the crimes had a cumulative effect of actually increasing his stress and therefore his emotional burden.

I advised the police that the unidentified offender more than likely had an arrest record involving crimes against property, such as burglary or breaking and entering; alcohol-related crimes, such as disorderliness or DWI; or "nuisance" sexual offenses, particularly window peeping, but also quite possibly obscene telephone calls.

His preoccupation with anal assault suggested the possibility that he had served time in jail or prison. But the anal rape also signified something else. Taken together with his profanity and physical violence, it reflected deep anger toward women.

His crimes reflected neither planning nor patience. None of his victims (all of whom were college students) believed that he was a student. Additionally, he used vulgar street language for the female anatomy, even when complimenting the women. All of this told me that me probably had no more than a high school education, if that.

Nothing about his crimes suggested a high intellect or even street-smart craftiness. He relied entirely on physical and verbal violence to control the victims. Nor did he seem to learn from previous crimes. For example, he never figured out a reliable way to hide his face. It would have been simple to bring a mask with him. He did seem to have some concern about fingerprints, but nevertheless left DNA evidence at each rape.

The victims were selected impulsively. He apparently acted without knowing anything about their habits, living arrangements, or personalities.

Everything about his crimes, from the victims to the weapons he used, stemmed from opportunity not forethought.

I felt that impulsiveness would be reflected in his consenting relationships, both in the beginning and ending of them. He would be the type of person who makes purchases without considering their long-term implications, including whether he could afford them. His credit rating would be poor. He would frequently change jobs as well as addresses.

His low tolerance for frustration was amply shown in his behavior in the Lory Taylor case. After unsuccessfully trying to capture her, he returned later and ransacked her bedroom, obviously in anger. After also failing to enter Beth Freedman's apartment, he took out his rage by using excessive, and unnecessary, violence against Frankie Burget. Similarly, following the interrupted assault on Marti Joseph, Mary Gilbert was violently assaulted.

I suggested that he had defective relations in his everyday life, that he was probably divorced, and that he collected pornography, especially material with bondage themes, as well as magazines and other materials emphasizing breasts and buttocks.

His anger toward women was increasing, and I believed

that the violence would continue escalating. If he had a consenting sexual partner, she would note that he was becoming more demanding, more sexually selfish, and more abusive, both physically and verbally.

He worked with his hands, probably outdoors. I doubted that he was employed at any job requiring more than vocational training and experience.

He seemed to be comfortable moving around the university campus. Of course, the college environment provided him with an attractive victim pool, but I thought he might have previously lived in the vicinity or perhaps worked there or maybe even regularly visited someone who lived there.

Finally, it was my belief that his own residence would be modest and poorly maintained, much like his vehicle. It might be an apartment, small rental house, or even a trailer.

A few months later the police notified me that the rapist had been captured in an adjoining state, where he had moved shortly after the attack against Ms. Gilbert. Predictably, he had continued committing sexual assaults. The routine work of establishing where the rapist had previously lived led investigators to the university town and its string of rapes. The DNA evidence solved the cases I'd been retained to analyze.

My inferential portrait of the rapist was accurate except for one detail: he lived in a nice house in an upper-middle-class neighborhood. When an officer told me this, I was amazed. The policeman let me stew for a moment and then said, "Oh, by the way, his father bought the place for him."

Although it was DNA that finally tripped up this offender, Mark Burget was extremely satisfied with my profile and the diligent work of the police department. In an evening that I will never forget, he treated the investigators and myself to a wonderful steak dinner.

At the conclusion of the evening, as we toasted all around, he said, "You know, guys, my daughter is still my hero."

10

JACK THE RIPPER

Profiling was developed to address here-and-now investigative issues. Yet the process has intriguing historical potential as well. As long as we can reliably identify an offender's behavior and gather sufficient information about the victim, we can profile any criminal, no matter when or where the crimes were committed.

In 1988, John Douglas was challenged to solve a notorious historical mystery. A television production company asked if he could profile Jack the Ripper for a two-hour live special marking the one hundredth anniversary of the Ripper's murders. The FBI approved the project, and John asked me to assist him.

Murder investigations in the late-nineteenth century weren't nearly as professional as they are today or as well documented. Procedure was especially deficient when the homicides were committed in slums like London's Whitechapel district and when the victims were streetwalkers, as was true in the Ripper cases.

John and I questioned whether enough hard facts were available a hundred years later for us to create a profile. We were happily surprised when the production company provided us with two volumes, each about three inches thick, of detailed information on the five murders.

The binders contained autopsy and police reports, a great

deal of background information on each of the victims, and maps detailing the area in which the murders occurred. They also held photographs of the victims after death.

Jack the Ripper killed five prostitutes from August 31, 1888, to November 9, 1888. Such a crime series is commonplace today, barely worth mention in the news. Yet despite his brief and unexceptional career as an aberrant offender, Jack the Ripper is perhaps the best-known serial killer in history.

What makes him so special?

For one thing, the newspapers gave him a memorable nickname, which made him sound more interesting, which in turn sold more papers, which generated more coverage. We sometimes see the echoes of such media attention in today's cases.

Another important factor was the sexual mutilation committed on his victims. Jack's postmortem slashing fueled the public's fascination with him and his crimes. The Ripper also was never positively identified, and as a result wild accusations and public speculation could continue indefinitely—just as they have in the aftermath of President Kennedy's assassination, which many people still think remains unsolved.

In the JFK case, government conspiracy has been a favorite explanation for what occurred. In Jack the Ripper's murders, conspiracy theorists predictably have singled out royalty for suspicion. Some have assigned guilt to a royal prince; others to the queen's physician. Even a cover-up was alleged.

We wanted to develop a profile based solely on facts. In the evidence binders we'd find the behavioral details we needed. We carefully pored over the two volumes, taking the murders step-by-step.

Jack the Ripper's first victim was Mary Ann Polly Nichols, forty-two, an alcoholic derelict last seen alive at 3:00 A.M.

Nichols was found dead on a narrow Whitechapel street called Bucks Row.

Her jaw was bruised and her throat had been cut from left to right. Two postmortem knife incisions had been made on her stomach in the shape of a reverse L, and she was disemboweled. Mary Nichols was missing two teeth, and her ring finger was abraded. Obviously, she was either stunned or rendered unconscious by the blow to her jaw. Her throat was then cut and mutilation ensued.

In profiling terms the Ripper was a disorganized lust murderer. He appears to have brought his own weapon with him, but the rest of his crime was highly impetuous. He apparently attacked and left his victim in an open area and made no effort to conceal his crime. The records show no documented evidence of penis penetration, so we can conclude that he did not rape his victim. Jack's instrument of psychosexual gratification was his knife.

Victim number two was "Dark Annie" Chapman, a forty-seven-year-old prostitute, also a drunk and a derelict. She was murdered in the early morning hours of September 8, 1888, and was found in the backyard of a building on Hanbury Street in Whitechapel, approximately six blocks from the scene of the Nichols murder.

Chapman was discovered on her back, clothed, with her head propped against the wall of the building. Like Mary Nichols, she was missing two teeth. Her killer had struck her in the right cheek, which was swollen, and cut her throat from left to right. Jack performed a long, linear incision on Chapman's front and rear torso, and she, too, had been disemboweled.

Her uterus, vagina, bladder, and intestines were found draped over her right shoulder. Her abdominal wall was missing, as were her ovaries. The area of her sternum was swollen. Her left hand lay across her breast. She also had an abraded ring finger.

The close similarities between these first two crimes quickly established in our minds a strong probability that the same killer was responsible for both. We discounted the fact that the victims were missing two teeth; this seemed more likely the consequence of chronic poor health, not Jack's fist or a club. The best explanation for the abraded fingers was that someone had torn rings from them. Whether Jack the Ripper took them, we couldn't say, but in my opinion the thief probably was a passerby. If Jack was taking souvenirs in this way, it seems that he would have continued to do so in the subsequent three killings. But he didn't.

After all, Whitechapel was hardly a quality neighborhood. Robbing the dead probably wasn't all that unusual.

Jack the Ripper's third victim was Elizabeth Stride, forty-five, also a prostitute and drunk. Stride was murdered in the early morning hours of September 30, 1888, in a courtyard off Benner Street, about six blocks from the first murder and slightly farther from where he killed Chapman.

The Ripper was interrupted by a horse and carriage that entered the courtyard, and he fled without being able to act out his grotesque mutilation fantasies on Stride. She was found fully clothed and lying on her back. Her shoulder and clavicle were bruised, and like the other victims, her throat had been cut from left to right.

John and I surmised that the postmortem mutilation was a physical manifestation of Jack's tremendous hatred and fear of women, common among lust killers. With the act of mutilation he achieved psychosexual relief and gratification.

With his third victim he was denied that sexual experience. The Ripper was unfulfilled. He could be expected, if possible, to immediately resume hunting for a victim to complete his objective. And that is what happened.

A short while later, that same morning in Mitre Square, about thirteen blocks away from the Hanbury Street address where Annie Chapman had been killed, he encountered victim number four, forty-three-year-old Katherine Eddowes.

Eddowes was discovered lying on her back with her clothing pulled up. Her throat had been cut from left to right. Her nose and one of her ears had been cut off. A diagonal incision was made across her abdomen, and a linear incision had been made down her back. Her left kidney was missing, and her intestines were drawn out. A portion of intestine lay beside her to the left. She also was stabbed in the liver. There were cuts to her scalp, and her face had been mutilated.

Jack the Ripper needed to finish the interrupted sexual experience he had begun with the murder of Elizabeth Stride. As is so frequently the case with aberrant murderers, Eddowes was a victim of opportunity, whose ill fortune it was to be alone and vulnerable when Jack found her.

Now we have four victims, all of a similar demographic type, and all killed within a rather small geographic area. What about the fact that they were all prostitutes?

It seems that whenever someone starts murdering prostitutes, some "expert" will tell the press, "The person who is perpetrating these heinous crimes is a man who has a great deal of anger and hostility toward females. He selects prostitutes because they symbolize the evil he perceives in some significant female in his life."

Such comments are of little use to investigators.

In my opinion, there are two reasons why serial killers select prostitutes as victims: They are available, and they are vulnerable. When I lecture about victim selection and why prostitutes so commonly are chosen, I ask my audiences to consider five key questions about street prostitutes:

1. With whom will a street prostitute go? Anyone.

2. Why will a street prostitute go with anyone? Money.

3. Where will a street prostitute go with anyone? Anywhere.

4. When will a street prostitute go with anyone? Anytime.

5. Who cares when street prostitutes are murdered? Hardly anyone.

For these reasons, prostitutes are an all-too-easy target group for violent offenders.

Jack committed his fifth and final murder on November 2, 1888, in Millers Court, within two blocks of the Chapman homicide. His victim, Mary Kelly, was also a prostitute, alcoholic, and derelict. But twenty-five-year-old Kelly was by far the youngest of Jack's murder victims.

The other departure in this murder was that the unfortunate woman entertained the Ripper in her one-room flat. For the first time Jack had a location where he could act out his aberrant fantasies at length and with little fear of being disturbed.

He brutalized Kelly's face and, as was his habit, cut his victim's throat from left to right. Then he cut off her ears and breasts and might even have attempted to skin her face and lower legs. He placed Kelly's heart and kidneys on a bedside table. Her liver lay by her right thigh. Her intestines were draped over a mirror.

After preparing the profile, John Douglas and I flew to Los Angeles. There we met the three additional participants on the program: William Eckerd (since deceased), a forensic pathologist whom John and I both knew; Anne Mallalieu, an English judge or "queen's counsel"; and William Waddell, a British criminologist and then curator of Scotland Yard's Black Museum, which houses relics of some of the darkest crimes in English history. The English actor Peter Ustinov would emcee the show.

A surprise awaited us the first day on the set. Besides producing the profile, we were to consider five suspects that the production company's investigative research had identified. They were:

1. DR. ROSLYN DONSTON, a journalist and self-

proclaimed satanist who had studied medicine and
lived in Whitechapel.

2. MONTAGUE JOHN DRUITT, an emotionally troubled schoolteacher and failed lawyer who committed
suicide seven weeks after the final murder. His father
and uncle were prominent surgeons.

3. SIR WILLIAM GULL, Queen Victoria's personal
physician and the central figure in what has come to
be known as "the royal conspiracy," an alleged plot
to eliminate prostitutes who were blackmailing members of the royal family.

4. PRINCE ALBERT VICTOR, the queen's twenty-
eight-year-old grandson and an avid hunter.

5. AARON KOSMINSKI, a psychotic Polish immigrant
and Whitechapel-area resident, known for his intense
hatred toward women.

Previous investigators of the case paid a lot of attention
to the "Dear Boss" letters, published in a London newspaper, in which Jack the Ripper allegedly claimed credit
for the killings. Yet Bill Waddell of Scotland Yard reported
on the program that the Home Office's forensic laboratory
had scientifically examined the "Dear Boss" letters and de-
clared them a hoax.

John Douglas added a behavioral analysis to the letters.
He explained that while some serial killers do communicate
with the police or the press in an effort to demonstrate their
superiority, lust murderers of Jack's type do not. After pe-
rusing the packet, we surmised that someone of superior
intelligence was attempting to assume Jack's voice. I added
that Jack probably didn't want to attract attention of any
sort and was more likely to have withdrawn into himself
for a period after each homicide.

During the program all five panelists were asked which

of the suspects we would eliminate immediately from consideration and why. Bill Eckerd said he would disregard Sir William Gull because the doctor had been ill during the time of the murders. He added that the mutilations did not appear to have been the work of a trained physician.

Bill Waddell eliminated Druitt. He did so based on information he said had only recently come to his attention and which he did not disclose.

Judge Mallalieu struck Prince Albert from the list on the strength of his strong alibis for three of them. She explained that during the Nichols and Chapman murders, the prince was grouse hunting in Scotland. At the time of Mary Kelly's killing, he was hunting pheasant in Norfolk.

I ruled out Dr. Gull as well but on behavioral grounds. First, he was fifty-two years old. In our experience, much younger men commit this type of crime. Second, Dr. Gull was too cultivated to have killed in the way Jack did. He would not have relished the blood and gore being splashed on him. A ligature was a much likelier weapon for him. Finally, Dr. Gull had suffered a stroke two years earlier in 1886 and was in poor physical condition. I didn't think he was physically strong enough to kill as Jack did.

John Douglas eliminated Dr. Donston, who had followed the Ripper investigation very closely and injected himself into the process with his opinions, behavior we often see in particular types of sexual killers. But as John explained, Dr. Donston was much too old to have committed the Ripper murders. Additionally, as an avid student of witchcraft, he could be expected to leave some sign of his satanic beliefs at the murder sites.

Both John and I believed Donston would have taken the women to some preselected location he preferred, rather than killing them opportunistically in the street or, in Mary Kelly's case, her flat. John also reiterated Dr. Eckerd's point that Jack the Ripper had no evident surgical skills.

After all the panel members explained which suspect they felt should be eliminated, I offered a brief introduction to profiling, explaining what materials and information are necessary. Then John began presenting the profile.

He explained that Jack was like a predatory animal who would be out nightly looking for weak and susceptible victims for his grotesque sexual fantasies. Douglas told the TV audience that with such a killer, you do not expect to see a definite time pattern because he kills as opportunity presents itself. He added that such killers return to the scenes of their successful crimes.

He surmised that Jack was a white male in his mid-to-late-twenties and of average intelligence. John and I agreed that Jack the Ripper wasn't nearly as clever as he was lucky.

I then said that we thought Jack was single, never married, and probably did not socialize with women at all. He would have had a great deal of difficulty interacting appropriately with anyone, but particularly women.

I said Jack lived very close to the crime scenes because we know that such offenders generally start killing within very close proximity to their homes. If Jack was employed, it would have been at menial work requiring little or no contact with others.

I went on to say that, as a child, Jack probably set fires and abused animals and that as an adult his erratic behavior would have brought him to the attention of the police at some point.

John added that Jack seemed to have come from a broken home and was raised by a dominant female who physically abused him, possibly even sexually abused him. Jack would have internalized this abuse rather than act it out toward those closest to him.

John described Jack as socially withdrawn, a loner, having poor personal hygiene, and a disheveled appearance. Such characteristics are hallmarks of this type of offender. He said that people who know this type of person often report he is nocturnal, preferring the hours of darkness to daytime. When he is out at night, he typically covers great distances on foot.

Peter Ustinov turned to me again. I said that Jack simultaneously hated and feared women. They intimidated him, and his feeling of inadequacy was evident in the way he killed. I noted that the Ripper had subdued and murdered his victims quickly. There was no evidence that he savored this part of his crime; he didn't torture the women or prolong their deaths. He attacked suddenly and without warning, quickly cutting their throats.

The psychosexually pleasurable part came for him in the acts following death. By displacing or removing his victims' sexual parts and organs, Jack was neutering or desexing them so that they were no longer women to be feared.

The television audience was invited to vote for their favorite suspect throughout the program. Many cast their votes within fifteen minutes of the beginning of the show, meaning that our discussion had minimal impact on their opinions. The results:

Donston—14%
Druitt—18%
Gull—25%
Prince Albert—23%
Kosminski—20%

Then Ustinov polled the panel. Dr. Eckerd said that based on his experience as a pathologist in similar crimes, the killer usually was someone with severe mental problems. Eckerd therefore chose Kosminski. Anne Mallalieu explained that while there was insufficient evidence to charge any one of the suspects, she felt that Kosminski was the strongest suspect, and listed four reasons:

1. He resided in Whitechapel and knew the district well.

2. His mental hospital records suggest strongly that he was a paranoid schizophrenic.

3. According to two investigating officers, Inspectors Anderson and Swanson, Kosminski was positively placed with Elizabeth Stride shortly before her murder.

4. Inspector Swanson reported that as soon as Kosminski was placed under surveillance and then hospitalized, the killings stopped.

I also felt that Kosminski was the strongest suspect. I cited the fact that of the five, he was least likely to care if he was sprayed with human blood. Additionally, his hatred of women was well documented.

Bill Waddell said that from a criminal investigator's point of view, Kosminski also was the primary suspect among the five.

John agreed with the rest of us and said of Kosminski, "If he didn't do it, then someone just like him, in Whitechapel, committed these crimes."

Although we'll probably never know Jack's identity for a certainty, our study of the cases was more than a busman's holiday for John Douglas and me. By showing the applicability of profiling, even in a century-old case, we were strengthening a valuable tool for today's and tomorrow's investigators to use in apprehending killers.

11

A SERIAL KILLER

Profiling, as the BSU originally conceived it, is the investigative technique of last resort, meant to be used after all else has failed. Only when all the traditional investigative avenues have been fully explored should police turn to a profiler for assistance.

A profile rarely solves the case by itself. In fact, I can think of only a few times when that happened. But a profile can kick start a stalled investigation, generating new ideas—as Szent-Györgyi put it, "thinking what nobody else has thought."

A case in point occurred in July 1997. I was asked by authorities in Wichita Falls, Texas, to analyze a series of homicide cases and provide a profile of their unidentified offender. Barry L. Macha, the Wichita County district attorney, said he didn't expect me to solve his case; he only wanted to see if I could connect a few dots. It turned out that I could, and the new insights led to fresh thinking, a lot of old-fashioned investigative legwork, a DNA breakthrough, and then an arrest, a confession, a death sentence, and a tangle of other surprises, too. The case vividly demonstrates how profiling can complement and amplify a wide range of other investigative disciplines.

Macha asked me to review three murders committed in Wichita Falls between December 1984 and September

1985. The first two killings already had been linked by
DNA analysis. The prosecutor wanted to know if I thought
the same person had committed all three homicides, and if
so, what sort of person was this UNSUB?

The victim in the first case was twenty-year-old Terry Lee
Sims, a nursing student and EKG technician at Wichita
Falls's Bethania Hospital, who was brutally stabbed to
death in the early morning hours of Friday, December 21,
1984.

Terry Sims lived with her great-grandmother, but often
stayed overnight with her friend Leza Boone. Boone was
also employed at Bethania Hospital. Both women worked
the night shift on December 20. When Leza learned that
she had been scheduled for a double shift, they decided that
Terry would spend the night at Leza's house.

Leza gave Terry her only house key, as she had in the
past, and last saw her friend alive as she drove away from
the two-bedroom residence to her second shift at the hospital. Terry was standing out on the small porch as Leza
left.

The next morning at 7:30, Terry did not respond to
Leza's knocks on the front door. Leza walked around to
the side of the house and discovered the kitchen light was
on. This was unusual because Terry always had remembered to turn it off in the past. Leza also found the sliding
glass door was securely locked.

Leza fetched a duplicate key from her landlord and let
herself in. She immediately saw an overturned stereo
speaker in the living room and blood splatters in the first
bedroom. Fearful of going farther, she summoned her landlord, who went inside to find Terry Sims naked except for
her socks, curled up in a fetal position on the bathroom
floor. She was dead.

There was no sign of forced entry, and Leza Boone reported no recent trouble with hang-up calls or prowlers. She
said that when spending the night, Terry's usual routine

was to change out of her hospital uniform the moment she came in from the night shift. Then she would turn on the stereo, get something to eat in the kitchen, and settle down in the living room to watch TV, listen to music, or study.

In front of the stereo speaker was Terry's uniform, a smock and a pullover shirt. Several items were found on the coffee table, including a blood-soaked yellow Kleenex. A pair of women's underpants, spotted with blood, were rolled up beneath the table. Also lying on the floor near the coffee table were the victim's glasses.

Police discovered a blood spot in the doorway leading to the first bedroom and more blood on the bedsheets and pillowcase, as well as on a pillow on the floor. A rag, resting on the corner of the bed, was soaked in blood.

Terry's purse and tan wallet were on the bed, and inside the handbag were two Swiss Army knives. The yellow extension cord used to connect the water bed heater to an electrical wall socket was cut and a length removed. Two buttons also were found on the bedroom floor.

The dead woman was lying on her left side in the bathroom, her hands tightly bound behind her with the yellow extension cord. Lab tests revealed semen in her mouth and vagina. There were bruises around her face consistent with being punched, bludgeoned, or possibly thrown against the floor or wall. Her attacker had stabbed Terry a dozen times in the chest and back. She had tried to fight back, according to the medical examiner, who found defensive wounds on both Terry's hands, as well as her upper left arm. Blood spatters were found on the front of the vanity, the sink, one wall, and the bathtub. There also was a large amount of blood on the rim of the tub. No murder weapon was recovered.

Terry Sims had lived in Wichita Falls her entire life. My interviews with people who knew her produced the portrait of a shy, quiet, somewhat insecure young woman who was naturally drawn to a helping profession such as nursing. She had a boyfriend who was out of the country at the time of her killing, and she was not known to be seeing anyone else.

Terry used to warn other nursing students to be careful going to and from their cars. She had taken classes in tae kwan do, and the martial arts school she attended even had used her picture in a newspaper advertisement.

She also collected sharp weapons, including bayonets, boot knives, knuckles knives, throwing knives, and pocket knives. It was an unusual hobby, to be sure, but her friends and family insisted there was no pathology attached to Terry's interest in knives. She just liked to collect them. One of her younger sisters planned to give her a knife for Christmas that year.

Besides her two Swiss Army knives, Terry was known to keep another knife in her purse, one disguised as a writing pen. It was missing the morning after her murder.

Terry Sims was neither combative nor unusually preoccupied with her own physical safety. Some people described her as naive and dependable. Her cousin Billy said that, in his view, Terry wasn't killed because of who she was but because of where she was. He couldn't imagine Terry provoking someone to murder. He believed she was killed because she could identify the man who attacked her.

Victim number two was Toni Gibbs, an attractive twenty-four-year-old nurse last seen around 7:30 on Saturday morning, January 19, 1985, as she left work at Wichita General Hospital. The next day Toni was reported missing.

On Tuesday morning, January 22, her white 1984 Camaro was discovered on a street approximately two blocks from Leza Boone's house, where Terry Sims had been murdered a month earlier. The car was legally parked and locked.

Toni's purse was found where she usually left it, under the passenger-side floor mat. Both bucket seats in the Camaro were positioned all the way to the rear. A small blood spot was detected on both the inside and outside of the driver's-side door. Also found were white scuff marks, presumably from shoe polish, on the emergency brake and center of the steering wheel. It appeared as though a person had been dragged or pulled across the front seat of the car.

On Friday, February 15, a utility worker discovered Toni Gibbs's naked body in a rural field approximately a mile south of the Wichita Falls city limits. The victim was lying on her back with her arms above her head. She had been stabbed numerous times and was wearing some moderately expensive jewelry that her killer had either overlooked or ignored.

Like Terry Sims, Toni Gibbs had sustained terrible injuries. The areas around her chest and left leg had multiple contusions and deep scratches, some of them inflicted postmortem. A knife blade at least six inches long had been used to stab her several times in the upper abdomen, left front shoulder, and left armpit, and three more times in the back. Seminal fluid was found in her mouth, vagina, and anus. As with Terry Sims, Ms. Gibbs had also suffered defense wounds to both hands. There was no evidence that she had been bound.

A hundred feet from her body was a derelict trolley car. Gibbs's blood-stained shoes, still tied, were found under the trolley floor, along with her blood-stained panty hose, bikini underpants, white uniform pants (one leg turned inside out), white uniform top, and her black leather jacket. The bloody uniform top, full of knife slits, was still buttoned up the back. Gibbs's bloody bra, still clasped, was also found inside the trolley.

There were blood stains on the trolley's inner walls and large blood drops on its floor. A rubber mat was soaked in blood.

Clearly, most of this horrific assault had taken place inside the trolley. But there were no drag marks anywhere on Toni Gibbs's body. The pathologist surmised that she walked or crawled from the trolley to where she was found in the field, nearly four weeks later.

I learned that Toni Gibbs was an extremely intelligent,

independent, outgoing young woman from a good family. She had been divorced for less than a year, lived alone in an apartment complex, and enjoyed going out to country and western bars with girlfriends.

Everyone agreed that Toni would not have picked up a hitchhiker or anyone she didn't know. She was in good physical shape, and she would have fought an attacker if she had any hope of prevailing.

More questioning elicited the information that she had been receiving obscene telephone calls over several weeks prior to her death. I learned from her brothers, Waldo and Jeff, that the caller told Toni exactly what she was wearing and where she had been on each day that he called. They reported that their sister was sincerely frightened about the incidents. As it turned out, these calls apparently had nothing to do with the crime. An investigator must remember that there are often circumstances in a crime that have no association with it.

The Gibbs investigation developed a viable suspect. Danny Wayne Laughlin was a strange young man who worked at the Stardust Club, one of the country and western clubs Toni frequented. His job as "bar back" was menial. Laughlin was sort of a gofer for the bartenders, responsible for keeping them supplied with liquor, wine, and beer, hauling ice, and running errands.

During routine police questioning of the Stardust Club's employees, Laughlin volunteered that he knew the victim. Then he showed up at police headquarters to say that on February 10 he had taken his dog out into the field where Toni Gibbs's body was found five days later.

That was a lie. On February 10 Danny Wayne Laughlin was in downtown Wichita Falls committing a burglary. The story he made up for the police was meant to be his alibi. In August he was tried and convicted of perjury and burglary and sentenced to two to seven years in prison.

Meanwhile, an informant whom Laughlin met in jail

claimed Laughlin had confessed the Gibbs killing to him. According to the informant, Laughlin described sharing drugs with Toni and then making sexual advances that she rebuffed. The source said Laughlin had told him that he became angry and killed Gibbs. A second witness also came forward to say she had seen Laughlin in the field with his dog, which, according to the witness, resembled a wolf.

Laughlin was indicted for the Gibbs murder in October 1985 and tried the following spring. When the jury was hung 11–1 in favor of acquittal, the prosecution declined to try him again. He was paroled the following year and died in a car crash near Cripple Creek, Colorado, in September 1993. Three years later, and a year before I entered the case as a consultant, DNA tests cleared Laughlin of Toni Gibbs's murder. They also showed that she and Terry Sims had been raped by the same man.

Now the story becomes even *more* complicated.

The third case that Barry Macha offered for analysis was that of Ellen Blau, twenty-one, who was last seen alive in the early morning hours of Thursday, September 19, 1985.

Ellen Blau was an intensely idealistic young woman, a strong-willed free spirit who was uncomfortable with her family's considerable wealth. Her parents told me Ellen left home in the Northeast at age seventeen to live with a young air force enlistee stationed at Wichita Falls. They brought her back home, but two days after completing high school, Ellen returned to Wichita Falls to be with her boyfriend.

She supported herself as a waitress or cook, refusing all offers of help from her parents, except for a 1980 Volkswagen Rabbit convertible they gave her a few months before her murder.

Her friends said Ellen was impulsive. Janie Ball, with whom Ellen was living at the time of her murder, reported her friend once drove to California with a truck driver, not bothering to inform Janie until she arrived on the West Coast. On the other hand, Ellen was not naive or easily frightened, according to her parents. They told me that she would probably resist an attacker unless he was armed.

The night of her disappearance, Ellen drank a few beers with friends at a Pizza Hut, then left unescorted in her Rabbit. She last was seen headed in the direction of downtown Wichita Falls. When she didn't show up the next morning at the Suds & Subs café where she worked as a cook, her boss telephoned both the police and Janie Ball.

Meantime, a bread truck driver who knew Ellen discovered her Rabbit parked behind a country store. Sensing something was wrong, the truck driver also called the police.

The VW was unlocked. The keys were in the ignition and at the "on" position. Both windows were rolled up. The victim's purse, containing $223 in cash, lay on the passenger-side floorboard near the hump. Her mother told me that Ellen would not voluntarily have left either the keys or her purse in the vehicle.

There was a small amount of blood on the driver's seat.

Three weeks later county employees found Blau's nude (except for one sock), mummified, and partially skeletonized body lying face down on a slope under a mesquite tree near a dirt road. Her tennis shoes, blue jeans, yellow-and-white shirt, bra, and other sock were recovered near a stock pond not far from the body. Her jeans were turned inside out.

Her yellow necklace, yellow bracelet, and yellow earrings were undisturbed, although two rings she was thought to have been wearing were gone. Her Lady's Rolex was found nine feet from her body.

A broken beer bottle near the body matched shards of a Michelob bottle in her car. Investigators believed the broken bottle had been her abductor's sharp-pointed weapon. Six .22-caliber bullet casings and one .22 round also were recovered nearby.

Because of extended exposure, Ellen's body yielded little in the way of forensic evidence. Animals had carried one of her arms almost two hundred feet away.

It did not appear that she had been bound. She had no head fractures or broken teeth. There was no evidence to suggest she was strangled and no evident wounds to the intact skin that remained. It was impossible to tell if she had been sexually assaulted.

Her official cause of death was "undetermined homicidal violence."

In my August 1997 report to Barry Macha, I concluded that because so little could be determined about the cause of Ellen Blau's death, I couldn't say conclusively that she had been killed by the same person who had killed Terry Sims and Toni Gibbs. Nor was there much about her personally, besides the women's ages and race, that really connected Ms. Blau to the other two victims.

But the killings did show some striking similarities. All three murders occurred in the morning hours. All three involved a sharp instrument (knives and the beer bottle). Despite their bloodiness and violence, none of the three homicides could be classified as "overkills" according to BSU criteria, in which the threshhold is twenty or more stab wounds.

None of the three women suffered head or facial fractures. All three apparently struggled with their attacker. There were no known thefts. All three victims were found naked, and their killer left their clothing behind. The victims' shoes were left tied in all three cases. At least one pant leg of each victim's clothing was turned inside out. Each of the women was alone when attacked, and in each case, the victim was left where she was killed.

Combining these similarities with the fact that all three homicides occurred within a very small geographic area and within nine months of one another, I wrote that "a strong possibility exists that the same person may be responsible for the three murders." I suggested therefore that the profile I had prepared could apply to all three investigations.

* * *

I wrote in my profile that the offender was a white male, twenty-four to thirty years of age at the time of the crimes. He almost certainly was less emotionally mature than his age and apt to react angrily at rejection, real or perceived. "He was a very selfish person," I went on, "who exhibited a lack of concern for the welfare or safety of others. . . . The killer would have projected a macho image to friends and associates."

It was obvious from the crimes that blood didn't bother him nor did killing in a very personal way with a knife (or broken bottle). That suggested to me that the killer's job involved working with his hands in a skilled or semiskilled position, and his job required physical exertion.

The absence of overkill indicated that his anger was controlled.

If he had served in the armed forces, he was unlikely to have completed his hitch because of a dislike for authority figures. He probably was, or had been, married, but was incapable of sexual fidelity.

He had a high school education and possibly had some trade or technical training. The lack of planning and sophistication in his crimes suggested no more than average intelligence.

At the time of the murders, he was socioeconomically in the lower- to lower-middle-class and resided in close proximity to Ms. Boone's residence.

He had a highly impulsive lifestyle.

At the time of the Sims murder, he was experiencing stress—occupational, health-related, financial, relational, family, or legal.

He would have had difficulties with the law since he was a teenager. His arrest record would reflect a variety of offenses and would probably include resisting arrest.

The murders had no effect on him, eliciting neither remorse nor guilt.

*   *   *

Prior to receiving my profile, the Wichita Falls authorities completed their investigation of a list of suspects in the three cases, clearing all of them. Then Barry Macha asked his investigator, John Little, to review the Sims, Gibbs, and Blau files again in light of my profile and the lack of a single credible suspect for all killings.

Right away Little noticed something previously overlooked. The name Faryion Edward Wardrip popped up in all three investigations. The police learned that Wardrip once lived with his wife and child in the same four-unit apartment building where Ellen Blau had lived with Janie Ball and her husband. The apartments were located two blocks from Leza Boone's house, site of the Sims murder. And Wardrip also had worked at Wichita General Hospital as an orderly at the same time that Toni Gibbs was employed as a nurse.

Detective Little dug deeper.

Faryion Wardrip was born in 1959 and grew up in Salem, Indiana. He was the fifth of nine children. His father was a machinist and his mother a telephone operator. According to his siblings, the family exhibited no dysfunction or deprivation.

Faryion was a poor student. He dropped out of high school in the eleventh grade and worked at mostly unskilled jobs until 1978, when he joined the Army National Guard. Six years later, just before the killings began, he received a less than honorable discharge in connection with an arrest for smoking dope.

In 1983, he married a Wichita Falls woman and fathered two children by her. He went to work as a janitor at Wichita General. In November 1983, he became an orderly at the hospital.

He soon thereafter separated from his wife. In 1985, four days after Toni Gibbs's body was found, he left his orderly's job at Wichita General. In December 1985, Wardrip and his wife separated for good.

Now a new victim enters the narrative.

Terry Sims was killed in December of 1984. Toni Gibbs's murder occurred one month later. Ellen Blau vanished in September of 1985. Then on May 6, 1986—one month after Danny Wayne Laughlin was unsuccessfully prosecuted for killing Toni Gibbs—twenty-one-year-old Tina Kimbrew of Wichita Falls was found dead in her apartment.

Kimbrew had been hit on the head and smothered with a pillow. Four days later, Faryion Wardrip arrived by bus in the Texas coastal city of Galveston where, he later would tell police, he intended to see the ocean before killing himself. Instead, he called the Galveston police and announced he had killed "a good friend" up in Wichita Falls—Tina Kimbrew.

Tina Kimbrew was a very pretty college student who supported herself by waiting tables. Wardrip claimed to have met her at the Stardust Club (Toni Gibbs's favorite) and became close with her. He said he took Kimbrew out to dinner at least once.

According to Wardrip, the murder occurred Tuesday morning, May 6, when he went to Kimbrew's apartment to ask if he could stay with her a few days. She said no. An argument ensued, and he killed her.

Police records show that as officers drove Wardrip back to Wichita Falls from Galveston, the prisoner mentioned that he knew Ellen Blau. No follow-up action was taken at that time. Apparently, no one thought to connect the Kimbrew case with any of the other three, unsolved, local homicides.

Wardrip acted deeply remorseful for the Kimbrew killing and pled guilty in exchange for a thirty-five-year sentence. He served eleven years before being paroled in December 1997. That was about four months after I had submitted my profile in the Sims, Gibbs, and Blau cases. The terms of Wardrip's parole included wearing an ankle bracelet to permit constant monitoring and a restriction on his movements to work, home, and church.

Upon his release, Wardrip moved to the little Texas town of Olney, where he had family members living. He went to work at the Olney Door and Screen Company, re-married, and became very active in the local Church of Christ. He began teaching Sunday school and told acquaintances he was studying for the ministry.

When the subject of his long imprisonment arose, Wardrip sometimes told people that the crime was a vehicular homicide. Other times he said the sentence had resulted from a tragic bar fight. "He'd climb a tree to lie before telling the truth on the ground," says Carlton Stowers, the Texas author who has written a book on the Wardrip case.

After developing this dossier, John Little proposed a search warrant for DNA. But prosecutor Macha declined, saying they still had too little probable cause to seek such a warrant. In order to get the necessary tissue sample, Little would have to secure his specimen the hard way. Under Texas's abandoned-property statute, anything someone discards—such as garbage put out for collection—is no longer considered private property and can legally be taken.

Detective Little drove to Olney and put Wardrip under surveillance, awaiting his chance. Because of Wardrip's restricted movements, opportunities were few. After several days of frustration, Little decided to settle in at a laundry across Olney's main street from the Door and Screen Company to await his chance.

A week passed. Then one day the new Mrs. Wardrip drove up during her husband's morning break. He got into the front seat with her and ate a snack of coffee and a package of peanut butter crackers. When break time was over, Wardrip exited the car, finished his coffee, and discarded the used paper cup in a blue trash barrel on his way back to work.

Here was Little's chance. The investigator, a snuff chewer, jammed a wad of tobacco in his mouth and then ran across the street. Pointing at the blue barrel, he asked Wardrip if he could fetch out his used coffee cup for a spit cup.

"Help yourself," said Wardrip, and John Little did. I admire innovative thinking, and Little's actions that day certainly earned my respect.

The DNA extracted from Faryion Wardrip's saliva in the paper coffee cup matched that of the person who had killed Terry Sims and Toni Gibbs. After fifteen long years, the cases finally were solved.

Authorities decided that the best way to bring Wardrip into custody was through his parole officer in Wichita Falls. He was asked to call Wardrip in Olney and request that Wardrip come to Wichita Falls for a meeting. Wardrip, who had been lobbying hard to have his ankle monitor removed, apparently thought the meeting would address that issue.

He showed up at the appointed hour on Saturday, February 13, 1999, and discovered John Little waiting for him. Later that day Wardrip was taken to the DA's office and arrested for the two murders.

In custody, Wardrip at first said nothing. Then his wife visited him with the news that a local paper was reporting the DNA match to Sims and Gibbs. After hearing that, Wardrip summoned John Little to the jail.

On the morning of February 16, 1999, Wardrip sat down in front of a tape recorder for fifty minutes with John Little and Paul Smith, an investigator for the Archer County district attorney. He had a lot to tell them.

After reading Wardrip his Miranda rights and other preliminaries, Little asked the prisoner about Terry Sims.

Wardrip began by explaining that he had been using intravenous drugs at the time of the Sims murder, and that he had been out walking that night after a fight with his wife. "As I was walking," he went on, "she [Sims] was at her door. I went up to the door and forced my way in. Well, [I] just ransacked her, just slung her all over the house in a violent rage. Stripped her down and murdered her."

Little asked Wardrip to explain his rage.

"I thought my family hated me. I hated them. My wife kept coming in and out of my life. She'd come to me when times were good, and then when times got hard she'd leave . . . I thought everybody was out to get me. The drugs made me paranoid . . . I would just reach a boiling point. But the crazy thing about it was, I was so mad at my wife [but] I never done [sic] anything to her. But I was just so mad and so angered."

Wardrip said he could remember very little about the crime, including whether he had sexually assaulted Sims or where he'd gotten the knife. All he knew for certain, he said, was that he had killed her.

Paul Smith asked about Toni Gibbs.

"Yeah," Wardrip replied. "Again I was out walking, been out walking all night. Somehow I was downtown . . . It was starting to get daylight and, uh, I was walking up toward the hospital and Toni knew me and she asked me if I wanted a ride and I said yeah.

"We got in the car and she gave me a ride and, uh, I started basically in on her. I started seeing images of anger and hatred and it just clicked off and I told her to drive out the road there. I don't remember which direction we were going. I just told her to drive."

Wardrip recalled it was cold that February dawn but claimed no recollection of the abandoned trolley where he killed Toni Gibbs. "When I'm in those rages, I just black out. I just don't remember. I don't remember that," he said.

"I just grabbed her and started trying to sling her around the car and she swerved off the side of the road . . . and she turned down a dirt road and I still had her by her jacket and I was just slinging her, just slinging her, and I was screaming as loud as I can at her and, uh, I told her to stop and she stopped. I did the same thing. I took off her clothes and I stabbed her."

"Did you have sex with Toni Gibbs?" Smith asked.

"I don't really remember. I remember screaming at her, screaming at her, screaming at her that I hate you. I don't remember if I had sex. I just remember screaming and screaming and screaming how much I hate you, how much I hated everybody."

John Little reminded Wardrip he had said he knew Toni Gibbs. "How did Toni know you?" Little asked.

"From the hospital," Wardrip replied. "She never had anything to do with me. I just knew her from there. It could have been anybody. She just happened to be in the wrong place at the wrong time ... I never set my sights on anybody. I would just get so mad and I would just get out and walk, be in such a rage. I would just scream at the sky, scream at the trees, scream at God.

"Then I would just lay down for a while and sleep, and then I'd see it on the news and [realize] that something must have happened real bad. I tricked myself [into] thinking it wasn't me ... I just blocked it out of my mind, wouldn't even want to think about it for a long, long, long time."

Little turned the conversation to Ellen Blau.

"Same thing," said Wardrip. "I'd just be out walking, just walking." He said he saw Blau turn her car into a store parking lot and followed her. "I asked her what she was doing. She said she was looking for somebody, and I just grabbed her and pushed her back into her car.

"We drove out to a road ... and I just started grabbing her and screaming at her, I hate you ... I had drug her out of the car and took her in a field and stripped her clothes off, but I don't remember how she died. I don't believe I raped her. I don't recall. She probably broke her neck because I sure was slinging her. I was just so mad and angry. ..."

Wardrip explained that he had seen his wife's face as he was assaulting the women. "I hated her so much. It's just like with Tina. I was screaming at her, and I had my arm across her throat. I was screaming at her bloody murder. I didn't see Tina's face; I saw hers. I was so consumed with hatred. I never hit them though. That's what really threw me. I wonder why I didn't, but I never struck. Just like my wife. I never hit her."

Wardrip wasn't finished. "There is one more," he told Little and Smith. "It ain't here though." He confessed to a fifth homicide, one for which he had not been a suspect, the March 25, 1985, murder in Fort Worth, Texas, of Debra Taylor, a wife and mother.

Wardrip said that following Terry Sims's murder he went to Fort Worth for a while looking for work. One night he met Taylor at a local honky-tonk.

"[She was] coming on to me," he insisted. "We went out to the parking lot around back and I made my advance toward her and she said no and she slapped my face, and when she did that I just snapped and I grabbed her and I slung her around and I done the same thing to her that she did to me. And I killed her."

"How did you kill her?" asked Little.

"I think I strangled her. I had her on the ground, and I think I used my forearm." Wardrip continued, "I put her in the car, took her up the interstate and found the first road and just, uh, threw her out."

One of the most remarkable aspects of this extraordinary story is the speed with which the UNSUB of a fifteen-year-old serial murder case was identified and brought to justice.

In early January 1999, when John Little had begun his cold-case review, Barry Macha had nothing more to go on than a DNA match between the Sims and Gibbs cases and my belief that Ellen Blau was killed by the same person. By early February John Little had obtained his DNA sample from Wardrip.

Within eleven days, Wardrip had confessed to four killings and had been charged with capital murder by a Wichita County Grand Jury in the Sims and Blau cases. On the first day of his trial for murdering Terry Sims, Wardrip entered a guilty plea and was sentenced to death by lethal injection.

By the end of the year, he was on death row, with life sentences in the three other homicides.

The wheels of justice may have been slow to grind in Faryion Wardrip's case, but once they got started, the outcome was satisfying, swift, and sure.

12

LINKAGE ANALYSIS

My report to the Wichita Falls prosecutor was a hybrid analysis; it combined a profile with related elements of what I call linkage analysis. Besides the portrait I drew of the UNSUB, I also analyzed the three murders for behavioral clues to see if they were linked, i.e., was the same killer responsible for all three homicides?

I always set high standards of behavioral proof for linkage analyses. I will not testify in court that two or more homicides are the work of a single killer unless I can document a unique combination of MO and ritual behaviors. The three Wichita Falls cases certainly had plenty of behavioral similarities, but without more complete forensic information in the Blau homicide, I wasn't prepared to make a definitive judgment.

At the time of the Wardrip matter, I had already worked on a large number of cases involving linkage analyses. In most instances there were at least three crimes to analyze, and generally they were grouped together, both geographically and chronologically. But not always. A midwestern state case offered an interesting challenge.

Several years ago I was retained by an attorney to conduct a linkage analysis in a civil liability suit that had grown out of a strange and savage murder. This homicide had a bizarre feature I hadn't seen before and haven't since—two of the victim's teeth had been taken from her mouth.

The case began just before 6:00 A.M. on a cold and snowy winter Saturday. As a police officer pulled into his station, he discovered a sports car parked improbably on the facility's front lawn. The driver's-side door was open, and a woman was lying on her back on the ground, her feet resting inside the car.

She was thirty-one-year-old Juliet Cruz,* and she had been shot with a handgun. She also had an extraordinary story to tell—after she was hospitalized—of how she had been shot, and why she was lying on the cold ground next to her car in front of a police station that Saturday morning.

The young woman explained that just a few minutes before the officer discovered her, she had been innocently driving along the highway on her way to visit her sick father. Cruz said that she had just turned onto the interstate when in the distance she saw a man exit the driver's side of a dark blue subcompact that was parked at the side of the road. He was headed across the highway toward a late-model sedan that had its emergency flashers on.

Then Juliet saw a woman jump out the passenger side of the blue car. She waved Juliet to a stop, got into the startled woman's car, and blurted out a harrowing tale.

Her name was Rose Morrison.* Two hours earlier, Morrison said, she had been driving along the same stretch of the interstate when the sedan suddenly had bumped her left front fender, running her off the road. The sedan's driver, a black man, at first behaved as if he wanted to help her. But then he drew a gun and took her to another location where, she said, he raped her for two hours and "used the gun on her during the rape," according to Juliet Cruz's later statement.

As Rose Morisson recounted her ordeal, Juliet cautiously steered her sports car back out onto the snow-covered highway—her top speed that morning was 40 mph—and headed north. When Juliet looked into her rearview mirror, she was stunned to see the sedan bearing down on her from behind.

The driver pulled abreast of her car and began shooting at Cruz with a handgun. Juliet drove onto an exit ramp, looking for a policeman. By this time the man had swung his car around to the other side of her vehicle and was shooting again.

One bullet hit Cruz, paralyzing her from the waist down. She saw the police station at the same moment and aimed her car straight for it, ending up on the front lawn.

The sedan was right behind. The man skidded to a stop in the middle of the street, ran over to Cruz's car, opened the passenger door, and dragged Rose Morrison out onto the snow. "This time you die, bitch!" he snarled.

Then he poked his head in the car once more, grabbed Rose's purse, and warned Cruz that if she said anything, he would kill her. He dragged Rose Morrison back to his car and vanished. The police officer arrived on the scene a few minutes later.

It was an incredible story, backed up by Juliet's paralyzing wound and the multiple bullet holes the police found in her car. Her descriptions of both her attacker and his sedan led to the arrest of twenty-nine-year-old Roland Smith,* a black man whom she later picked out of a police lineup.

Rose Morrison's fate wasn't known for seventeen days. A witness, John Jones,* came forth with the news that he had found a woman's body hidden under a low bridge approximately twenty miles from the police station. Her blouse and one of her boots also were recovered. There was a large pool of blood nearby, and a bullet lay underneath the body.

Jones reported that, while driving by, he had noticed a woman's white slip. When he stopped for a closer look, he saw a woman's leather coat on the ground by the roadway. Near it was a package of condoms. Police would later find another condom package at the same site as well as two empty cigarette packs.

Rose Morrison's battered, nude body was secreted under the bridge a little farther on. She had been horribly beaten all over her body with blunt force. Her nose was fractured in several places, as were several other facial bones and her skull. The left side of her face had taken the brunt of the assault. It was deformed from his blows.

The blunt-force injuries caused Morrison's death, but her killer had also shot her in the left forehead and shoulder. A piece of shrapnel pierced her right hip.

No drugs or alcohol were found in her system. Her body bore no defensive wounds or ligature marks. No semen was recovered. A lubricant had been applied to her vagina and anus. It appeared that Morrison had been anally raped after she died.

Strangest and most gruesome of all, two of her upper incisors, the left mid and left laterial, had been taken from their sockets, which the medical examiner described as open and bloody. The teeth were never recovered.

My participation in the case evolved around the pivotal issue of whether Smith had committed a similar crime four years earlier. I was asked to render my professional opinion as to whether the two crimes in fact were linked. I started by examining the facts of the earlier case.

On a Friday night in November, twenty-one-year-old Maria Rodriguez* left a local nightclub about 11:45. A couple returning home from a movie that night reported seeing her at an intersection not long thereafter. They said that a white car, occupied by a single male, and a blue car were right behind her. The male in the white car appeared extremely angry.

A short while later, residents in a nearby, middle-class subdivision heard the sounds of a collision, followed by approximately ten minutes of excited yelling in the street.

Two or three male voices were heard. Car doors were repeatedly opened and slammed shut.

Maria Rodriguez's vehicle was later recovered in the vicinity. It was locked. Her flashers were on. The left front had minor scratches, and the left turn signal lens was broken out.

The next day, on a mountain highway an hour's drive northwest from where her car was found, Maria's battered, naked body was discovered at the bottom of an embankment at a roadside rest area. Evidence at the scene suggested that a vehicle had been backed to the edge of the embankment, and that two people had gotten out and thrown her over the edge. Footprints indicated that a third individual had walked from the car over to the highway, probably to keep watch.

Her bloody sweatpants and torn underwear were found along the roadside three miles away. Her car keys were recovered seven miles from the body disposal site. Police did not recover the necklace that Maria Rodriguez wore that night, or her watch, driver's license, or credit cards.

The victim's cause of death was listed as "central nervous system contusions and acute blood loss." She had been beaten to death and her throat cut three times. Her entire body was covered in injuries from blunt-force trauma. Her nose was fractured, and a single huge contusion covered the left side of her face.

No semen was detected, nor was there any indication of direct injury to Maria's sexual organs. No defensive wounds or ligature marks were noted in the autopsy. The medical examiner did describe extensive bruising of her pubic area and breasts. The most remarkable injury, however, was to her mouth.

Maria Rodriguez's upper right mid incisors and left middle incisor—three teeth in all—had been taken.

In linkage analysis I must examine the differences between crimes as carefully as the similarities. In the Rose Morrison and Maria Rodriguez cases, these differences began with the fact that one victim was an Anglo and the other Hispanic. Also, a gun was used in the Morrison murder, while Maria's killer used a knife.

Morrison hadn't been robbed; Rodriguez had. Only a single offender had attacked Rose; it was believed that several males were involved in Maria's abduction.

The presence of the lubricant and evidence of postmortem anal tearing support the conclusion that Rose Morrison was sexually violated after death. There was no medical evidence that Maria Rodriguez was raped.

However, these dissimilarities did not rule out the possibility that one man had been involved in both women's deaths. I believed some of them stemmed from the killer's moving up the learning curve, as successful offenders generally do. It is not unusual for a serial offender to commit his first crime, or crimes, with accomplices then graduate to committing them on his own. Kenneth Bianchi—known together with his cousin, Angelo Buono, as the Hillside Strangler—is a notable example of this pattern of progression.

A serial offender has several reasons for preferring to act alone. Maria Rodriguez's killer probably realized he was safer without fellow offenders who could become witnesses against him. He would also recognize the danger of being seen and identified in the suburban neighborhood where Maria was abducted. The interstate was a safer place to operate. Likewise, a gun is a more useful weapon than a knife.

He also did a better job of hiding the second victim's body. Rodriguez was discovered within twenty-four hours; Morrison's remains weren't found for seventeen days. Finally, by stealing Rodriguez's personal possessions, he had heightened his risk of being connected to her murder. Nothing belonging to Rose Morrison was known to have been stolen except her two teeth.

Investigators should always bear in mind that there will be differences between two crimes, even if the same person

committed them. The variables responsible for these incon-
sistencies include the circumstances, victim behavior, the
amount of time the offender has, and his mood.

Next I focused on the similarities. Both victims were
females in their early twenties, and both had been out alone
in their cars in the early hours of a Saturday. Both were
abducted after incidents in which the left front portions of
their vehicles received minor damage. There were no witnesses to either collision.

Both victims' cars were left where they had been abducted. Both women eventually were transported elsewhere
in their assailants' vehicles.

Both cases featured multiple crime scenes, and both victims' possessions were found scattered in different locations. Both were found nude, near a rural roadside, and in
both instances care had been taken to conceal the body. No
victim clothing was found near the disposal site.

Both murders appeared to be anger motivated. The victims had been severely beaten over their entire bodies, sus-
taining injuries far in excess to those necessary to cause
death. Both murders were examples of overkill.

Recall that none of Faryion Wardrip's Texas homicides,
bloody though they were, met the overkill criterion. These
two homicides, however, passed the threshold of excess-
iveness.

Both women suffered blunt trauma, primarily to the left
sides of their faces, and both had been kept by their captors
at least two hours.

No seminal fluid was found in connection with either
homicide.

There were no defensive wounds nor ligature marks on
either body.

Both victims had their noses fractured.

And the killer had extracted and kept upper incisors
from both of them.

Although four years separated the two crimes, I had little
trouble concluding that the same killer had committed both.
The extracted teeth were compelling evidence, of course.

But since this aspect was totally new in my experience, I advised my client to secure a second expert's opinion.

My recommendation was Dr. Lowell Levine, the eminent forensic odontologist and director of the New York State Police's Medicolegal Investigations Unit. Dr. Levine said that he, too, believed the teeth in both cases were intentionally removed. Dr. Levine also could not recall a similar case of deliberately excised upper teeth.

Roland Smith was sentenced to prison in the Rose Morrison case, thanks to Juliet Cruz's bravery and quick wits.

Linkage analysis can be a useful tool for isolating the probability that one person was, or was not, involved in multiple offenses. In cases where no reliable witnesses, or physical evidence, are available, it can be a critical factor in establishing guilt or innocence. Sometimes, as in the Wardrip case, it has the same sort of value that a good profile has. It helps the police focus their investigation, to perhaps discard unpromising ideas and pursue potentially valuable ones that they hadn't previously considered.

In this case my analysis did provide survivors with a sense of justice completed. It seemed certain that Smith had indeed murdered both women, and just as certainly he's serving time for committing the crimes.

13

EQUIVOCAL DEATHS

Sometimes my job as an investigator is not to help identify the person most likely to have committed an unsolved crime. Instead, the task may be to determine just what happened when a person's manner of death is unclear or in dispute. This facet of my work is known as equivocal death analysis or EDA.

Equivocal death analysis is by far the most demanding work I do. Unlike a profile, in which I paint a word picture of an UNSUB, in an EDA my quest isn't who but what. Was the death a homicide, a suicide, or an accident? Besides having broad experience with all three manners of death, the equivocal death analyst requires extensive information about the victim and the circumstances surrounding his or her demise before rendering an opinion.

Finding out just what happened to the deceased is, of course, of vital interest to the victim's loved ones. In addition, a question of suicide versus accidental death can have profound religious significance—as well as insurance implications.

Then there is the stigma attached to certain deaths. I know of two instances in which parents of boys who died during dangerous autoerotic episodes sought to have their sons' death certificates altered—one to show the cause of death as an accident, the other to list it as murder—in order to avoid embarrassment.

In this chapter you will read about three cases that illustrate some of the many obstacles that a person preparing an EDA faces.

THE MYSTERIOUS WATCH

Eighteen-year-old Patrick Mahan* died in an unusual way, in an unusual position, at an unusual location. Three days after disappearing from his home, the young man was found hanging from a metal ladder inside a vertical sewer pipe, with a plastic-coated bicycle cable snug around his neck.

Mahan was totally nude except for a rosary around his neck and a bracelet with a cross on his right wrist. His mouth and eyes were wrapped with a single, continuous piece of duct tape, which had prevented the teenager from seeing or speaking, but did permit him to breathe through his nose.

His body was partially visible from a slotted manhole cover above him. But Mahan arrived at the site where he was found from below, via a horizontal sewer main that ran twenty-five feet directly beneath his suspended body. The teenager's clothes were discovered at the mouth of the horizontal pipe. A partially used roll of duct tape was found another fifteen feet away.

The bicycle chain was looped through the third topmost rung of the metal ladder, then under his left arm and around his neck in a bizarre configuration. A lock—its keyhole facing up and toward Mahan—secured the ends of the chain. The key later was discovered directly below the victim in the horizontal pipe, lying in five inches of sewer water.

Mahan's hands and feet were free and unmarked, though dirty with debris from the ladder. His body showed no injuries other than that caused by the bicycle cable. Strangest

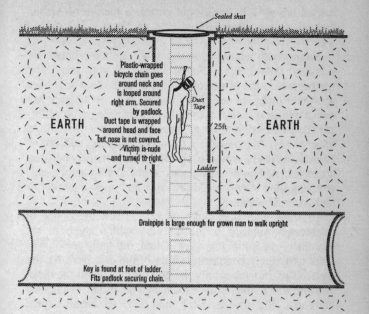

Sealed shut

Plastic-wrapped
bicycle chain goes
around neck and
is looped around
right arm. Secured
by padlock.
Duct tape is wrapped
around head and face
but nose is not covered.
Victim is nude
and turned to right.

Duct Tape

EARTH   25ft   EARTH

Ladder

Drainpipe is large enough for grown man to walk upright

Key is found at foot of ladder.
Fits padlock securing chain.

THIS IS AN INVERTED "T" SITUATION

of all, Patrick Mahan's most prized possession, his grand-father's pocket watch, was discovered in his mouth.

Local authorities spent a year investigating this death. Among themselves they debated what to call it—a homicide, a suicide, or perhaps an accident—before the District Attorney's Office contacted the BSU to request an equivocal death analysis.

Knowledge of the victim's personality and behavior is critical to an EDA. In this case our sources of information would be a wide selection of Mahan's family, friends, and acquaintances, a real cross section of those who knew him. Each sat down for a structured interview with a police officer, who asked the witnesses a number of questions I had provided in the order I had listed them. These procedures helped ensure a balanced and detached picture of Mahan and not just a general discussion of "how wonderful he was."

Subjectivity among witnesses is a common problem for criminal investigators. For example, if you asked my mother what kind of person I am, I believe she would have answered that God personally chose me to be her son. My own three sons would each tell you something a bit different about me. I don't care to guess what my first wife would have to say. My neighbors, business partners, and fellow church members would each have their independent perspectives. Although their views might differ sharply, collectively their views would probably add up to a pretty fair and accurate appraisal.

In some equivocal death analyses I ask the police to reinterview subjects a second time within three to six months of the initial interview. Often, the same person will offer two highly contrasting views of the deceased. At first we tend to remember only the good things about the dead. "Oh, he was a wonderful husband and neighbor" is a typical comment. Six months later, however, the same source might say, "I know I told you what a great guy he was, but he could be arrogant at times. He could really irritate people."

In the Mahan case, the police conducted excellent interviews with a large number of people who knew the young man in various ways and obtained for me a well-balanced description of the victim.

Patrick Mahan lived in a small northeastern community and attended a vocational high school. His teachers said he paid attention to his studies. Until just before his death he had done well in class. Patrick resided alone with his mother, who was separated from her husband, Patrick's stepfather. Mrs. Mahan told police her son was highly inquisitive and easily bored by any sort of routine. She also said that he was a very observant Catholic.

The teenager was physically well developed and lean, about five feet, six inches tall, and very athletic. He participated in a variety of sports, from swimming, karate, soccer, and weight lifting to football and baseball. Patrick moved in a small circle of close friends. These boys and girls said that Mahan did not go out on many dates but wanted to. There was also a rumor that he had fathered a child, they said, but the police were unable to verify this allegation.

He had a collection of ornamental swords that he recently had destroyed and discarded after using one of the weapons to decapitate a cat—or so I was told. The incident was not described more fully. Mahan kept the rest of his prized possessions, including his grandfather's pocket watch, in a locked chest in his room.

The goal of an equivocal death analysis is not to prove the manner of death, but to arrive at an informed opinion whether homicide, suicide, or an accident most likely occurred. To remain as unbiased as possible, I identify and list every material fact or instance of behavior that is consistent, or inconsistent, with homicide, suicide, or an accident. What results is a kind of evidence tally sheet, a three-column graph of all relevant data.

In the Mahan case I focused first on the possibility of homicide. I found four factors consistent with this hypothesis. First, two sources told the police that the young man may have owed money to drug dealers. The rumored amounts ran from two thousand dollars to two hundred thousand. Further investigation failed to verify any such drug connection in Mahan's life. Nevertheless, we had to consider the reports as elements consistent with murder.

Second, one of the victim's female friends reported she had observed Mahan speaking to a person in a white car with tinted windows shortly before his death. She said Patrick had ignored her as she walked by. The alleged incident further fueled conjecture that Mahan was involved with drug dealing.

The third factor was a report to the police that the victim was part of a male prostitution ring. He allegedly was seen riding in a car belonging to the group's pimp on the evening he disappeared. The pimp, if he existed at all, was never identified.

Some pretty far-fetched stories of this nature can surface in the course of a criminal investigation. Usually they are based on nothing more than hearsay. However, the people reporting such tales often sincerely believe them to be true and can be quite convincing in reporting them. All such leads must be investigated.

In Patrick Mahan's case, the police found no evidence to suggest the victim was a prostitute or that such a ring even existed. Additionally, the pathologist who conducted Mahan's autopsy found no medical evidence that he was engaged in homosexual practices.

Another intriguing bit of evidence was a red mark, wider than the bicycle chain, around the victim's neck. Although this discovery caused some concern initially, it was determined to be the result of livor mortis, a common case of tissue discoloration due to the settling of the victim's blood after death. The mark was consistent with blood pooling above the noose, which had impeded its normal postmortem flow to the lower parts of the body.

Seven factors in the case were inconsistent with homicide.

To begin with, the victim was found completely unclothed, which suggested a sexual component to Patrick Mahan's death. Nudity is rarely associated with homicides committed to silence the victim or for reasons of personal gain. Yet the autopsy revealed no injury to the anus, and the penis was free of foreign material. While this did not rule out a murder, the nudity—taken together with the autopsy results, the body's position and location, as well as the complexity of the hanging apparatus—made homicide seem improbable.

Second, the neighborhood in which the young man's body was found was popular with teens. This meant that

Mahan's clothes and the roll of duct tape left near the sewer pipe opening were likely to be noticed quickly. In fact, this is just what happened, since a search was mounted for the teen in the immediate wake of his disappearance. In my experience with homicide, anyone who had gone to the lengths necessary to murder Patrick in the extraordinary way and place he died would not have called attention to the body's location by casually discarding the clothes in that way.

Third, I have never seen, heard, or read about a homicidal strangulation featuring such a complex apparatus. Wrapping the cable around Mahan's arm as well as his neck did not facilitate death; on the contrary, it would have greatly impeded that goal.

Fourth, I thought it highly improbable that a killer would take Patrick Mahan to the top of the narrow, twenty-five-foot vertical drainpipe in order to hang him. No matter what the victim's physical condition, doing so would have been extremely difficult, as well as unnecessary, if the objective was to kill the young man.

I reflected at length on this part of the puzzle, searching for a hole in my logic. If Mahan was conscious, why weren't any defensive wounds found on his body, scrapes and bruises consistent with a struggle to defend himself? If he was unconscious, why was there no evidence of his body being dragged or carried to the sewer pipe? There were no ligature marks (save for the one from the bicycle chain) on his body; no evidence of a blow to the head or other injury that would have rendered him unconscious; no toxicological evidence of incapacity due to drugs or alcohol.

If this was a homicide, the victim either undressed himself or let the killer undress him, and then did not resist being taken or carried up the drainpipe, where the cable was arranged around his neck and fastened by means of a lock. All of this was beginning to sound very unlikely to me.

Fifth, we knew from his mother that Mahan kept the bicycle chain and lock in the garage at home. If this was a

homicide, the killer must have taken these two highly unusual "weapons" to the drainpipe with the intent of using
them to kill Patrick. Once more, the pieces weren't adding
up in my mind.

Sixth, the victim was allegedly killed because of his association with a ring of homosexual prostitutes. In my experience, homosexually related murders are highly personal
and violent crimes. An investigator can expect to find multiple injuries to the victim's face, neck, heart, or genitalia.
Patrick Mahan was virtually unmarked.

Finally, his grandfather's pocket watch was found taped
within the victim's mouth. An extraordinary—and, in my
experience, unique—feature of this case, the watch's placement is inconsistent with homicide. If anything, I would
have expected Patrick Mahan's killer to destroy the cherished article not preserve it.

So I was inclined to rule out homicide as the cause of
Patrick Mahan's death.

I next examined the evidence for and against a conclusion
of suicide.

When people contemplate taking their own lives, they
often give away, or destroy, personal possessions, including
items of great sentimental value. Remember that Mahan
reportedly broke and threw away his sword collection after
beheading a cat. We learned that he also collected precious
coins. These were missing from his locked trunk, and it is
possible that he gave them away or disposed of them in
another manner.

The second factor consistent with suicide was the victim's frame of mind. His mother and others reported that
Patrick was depressed and anxious about the future. Mrs.
Mahan said her son feared the possibility of World War III
or a nonsurvivable nuclear war. He was unhappy over the
lack of contact with his biological father, and he reportedly
was using both alcohol and drugs. Recently, his grades at
school had declined, too.

Third, prospective suicides often distance themselves from close friends and family just prior to taking their own lives. Patrick had recently severed his close relationship with another boy, whom people described as "like a brother" to him. He also had broken up with his girlfriend.

Fourth, his mother and a few of his friends told police that the victim had discussed suicide with them.

Fifth, Mahan died in an isolated and secluded spot. Serious suicides typically pick out such locations in order to kill themselves undisturbed.

So a viable argument could be made that Patrick Mahan was a suicide. More persuasive, however, were the seven factors I isolated that argued against that conclusion.

First and foremost, the victim was a Roman Catholic who, according to his mother, took his faith very seriously. Catholic doctrine, which forbids suicides from burial in hallowed ground, would have presented a strong deterrent in Mahan's mind.

Second, nudity and suicide don't mix. Outside of prisons, jails, mental institutions, or juvenile facilities, it is rare for someone to commit suicide by hanging himself in the nude. Call it a peculiarity of the human psyche. Every fatal, naked hanging I have ever seen, outside an institution, occurred in the course of an autoerotic misadventure.

Furthermore, Patrick's mother told police her son was meticulous about his clothes and grooming. Had he intended to commit suicide, he probably would have showered, shaved, and dressed beforehand.

Fourth, hanging himself from the third highest rung of the metal ladder was inconsistent with suicide. A much lower rung would have served Mahan's purposes just as well.

Fifth, the configuration of the bicycle chain ligature made as little sense for a suicide as for a homicide. As mentioned before, the complex looping actually would have impeded Mahan's death.

Sixth, the duct tape and watch were inconsistent with a suicide. The tape covering his eyes and mouth were a form of sexual bondage, for which there is no reasonable explanation in a suicide. Likewise, placing the watch in his mouth served no useful function if the young man's intent was to kill himself.

Seventh, though the victim had discussed suicide on a number of occasions, he had not initiated the conversations, according to the witnesses. His friends also said Mahan pointedly had dismissed suicide as "stupid." He reportedly told one group, "If I want to kill myself, I'm not going to do it by hanging or suffocation. I'd blow my brains out."

The evidence was convincing to me. Patrick Mahan was not a suicide.

I could not feel confident in concluding that Patrick Mahan had died as a result of dangerous autoeroticism, simply because both homicide and suicide seemed unlikely. I had to let the evidence persuade me that his death fell into this category. Having studied and written about the subject for two decades, I knew it was full of complexities. In assessing this possible explanation for Patrick Mahan's death, I had eleven factors to consider.

The first was the statistical profile of an autoerotic death. Victims of this type of fatality typically are of average or higher intelligence. They possess strong imaginations, are easily bored, and usually have no known history of sexual or mental disorders. The overwhelming majority of them are white males, and a significant number are roughly Patrick Mahan's age. Also, what the police learned about his temperament suggested to me that the young man liked to take chances. Being a thrill seeker was also consistent with being a seeker of autoerotic gratification. In sum, Mahan matched the profile of a person who accidentally kills himself during dangerous autoeroticism.

Second, I always examine suspected autoerotic death scenes for evidence that the victims provided themselves escape or release mechanisms. They invariably do so. In this case, I could identify at least three:

1. The ladder was mere inches from Mahan's feet. All he had to do to relieve the cable's pressure on his neck was step back and stand up.

2. The bicycle cable's odd loop around Mahan's arm, unnecessary for simple suspension, would have been a very handy pressure-release device. All he needed to do was simply shift his arm.

3. From the keyhole's position, I believed Mahan deliberately placed the lock right in front of him to make it easy to open in an emergency. My opinion is that he was holding the key, and as he lost consciousness, it dropped from his hand into the sewer water below.

So the question became: If he had all these safety options available, why didn't he use one to save himself?

The answer lies in the practice itself. The key element in dangerous autoeroticism by neck compression is restriction of blood flow to and from the brain. Hypoxia, or oxygen deprivation, ensues, inducing one desired effect—euphoria. Hypoxia is associated with enhanced sexual sensation as well. The problem is, it also can impair a person's judgment.

Hypoxia clearly puts the autoerotic practitioner in a vulnerable, dangerous state. From the notes and diaries these victims leave, I have learned that they also concentrate intently on their fantasy—whatever it may be—even as the hypoxia alters their perceptions. In this condition, they eventually lose consciousness and slump into total suspension. Unless they are rescued, they will die due to asphyxiation.

Third, Patrick Mahan was naked, which is consistent with autoeroticism, but not with homicide or suicide. Fully a third of the victims I studied with Park Dietz and Ann Burgess for our textbook, *Autoerotic Fatalities,* were discovered nude.

Fourth, his hidden and protected location also was con-

sistent with the sort of place that a practitioner of autoeroticism seeks out. In Mahan's case, his age and relative
immobility had to be taken into account, too. The site could
be reached on foot. In addition, the victim was very familiar
with the general area where he was found.

Fifth, hanging is the most common method autoerotic
practitioners use to induce hypoxia.

Sixth, I believe the application of the duct tape to his
eyes and mouth was meant to achieve sensory deprivation,
a form of sexual bondage commonly associated with autoeroticism.

Seventh, easily the most fascinating aspect of this sad
case was the watch in Patrick Mahan's mouth.

Here are three plausible reasons for it:

1. By securing it in his mouth, Mahan was making sure
   he would not lose or damage the treasured item.

2. He may have kept track of time by it, measuring the
   minutes and seconds by the sensory sensation of the
   ticking against the sensitive interior tissues of his
   mouth. In other autoeroticism cases the victims used
   cooking timers, stopwatches, and even alarms to alert
   them to the passage of time.

3. The ticking may also have enhanced the thrill of the
   experience, allowing Mahan to fantasize the dangers
   of his life literally "ticking away."

Reasons 2 and 3, I think, are the most likely explanations. The watch could have possibly had some other purpose altogether, a secret that died with Patrick Mahan.

Eighth, the debris on the victim's hands and feet strongly
suggest that he climbed the drainpipe ladder on his own,
which is consistent with autoeroticism.

Ninth, his high perch didn't make sense for either murder or suicide, but it may have added a thrilling extra element of danger to solo sex. Again, his fantasy was as

important as any element in his decision to scale the ladder.

Tenth, his elaborate preparations and equipment, position, props, and bindings suggested that Mahan had been perfecting his technique over time. That he had previously practiced autoeroticism seemed evident.

Finally, a short while prior to accepting this case, I had become familiar with an oddly similar autoerotic death in England. A white male had crawled through a sewer pipe and, like Patrick Mahan, had hanged himself from the rungs of a ladder leading up a drainpipe. It, too, formed an inverted T with a horizontal main. I found these parallels too striking to ignore.

After carefully weighing the pros and cons of each explanation, I presented the authorities with my opinion that Patrick Mahan died as a result of dangerous autoeroticism. I also provided them with a likely reconstruction of the events leading up to his death.

His mother said he left home about 10:00 P.M. I believed he chose a familiar destination, knowing that the hidden subterranean drain would provide him both the necessary privacy and the thrill he sought in his autoerotic practice. He disrobed outside the horizontal sewer main and left his clothes there so that they would not become soiled in the dirty water flowing through the pipe. Remember, Patrick was a neat young man. He probably didn't bother to hide his clothes because he planned to get dressed again at the same spot.

After tearing off the length of duct tape, Mahan walked into the pipe carrying his grandfather's watch and the bicycle chain and lock—all necessary props for what he intended to do.

He then climbed nearly to the top of the twenty-five-foot vertical drain, where he placed the timepiece in his mouth and secured it with the length of duct tape, which he also used to cover his eyes.

Next, he wrapped the plastic-coated chain around his

arm and neck, making certain by sense of touch that the keyhole was facing him.

With all these preparations in place, it was time for the fantasy to commence. I believe Mahan stepped gently off the ladder and soon was lost in his private dream world. He eventually lost consciousness, dropped the key, and expired in midair.

The conclusions I reached in my equivocal death analysis allowed the authorities to close a case that had remained perplexingly unsolved for a year. Classifying it as a tragic episode of dangerous autoeroticism prevented any possibility of an innocent party being erroneously charged with a homicide. It relieved the family of the psychological burden that survivors of suicide victims typically experience. And since Patrick was a devout Catholic, it clarified his eligibility for burial in a church-sanctioned facility. Although the young man's death was undeniably heartrending, the EDA brought some measure of closure to all concerned.

DYING FOR ATTENTION

In the popular imagination the practice of dangerous autoeroticism is usually considered an exclusively male behavior. But in preparing an equivocal death analysis, it is important not to overlook any valuable avenues of research. In the case of a young woman, Maggie Thomas,* the possibility of autoerotic aspyhxia featured prominently in the investigation of her death.

Maggie Thomas's world was painful and joyless. Born out of wedlock, she was raised by her single mother to age thirteen, when an adult male took her in and forced her to become a prostitute. Over the next three years she repeatedly was in trouble with the law, and she became pregnant three times. The first two pregnancies ended with abortions. When she was sixteen, Maggie miscarried her third fetus after being committed to the California Youth Authority (CYA) facility at Ventura in February 1984.

Ten months later, on December 13, she was discovered unconscious in her cottage room at CYA. She died after being rushed to the hospital.

The case was brought to my attention when a difference of opinion arose as to whether Maggie Thomas had committed suicide or died by accident while practicing dangerous autoeroticism.

As always, I analyzed all the information in the case, including investigative reports, toxicology results, hospital records, death scene photos, and questionnaires I prepared and distributed to those who knew Maggie at the CYA.

Of particular interest was a psychiatric report, dated July 1983, in which she was diagnosed with histrionic personality disorder. According to DSM IV, (*Diagnostic and Statistical Manual*, 4th edition), the histrionic personality is typified by "a pattern of excessive emotionality and attention seeking."

DSM IV lists the following behavior as common to the histrionic personality: " . . . an incessant need for attention, may do something dramatic to draw the focus of attention to themselves, rapidly shifting and shallow expressions of emotion, often inappropriately sexually provocative or seductive, a craving for action and excitement, overreaction to minor events, and irrational, angry outbursts or tantrums."

Others tend to view the histrionic individual as shallow and fake, even if he or she is superficially warm and charming.

"Clinical experience suggests that individuals with this disorder are at increased risk for suicidal gestures and threats to get attention and coerce better caregiving."

Witnesses reported that Maggie Thomas was involved in two separate lesbian relationships at CYA and was caught on one occasion in the boys' dormitory. She reportedly used drugs while at the facility and had in the past made suicide threats.

Maggie was described as moody, with low self-esteem. She was a behavior problem for the staff and consequently received far more attention from them than did the other girls in her cottage.

In the spring of 1984, according to her grandmother, Maggie attempted suicide by slitting her wrists. The grandmother described the incident as a ploy to gain attention.

The following October Maggie told her psychologist, "When I feel like nothing, I feel like killing (or hitting) myself." Yet witnesses also reported that the following month the teenager had suggested that such life-threatening behavior was unacceptable to her because she had too much to live for.

Two weeks before her death, Maggie reportedly slit her wrists once again. She told one associate that she was depressed over her poor relations with her mother and a recent breakup with a female lover. According to her psychologist's notes, she said in early December that she was "giving up and didn't want to go through the pain."

A few days later Maggie Thomas asked that her pending December 16 release be postponed until July 1985, explaining that she did not want to be supervised on the outside. The request was denied when authorities discovered that Remi Barstow,* Maggie's lesbian lover, was also scheduled for release in July.

On the afternoon of December 13, Barstow sent Maggie a note, informing her that their relationship was over. Maggie previously had threatened suicide if this happened. Shortly after three that afternoon, Maggie was sent to her room as punishment for a rules infraction.

Within the next hour, she was visited there by another onetime lover, Diedre Lane,* who found Maggie depressed over her estrangement from her mother. Maggie told Lane she was tired of people hurting her and said "I love you" and "good-bye." Lane did not, however, think Maggie actually was going to harm herself.

Approximately a half hour later, Maggie Thomas was discovered hanging from a knotted bedsheet, suspended from a clothes rod inside her wardrobe. The door to her room had been closed but left unlocked. The door to the wardrobe was open.

She was fully clothed, although her pants were unbuttoned. Her chin rested on the loose loop she had tied in the knot. Her knees were bent slightly, and her feet brushed the floor. Her arms hung straight at her sides.

Maggie was rushed to the hospital where she died late the next day.

Although some evidence at the scene superficially suggested that the victim had accidentally died in the midst of dangerous autoeroticism, I believed otherwise. Three major factors were inconsistent with autoeroticism.

First, Maggie made almost no effort to avoid being interrupted or discovered. She was in a room anyone could enter and often did. The practitioner of dangerous autoeroticism habitually seeks a private, secluded location.

Second, Maggie had a lengthy history of depression and reportedly was feeling low on the day of her death. Victims of dangerous autoeroticism typically are in good spirits just prior to their death and have no history of depression.

Third, victims of dangerous autoeroticism have no known history of sexual or mental problems. Maggie had become a prostitute at a very early age and was engaged in at least two lesbian relationships. Later, she was diagnosed with histrionic personality disorder.

Factors weakly consistent with autoeroticism were: the fact that Maggie was not totally suspended; her use of a wide, soft ligature; and her unbuttoned pants. However, the clear preponderance of the evidence pointed away from dangerous autoeroticism.

Did she die on purpose or by accident? In my opinion, Maggie's death was accidental but not related to autoeroticism. Here's why.

First, threats of suicide and pseudoattempts at suicide are not uncommon among institutionalized juveniles who seek attention and sympathy from both the authorities and their peers.

In addition, her grandmother's report of a suicide attempt the preceding spring was accompanied by the opinion that Maggie was seeking sympathy not death. If so, this indicates that her December 14 demise resulted from accident not intent.

Third, Maggie's histrionic personality disorder predisposed her to "self-dramatization, theatricality, and an exaggerated expression of emotion." (DSM IV) The following information provided by her counselor tends to substantiate that diagnosis:

A. Witnesses said she was prone to temper tantrums and would "stomp" from a room if her wishes were not met.
B. She was given to hysterical fits of yelling and crying. If the staff or the other girls disagreed with her, Maggie often would shrug that she "didn't care anymore."
C. The staff reported she was loud, defensive, and very demanding. This behavior created a great deal of tension in her relations with the other residents.
D. Maggie was extremely self-centered, demanding, and bossy around the other residents, often ordering them to do her work for her.
E. As a result of this behavior, she required at least ten times the staff attention that other girls received, which created even more resentment.
F. In addition, DSM IV describes the histrionic personality as being "at increased risk for suicidal gestures and threats to get attention . . ." which from witness reports Maggie did on at least two occasions before her death.

Fourth, her choice of ligature was inconsistent with suicide. In my experience, those seriously intending to take their own lives by hanging do so with a ligature tied tightly around the neck and secured with a knot. Thomas had access to belts, shoestrings, and rope.

I believe that she fashioned a loose sheet knot in the belief that if she lost consciousness, her head would slip and she would fall to the floor before she died.

Fifth, she had made several suicide threats in the past, which apparently no one took seriously. The reason was that her penchant for dramatic gestures made others discount the seriousness of her threats.

Sixth, her choice of time and place called into question her intent. The supervisor of her living unit made room checks every fifteen to twenty minutes. Maggie Thomas had reason to expect she would be discovered.

Seventh, Maggie told Diedre Lane "good-bye" approximately thirty minutes before she was found in her wardrobe. The victim had reason to believe Lane would report this conversation at once, and that someone would soon come by to check on her. As it turned out, that is exactly what occurred. Unfortunately, not in time.

Maggie clearly did not recognize the dangers of feigning a suicide attempt via neck compression. Obviously, she thought that if she remained on her feet and used a soft, loosely tied loop, she was in no peril. However, as little as 4.4 pounds of pressure may interrupt the flow of oxygen to the brain. Once that occurs, unconsciousness rapidly follows.

After she lost consciousness, Maggie Thomas's entire body weight was totally suspended from the loop, and she died by accident. She was not a victim of dangerous autoeroticism. Still, in her case, the theory was worthy of exploration. Sadly, this sexual practice claims victims of every age, gender, and social status.

THE MISFIT

The death of a loved one is always hard to bear. But sometimes the motive behind that death can be even more difficult to accept. Both dangerous autoeroticism and suicide carry social stigma, and the victims' families often go to great lengths to avoid facing the facts. Ironically, many people would rather believe that their loved one's death was intentionally caused by a fellow human being than accept another explanation.

In the following case, a family's insistence that their son had been murdered led directly to my involvement. Coincidentally, the analysis and adjudication of this equivocal death made a bit of legal history.

I first learned about the death of James Stanley Harrison in mid-April 1992 while attending a violent crime conference at the University of Windsor, Ontario, just across the river from Detroit. Among the other speakers at the conference were Sgt. Kate Lines of the Ontario Provincial Police and Insp. Ron Mackay of the Royal Canadian Mounted Police's Violent Crime Analysis Branch. Lines and Mackay are the only two FBI-trained profilers in all of Canada. I'm proud to say that I helped train them both.

Kate Lines approached Ron and me with a request for professional assistance. Sixteen months earlier, a second-year student at the University of Guelph, near Toronto, had plummeted to his death down a dormitory stairwell. The initial investigation quickly concluded that a despondent Jamie Harrison had taken his own life, but the boy's family strongly disagreed. As a result of the controversy, a coroner's jury was to be held on April 30. Kate Lines asked if I would undertake an equivocal death analysis with her and Ron Mackay.

The documentation in the case was extensive. Four hundred pages of single-spaced reports and interviews, plus photos. I could tell right away that the biggest challenge would be to master all that detail in such a short period of time. I have rarely worked harder on an analysis than we did on Jamie Harrison's death. By the time I took the witness chair, the three of us had devoted a collective 150 hours to the case. My thirty-page report took three hours to present to the five-person jury.

First, I covered what was known generally about Jamie Harrison. He was six-one, 195 pounds, and wore glasses. He and his sister, Marnie, had been adopted as infants by the Harrison family of Peterborough, Ontario. One grandmother described him as a careful boy. For example, she said that after Jamie got his driver's license, the teenager was ever alert to other motorists' mistakes and made a habit of pointing them out. Jamie also told his grandmother that he was thinking of studying German because he believed his natural father might have been German.

Marnie Harrison said her brother shunned physical confrontation. "He would go to his room rather than take a verbal argument to a physical conclusion," she said.

Elizabeth Davies, a Guelph coed for whom Jamie conceived an unrequited romance, was a member of the College Games Club with him. She described Harrison as the friendliest, most outgoing member of the group. But Davies, who was seeing another student, Paul Garster, liked Jamie Harrison as a brother not a boyfriend.

One male student at Guelph recalled that the victim had trouble talking to girls and even to other males. "It was like he didn't know how to talk to people," he said. "He told me he was adopted. It kind of made me realize why he felt unsure of himself." Jamie's two roommates from his first year at Guelph told investigators he was a loner, very bright and arrogant about his intellect. He had no friends outside the games club, they said.

These two disliked Jamie and harassed him. They put Jell-O powder in his bed and locked him out of the room. Just before Christmas of his first year, Harrison abruptly transferred to a single room in the dorm.

Some students recalled that Jamie spent a lot of time alone: in his room, at meals, and late at night, watching television. He was a fan of *Star Trek* and read tarot (fortune-telling) cards. Several people mentioned that he was fascinated with a particular card, the one bearing the figure of Death.

A fellow student named Herminda Peeling-Dykman said Harrison was friendly, laughed a lot, and made her welcome to the games club in 1989. "But he was an introvert, like most of the games club," she said. "Being with others would be an effort to him."

"He was what is generally referred to as a square, or geek," remarked another acquaintance.

I next addressed what the witnesses recalled of Jamie Harrison's final days.

Student Fiona Beatlestone remembered Jamie joined in a snowball fight three days before his death. "It was odd because he usually didn't participate in them," she said.

"Jamie," said Thomas Cook, "was very prone to mood swings. When he was at the games club office he was very upbeat. Once outside he would act in a more depressed way. In the week prior to the day he died, I felt he was more involved in pronounced ups and downs. The day prior to his death, I was in the office during the afternoon with Jamie and several others. He was in a good mood. We threw a Frisbee back and forth."

Elizabeth Davies saw the victim at the games club the night of his death. She beat him in a game of Uno. "Jamie seemed angry that I won," she said. "I had a nickname, 'the superbitch from hell.' When he called me that this time, he seemed really angry." Harrison also told Liz that he had just taken an exam and feared that he had failed it. "I think my beating him in Uno just added to him being upset," she said.

Jamie Harrison went to dinner and a movie that night with Liz Davies and others. Student Michael Porter recalled that during the movie Liz kissed Paul Garster. "Jamie was there to see this," Porter said. "[He] might have realized at that point he had no further chance with Liz."

After the movie and back in the dorm, Davies and Garster said they were going for a drink of water. "I guess I know what you guys want," Harrison said, as he walked away. Davies called, "Wait," but he didn't respond. It was the last either of them saw of Jamie Harrison.

Shortly thereafter he appeared alone in the student lounge, where he sat on a couch, his feet propped on a table, for fifteen to twenty minutes, saying nothing. Then he stood up and walked off in the direction of his room.

Next, I listed for the jurors all the things that Kate, Ron, and I had determined Jamie Harrison was looking forward to in the future. The more positively focused on the future a person is, the less likely he is to be overcome by a momentary depression. We could document only four anticipated events. According to his grandmother, Jamie was looking forward to Christmas shopping with his mother. Fellow members of the games club described him as deeply involved in preparations for an upcoming games tournament called Gryphcon, which was to be held the following March. He had a game date for the following morning, and he had paid his tuition for the next semester.

When preparing an equivocal death analysis, I try to establish whether anyone had a motive for murdering the deceased. I told the jurors that apparently there was no deep ill will between Harrison and any of his fellow students. "I can't really think of anyone who hated him," said Thomas Clarke.

Everyone in the dorm agreed on one significant fact: Jamie Harrison was afraid of heights. Fourteen out of fourteen people interviewed said they knew, or had heard, about his phobia. However, both his grandmother and his sister denied it.

Then I detailed for the court a list of reasons why Jamie Harrison's death appeared not to have been an accident.

His reported fear of heights was first. Harrison would have been extra cautious not to trip or stumble at the top of a stairwell, especially this one, which had a low guard rail.

Second, his glasses were discovered upside down on the

top-floor landing. Lab tests indicated they were un-scratched. It appeared that they had been carefully placed where they later were found. They weren't dropped. And they didn't fall.

Suicides, especially jumpers, often leave a personal possession such as glasses, a billfold, or watch at the place from which they leap.

It was cold that night and the concrete dorm stairwell, although enclosed, was not heated. Jamie Harrison, who had no known reason for being on the top-floor landing that night, was not dressed for the cold.

The lighting was adequate, if dim, and Harrison was wearing sneakers. He was unlikely to have slipped on the concrete floor. Jamie showed no evidence of mental impairment from drinking, drugs, or illness.

Six students lived close enough to the stairwell to have heard Harrison if he had made a sound that night. None of them reported hearing any noise at all.

No forensic evidence suggested that the young man attempted to regain his balance, for example, by grasping the wall. He had no torn fingernails or bits of concrete under his nails.

Factors consistent with an accidental death included the lack of witnesses or forensic evidence that conclusively proved either suicide or homicide. There was that low railing, and Harrison was known to have been preoccupied with other matters, including Christmas and his exams. He might not have been paying as close attention as he usually would. Also, his fatal injuries were consistent with those normally suffered in such a fall, no matter what its cause.

We found an impressive number of reasons to doubt that Jamie Harrison's death was a homicide.

As I noted above, the victim didn't have many close friends, but no one seemed to dislike him enough to kill him. No theft was associated with the death. Harrison had no known involvement with criminals and did not gamble, use drugs, or have any reported sexual problems.

No signs of a struggle were found either in his room or

at the top of the staircase. His body had no defensive wounds. All of the injuries he suffered were consistent with a fall. Harrison had not tried to break his fall or grasp anything to save his life.

No evidence pointed to the presence of anyone else in the stairwell at the same time, and no trace of any weapon was recovered. However, at the bottom of another, identical, stairwell, investigators found a large brick. It's discovery prompted speculation that whoever was responsible for Harrison's death had pretested the incident using the brick as a surrogate victim or to determine if its noise would attract attention.

Harrison surely would have screamed if someone had pushed him off the top of the stairs. What's more, the staircase would have acted as an echo chamber, amplifying his cry. Yet no one heard a thing.

Anyone intent on pushing Jamie Harrison down that stairwell ran a high risk of being detected. It was exam time, and many students were up late. Escaping unnoticed would have been difficult.

Finally, Jamie Harrison survived his fall for a time. If his death had been a homicide, the killer surely would have checked to make sure his victim was dead if for no other reason than to preclude the possibility of being identified.

I told the coroner's jury that only two factors were consistent with murder. One was the victim's fear of heights, although you might argue that he could have been coerced into climbing to the top of the stairwell because he would never do it on his own. The second was the way he died—from a fall. Such a death is open to misinterpretation; it can look like an accident, suicide, or a homicide.

Factors inconsistent with suicide included Harrison's future plans. We knew he was looking forward to Christmas and to the games tournament in the spring. He even had a game-playing appointment for the next morning. Also, the young man had paid for his next semester's tuition with a postdated check.

As far as we knew, he had never attempted suicide in

the past, nor did Jamie Harrison give away any prized possessions in the period just prior to his death. There was no suicide note, although investigators did find a deleted message on his computer. It was an enigmatic and unclear note that began "Try this twist" and was focused on death throughout.

None of the stress factors commonly associated with suicide were present. Harrison had no health problems as far as anyone knew; there had been no sudden disruptions in his intimate relationships; he showed no symptoms of internalized stress, such as disturbed sleep, or vomiting; and he had no urgent financial problems.

Jamie Harrison's death was subject to a number of interpretations. But after looking at all of them carefully, my colleagues and I concluded that this young man had killed himself. Here is our reasoning:

1. Harrison was an introvert with poor social skills who spent a great deal of time alone.

2. Consequently, he had few close friends. Not one of his dorm mates whom we interviewed considered himself Jamie's confidant. He had no one to turn to in time of emotional need.

3. He was having difficulty adapting to the university social environment. In his first year he couldn't get along with his roommates and moved out to live alone. He also unsuccessfully ran for student office three times as a freshman. In his sophomore year, Jamie's application to be a dormitory resident adviser was rejected. He did not date, and the only female in whom he showed interest, Elizabeth Davies, clearly preferred another.

4. The foundation of Harrison's precarious self-image

was his record of intelligence and scholastic accomplishments, and this part of his world was crumbling. His grades had steadily declined since he entered the University of Guelph. His first-semester grade average was 79.4. His second-semester average dropped to 65, and he lost his academic scholarship.

In his sophomore year, he had scored just 53 on his first chemistry midterm, and 50 on his second. Classmates reported that his study habits were poor, and that he expressed concern over his teetering academic career. "That was one thing he could feel superior about," said fellow student Pamela J. Livingston. "Now that was gone. He couldn't get by just listening in class anymore."

5. Harrison thought a great deal about death. A female acquaintance recalled that he read the tarot cards for her from time to time. "The things he would say for me were so positive," she remembered. "But every time he did himself he seemed to turn up the death card or say he'd have to die here." Another student recalled how Jamie Harrison always "flipped out" whenever the death card appeared.

Death was also the principal subject of the obscure note left on the victim's computer.

"He liked to make twisted, sarcastic comments that no one could answer," said Pamela Livingston. "I think that made him feel superior, too. He liked to be mysterious."

For instance, Harrison sometimes used a standard poker deck as tarot cards. In it the jokers represented the fool in tarot. Harrison told his acquaintances that the fool could be thought of as a person standing on a cliff with his back to the edge, weighing the choice of stepping forward or backward.

Joker cards were found in his dorm bed. Unofficially, I believed Harrison was acting out the role of the fool. I also believed that "try this twist" was a parting attempt to play games with his friends, to toy with them.

Similarly, as Harrison explained to an acquaintance, the ace of hearts is equivalent to a particular tarot card, the cup card, that is suggestive of great hope and love, he said. A ripped ace of hearts was discovered in Jamie's deck.

It's impossible to quantify the sense of alienation Jamie Harrison felt or to measure how wounded he was by other students' rejection. But it was clear from the interviews that he had had a difficult time at Guelph.

The female students especially dwelled on how his roommates had harassed Jamie until he finally moved into a room by himself.

Pamela Livingston believed Jamie's penchant for the occasional odd comment contributed to his isolation, too. "People thought he was bizarre," she said, "so he learned not to say anything."

Yet at times Jamie Harrison seemed to crave even negative attention. When he grew a beard, acquaintances said he looked better without facial hair, but he kept the beard anyway. When he finally shaved it off and was told that he looked better, he promptly grew it back.

In all, the weight of the witnesses' evidence clearly supported the conclusion that Jamie Harrison had taken his own life. That is the finding that I told the coroner's jury, and they agreed.

For Kate Lines, Ron Mackay, and me, the hard work in preparing the equivocal death analysis brought an unexpected reward. Never before in a Canadian court had behavioral testimony been allowed as evidence. Out of the sad duty of explaining why I believed this troubled young man had taken his own life had come a form of formal legal sanction for an investigative technique I had pioneered years before at the BSU.

We appreciated the historical nature of the occasion and hoped that, as a precedent, it would allow other authorities and families to find the answers they sought in solving unexplained deaths.

14

REVENGE MURDER

At 2:10 A.M. on a rainy Tuesday night, Langford Hall on the campus of Montana State University in Bozeman was quiet. It was May 15, 1990.

Then four thunderous shotgun blasts shattered the calm, followed by screams from Room 130 of the dormitory. Students hurried to the scene. One of the first to arrive was resident adviser, Larry Vaught, who discovered a student named James Clevenger standing in the hallway, clutching his lower abdomen, a dark trail of his blood leading back into the room.

Student Richard Mickelson ran into 130 and found Brian Boeder lying on the floor in the middle of the room, one arm outstretched. Boeder was wounded in his right arm, upper thigh, and buttocks. The shotgun used against Clevenger and Boeder lay on the floor nearby, partially covered by a pillow and a blue blanket. Mickelson also saw two expended shotgun shells on the floor.

Though mortally injured, Clevenger and Boeder were lucid as they waited for the ambulance. They told officers Michael B. Murphy and Rex Duncan of the MSU Campus Police that they had been quietly chatting in Boeder's room when a knock came at the door.

"Come in," said Boeder casually.

In strode a red-haired, freckle-faced, young man they

both knew by sight but not by name. Saying nothing, he raised a sawed-off Marlin shotgun, pointed the weapon at the two friends, and squeezed off four rounds. Clevenger and Boeder lunged at the intruder, knocking the weapon out of his hands. He then fled out the door.

Moments later, resident adviser Tim Kluesner stepped out of his room, number 113, to encounter student Brett Byers, a red-haired sophomore who lived in 103.

Mark Baxter looked out his door as they met.

"You need to call the police, Tim," said Byers, as he lightly jogged on down the corridor. "There's been a murder."

Kluesner would later remember that the young man seemed intense, excited, but not scared.

Back at the crime scene, both victims described their assailant to the officers. Their mention of his red hair made Officer Duncan think immediately of Brett Byers, whom he knew.

In recent months Byers had complained repeatedly to Duncan of vandalism to his pickup, which was his most cherished possession. Duncan was therefore familiar with the vehicle; he had noticed it in the parking lot earlier that night. Now he walked over to the window, looked out, and saw that the truck was missing.

After consulting with Tim Kluesner, Officer Duncan prepared an all-points bulletin for Brett Byers's arrest.

Paramedics meantime had placed James Clevenger and Brian Boeder in an ambulance.

"Do you think we're going to make it?" one of the young men was heard to ask.

"No," his friend answered.

Brian Boeder died at 4:45 A.M.; James Clevenger succumbed to his injuries a half hour later.

Their killer, meanwhile, was fleeing northwest toward his home in Great Falls. Brett Byers stopped along the way in the little community of Townsend, on U.S. 287, where he broke a store window in order to steal a Coke and candy bar. He was intercepted north of Townsend by Dep. Everard Creek of the Lewis and Clark County Sheriff's Office.

Deputy Creek would testify that Byers was traveling about fifty-five miles per hour when he pulled his police car in behind the pickup. The truck then slowed to forty-five, said Creek. When he turned on his flashing lights and sirens, Byers accelerated.

A highway roadblock was in place to the north in East Helena. Creek estimated that Brett Byers was driving in excess of eighty miles per hour when he saw the police vehicles with their flashing lights ahead. The subject immediately jerked his pickup off the highway, through a ditch and cyclone fence, and headed overland for the gas pumps at a Circle K convenience store and station. Byers seemed to smash his truck deliberately straight into one of the pumps. He then bounced into another vehicle, flipping over his pickup before it came to a rest.

There was never any question that Brett Byers murdered James Clevenger and Brian Boeder. In 1991, a jury found Byers guilty of the killings, and he was sentenced to 165 years in prison. He would be eligible for parole after 35 years. But a separate civil issue was raised in lawsuits filed against the university by the Clevenger and Boeder families. Were these killings foreseeable and could they have been prevented?

That was the question posed to me in a March 1994 letter from Last Chance Gulch in Helena, the street address for G. Curtis Drake, an attorney representing MSU in the litigation. Drake supplied me with all the necessary background material—everything from Langford Hall's floor plan to psychiatric and psychological evaluations of Byers—and I began to analyze the information.

It was critical for me to learn as much as possible about the circumstances that helped shape Brett Byers's outlook and behavior. One source was his older sister, Sloan, who testified at her brother's trial. She told the court that Brett had emotional problems that had begun in his earliest childhood. He'd started lighting grass fires at age four or five, Sloan said. By the fourth grade her younger brother also was having nightmares of being chased and killed.

Sloan described her early relationship with Brett as closer than many of her friends seemed to be with their brothers. But they started pulling apart in junior high. About that time, her brother also started having trouble with their mother, an elementary schoolteacher. Brett complained that she was too demanding.

Sloan testified that in time Brett came to avoid their mother whenever possible. She didn't think her brother was ever close to their father either. When he came home to Great Falls from Bozeman for Christmas, for example, Brett spent two nights at a friend's house without even telling his parents he was in town.

In high school Brett started gambling and drinking. Both habits would spiral out of control once he got to MSU (where Sloan also studied). Something else changed, too—his personality. At MSU Sloan noticed that Brett began having severe and sudden mood swings. He had trouble controlling his temper and sometimes broke down in tears.

He got a little crazy behind the wheel, too. Brett had always been a risk taker, she said, but in college his driving became scary. Sloan was sometimes afraid to ride with Brett in his beloved pickup.

Sloan Byers was not alone in her apprehension. Several friends and acquaintances testified that her brother was a reckless driver. Several also mentioned the sawed-off shotgun he kept in the truck.

Brett seemed nearly as attached to his gun as he was to his truck, they said, and just as rash and foolhardy with it. In the autumn of 1989, for example, he had produced the weapon at an outdoor party to shoot kindling branches out of a tree. A number of fellow students were angered by the incident.

He was not a responsible young man.

Sloan Byers said her brother kept to himself at MSU. If Brett wasn't at his job as a restaurant waiter, he was in his room. He seldom went to class or even to the cafeteria. He took showers at odd hours to avoid other dorm residents.

Witness Shane Tanberg told the court he had known Brett Byers since the first grade. The two boys were part of a tight group of five or six close friends. Tanberg, too, said that Brett changed in high school. His friends began to find him annoying and hyper. In Tanberg's view, Byers wasn't maturing along with the rest of the group, and as a result he alienated his friends.

Brett's parents, said Tanberg, had always treated him as a child; Mr. Byers's nickname for his son was "Bretty Boy."

According to Tanberg, Byers feared his parents and came to hate them, especially his mother. If Brett ever was late getting home, Tanberg explained, he would panic. "My mom's going to yell at me," he would say. "She's going to rip my head off."

One time Brett put a small dent in the tailgate of his pickup. Rather than risk his mother's wrath, he removed the tailgate, threw it into a river, and told his mother it had been stolen while he and Shane were at the movies.

Shane Tanberg also confirmed that Brett was prone to mood swings and depressions, which grew more pronounced in college, and that he was drinking a great deal.

A psychiatrist and a psychologist who interviewed Byers described him as impulsive, immature, and unstable. But neither believed the young man suffered from any mental disease or defect.

One stress factor in Byers's life was an unfortunate gaffe he committed early in the 1989 autumn term. At a meeting of Langford residents, Byers joked that he chose Langford because he liked living with guys. The line was supposed to be funny, but it fell flat. Instead, some of his fellow residents wondered what Byers really meant. Others teased him.

At the trial Byers's acquaintances testified that he was obsessed with the fear that others believed he was homosexual because of the remark. Shane Tanberg told the court that two weeks after the meeting, Byers confided that the previous evening he had loaded a firearm and held it to his head, intent on taking his own life. When Tanberg inquired why, Byers answered, "I can't talk about it. You'll make fun of me."

Said Tanberg, "It devastated Brett that he screwed up a joke because he was just trying to make some people laugh. And now they all hated him"—or at least that's how Byers saw it.

He told essentially the same story to another student as well.

Byers's grades were another problem. In the fall quarter, he had failed algebra and a course in computer literacy and received a D in economics. In the winter quarter, the best grade he had managed was a C in a course called "Mysteries of the Sky."

Then there was his gambling. Byers bet away four thousand dollars during the fall quarter. Broke, he was forced to turn to his parents for tuition and room and board money.

But the nexus of Brett Byers's deepening emotional crisis was his pickup truck. So important was the vehicle to him that as he sat upside down in the gas station outside Helena, after very nearly killing himself and now awaiting arrest for murder, Byers's first words to Deputy Creek were, "How's my truck?"

I remember being particularly struck when I read that quote. He was concerned about his truck but not the two humans he had just murdered.

Because of his poor grades and a pile of traffic citations, Byers had been worried that his mother would take away the truck. Even if she didn't, his reckless driving and consequent tickets put his insurance policy in jeopardy.

Above all, however, he complained about the maddening vandalism. Throughout 1989 and 1990, Byers's truck was repeatedly damaged. Vandals scratched its paint, broke mirrors and lights, snapped off his windshield wipers and hood ornament, and repeatedly deflated his tires. Apparently a good deal of vehicle vandalism was occurring at this time around the MSU campus. It is unclear whether Brett Byers was being singled out, or if the repeated damage to his truck was entirely coincidental, a problem that he shared with other student drivers.

Whatever the case, the vandalism drove Byers to distraction. "It was like beating Brett up," said Shane Tranberg. "Every time they vandalized his truck, it took a part of him."

Byers swore on several occasions that he would kill the person or persons responsible. No one took him seriously. Leslie Busby, who didn't know Byers well, described him as solitary and occasionally depressed. But Busby also never saw Byers get mad, start a fight, or do anything to suggest he was potentially violent. When Busby was told Byers was under arrest for the shotgun killings, he thought a mistake had been made.

Similarly, student Jeff Nygard, who had known Byers since the start of the year, was amazed. Nygard knew Byers as hot-tempered, hyperactive, hungry for friendship, and often obnoxious. But murder was out of the question. "He was capable of a lot of things," said Nygard, "but not that."

Byers tried to protect his truck by parking it in the most exposed, well-lit spaces he could find. He would watch it all night from the dorm. Some nights he slept in it. At one point he even offered a reward for information leading to the arrest of the vandals.

Sometime during this emotionally charged process, he also conceived the dangerous and wholly erroneous idea that Brian Boeder in Room 130 was his chief tormentor. Never mind that the two young men weren't even acquainted, let alone enemies. This was pure paranoia.

Byers told very few people of his suspicion. But there was much about Brett Byers that was deeply hidden, contradictory psychological currents churning toward eruption.

Among Brett's MSU acquaintances were Mark Weirich and Dan Evans, roommates in Hedges Hall. Both had met Byers at the start of the fall quarter, and both knew he was interested in firearms and weapons. Weirich had seen the sawed-off Marlin; Byers had brought the gun into Hedges under his trenchcoat. ˋ

Byers also showed Evans a bomb he had made to get even with the people responsible for damaging his truck. He said he was going to throw the device through their window. Evans testified that he eventually took the bomb from Byers and disposed of it.

This was sometime in the fall of 1989. Not long thereafter, Evans went out drinking with Byers and a couple of other students at a local bar called Molly Brown's. While they were inside, his truck again was vandalized. A rear taillight was broken out, and a tire stem was jammed in, causing the tire to go flat.

A few days later Byers led a small vigilante squad to Boeder's room, allegedly to beat him up. When Byers knocked and no one answered, he entered the room and stole a three-hundred-dollar stereo as an act of retribution.

Brian Goetz, one of the resident advisers at Langford Hall, was another of Brett Byers's longtime friends. Goetz testified that he was surprised to learn from Byers of the stereo theft. Goetz didn't think Byers was capable of an act of this nature.

He told the court Byers said that he felt guilty about taking the stereo but couldn't give it back because he had sold it.

The night of the murders, Byers came home from work with a magnum of German wine, which he had with him

at nine o'clock when he visited his friends, James Hesterberg and Jeff Nygard, in their room, 327. He offered the
bottle around, but neither Hesterberg, Nygard, nor a fourth
student in the room, Scott Strobel, was drinking that night.
So Byers drank the wine by himself.

The friends listened to music, played computer games,
and watched television together. According to Strobel,
around midnight they moved the gathering to his room.
Around one, Hesterberg and Nygard left. Byers, who by
now had finished the wine, was visibly drunk.

He and Strobel started playing low-stakes blackjack.
Byers lost about three dollars over the next hour. Near two,
he suddenly offered to bet his truck against a penny. Scott
Strobel wanted nothing to do with the bet.

"I was very reluctant," he testified. "In his condition, he
would have given me the keys, and I didn't want to take
them." Instead, Strobel asked Byers to leave, explaining
that he needed to get some schoolwork done. Byers rose,
said, "Good night," and departed.

"He was real passive," Strobel explained in court. "He
was drunk when he left. He was staggering slightly."

Scott Strobel assumed his friend was headed for bed.

Instead, Brett Byers headed for the parking lot to move his
truck from a restricted area so that he wouldn't get a ticket.
As he later recounted to Dr. William D. Stratford, the
pickup fishtailed as he hit the gas and swung into a black
truck parked nearby.

This incident sent Brett Byers over the edge.

As Dr. Stratford would testify, he grabbed his sawed-off
Marlin out of the pickup, walked over to the black truck
with it, and smashed the driver's side window. From there
Byers headed on foot for Langford Hall. On the way, he
used the shotgun to break out the passenger window on a
white truck. Then he entered the dormitory, walked down
to room 130, and murdered Brian Boeder and James Clevenger.

*   *   *

I don't believe there was any practical way this double murder could have been anticipated or prevented.

In my report and testimony, I classified the crime as a revenge murder, as defined in the *Crime Classification Manual* to which I was a contributing author. Revenge-motivated murderers kill in retaliation for a wrong, real or imagined, committed against themselves or someone close to them. This killer may stalk an intended victim for years or may act out spontaneously, as I believe Brett Byers did.

Here is a list of factors commonly seen in revenge killings, taken directly from the manual and compared against the facts of the Boeder-Clevenger slayings.

A significant event links the offender and the victims(s).

Brett's truck had been the target of numerous acts of vandalism. He erroneously believed that Brian Boeder was responsible for the damage. Recall that he also went to Boeder's room and stole the stereo.

The revenge motive that grows out of this event may be unknown to the victim or to the victim's family or friends.

Students and officers responding to the shotgun blasts reported that neither Byers nor Clevenger was aware of why they had been attacked, even though they both had seen and physically described their attacker.

This element of secrecy is a major reason why revenge murders are so difficult to prevent. Prospective victims, unaware of their potential peril, can do nothing to avert it or to protect themselves.

Multiple victims may be involved.

Byers went to Boeder's room unaware that James Clevenger also would be there. In revenge-motivated

killings, it is not uncommon for innocent parties to
be killed if they are present when the intended target
is attacked. For this reason, children or other relatives
or visitors are often killed in domestic murders.

*The precipitating event and the killing that follows
often occur in separate locations.*

In this case, the precipitating events (truck vandalism) occurred in the campus parking areas. The
murders occurred in Room 130 of Langford Hall.

*A so-called "mission-oriented" killer may have no
criminal background.*

Byers clearly didn't.

*The offender is apt to be in a highly charged emo-
tional state at the time of the killing.*

Byers was extremely agitated. His truck repeatedly
had been vandalized, and he believed he knew the
individual responsible. He feared that he might soon
lose his driving privileges due to traffic tickets and
bad grades. He chronically gambled and lost. He was
drunk the night of the offense. He offered to bet his
truck against one penny. He went out in the rain to
move his pickup to a legal parking position. In the
process, he damaged his most prized possession, the
truck.

As further evidence of his irrational frame of
mind, his crime carried a high risk of detection, and
he left evidence (the shotgun and expended shells)
linking himself to the crime scene.

*The crime may exhibit a clear shift from organized
to disorganized behavior, possibly manifested by a
skillful approach to the crime scene and then a blitz-
style of attack followed by a rapid exit.*

Byers entered the dormitory at a time when most
residents were in their rooms, asleep or studying. No

one realized he was about to kill his "enemy." After being invited to come in, he entered the room firing the shotgun. That was disorganized. Though armed with a lethal weapon, he didn't control the victims; they physically attacked him. He also left physical evidence in the room and encountered an acquaintance on the way to his truck.

Because vengeance is the point of a revenge-motivated murder, the killer often gives no thought to an escape plan.

Brett Byers clearly had not thought beyond the killings. Earlier in the evening he had very nearly gambled away his only means of transportation. After the murders he departed MSU in his truck with no obvious plan to hide out or avoid detection. He apparently was headed for his hometown when he was observed, pursued, and captured.

The murder weapon is most often a weapon of choice brought to the scene. It may be left there.

From all accounts, the sawed-off Marlin was Byers's second most prized possession after his truck. Yet he left the shotgun at the murder scene, where his victims knocked it from his hands. This haste and poor planning are indicative of disorganized behavior.

The revenge-motivated homicide often is opportunistic and spontaneous.

I have no question that this was an impulsive crime. Byers's behavior belied nothing out of the ordinary that evening. He seemed the same as usual to everyone. It seems clear that the idea to kill Brian Boeder came to him after he damaged his truck. Something snapped.

There is no evidence of premeditation. All he seemed to have on his mind was the intended victim, the location, and the means, which required no reflection at all. He had no plan for escape and/or a location to "hide out" following the crime. Also, he left the weapon at the scene and was observed by at least two acquaintances departing the vicinity of the crime scene.

The killing commonly is committed at close range and is confrontational.

Byers walked in, pointed the shotgun, and started shooting.

The offender derives satisfaction at rendering "justice."

Following the murder, Byers was observed by two dormitory residents. "Tim," he said to one of them, "call the police. There's been a murder." Neither witness reported that he was distraught. I believe his lack of appropriate concern reflects Byers's sense that he was justified in killing the two victims. When he was arrested, he did not first ask how Clevenger and Boeder were but if his truck was damaged.

After the homicide, the offender often feels relief. Mission accomplished. He may stay at the scene or make no attempt to conceal himself or his identity.

While Byers did not remain at the scene, he made no apparent effort to avoid being observed. Two witnesses positively identified him in the hallway; he spoke to one of them.

The precipitating event is the key to understanding revenge-motivated murder. However, it may hold significance only to the offender.

As previously noted, neither victim understood why he had been attacked. Friends and acquaintances of Byers couldn't believe that he had committed murder.

*   *   *

Ken Baker, an old friend and partner in the Academy Group, testified that in his opinion the untrained eye could not have detected behavioral indicators that Brett Byers was about to commit a homicide. No one claimed that they had. Also in Ken's opinion, Byers himself did not know he was going to commit murder until minutes before he did so.

I testified that I did not believe these murders would have been prevented by more stringent security measures unless they included armed guards and metal detectors at all dormitory entrances twenty-four hours a day. Even that would have been no guarantee of safety.

Brett Byers was a legitimate resident of Langford Hall dormitory with authorized access to the building. Had the doors been locked or "card accessed" that night, Byers would still have gotten inside. If the building had security guards, they would have admitted him. Because the murder weapon was compact, he could have easily hidden it within a container or otherwise gotten it past security. As for metal detectors, Byers had a first-floor room. He could have tossed the shotgun through his window, just as he talked of flipping his homemade bomb through a window.

If weapons were not allowed on campus (they were), he still could have concealed the weapon in his truck, as was the case.

Psychological testing might have identified Byers's potential for endangering others; but with no history of committing violence, tests alone would not have been sufficient to deny him enrollment at MSU and probably would be unconstitutional anyway.

The survivors' lawsuits were argued in front of a jury in Helena for seven full days in June 1995. After ten hours of deliberation, the jurors voted unanimously that Montana State University bore no responsibility in the murders.

Afterward, one of the plaintiffs' attorneys approached me outside the courtroom, offered his hand, and said that although the verdict was a disappointment, he believed that Ken and I had given honest testimony and that he respected our point of view.

I deeply appreciated the gesture and told him so.

15

A COMPLETE KILLER

Christine Burgerhof was a secretive young woman. Her parents believed their married daughter was a receptionist at a local school for the deaf. But when Christine was brutally murdered in early April 1996, their pain at her sudden, violent death was compounded by the surprise discovery that twenty-four-year-old Christine had been working in a massage parlor.

Henry and Donna Negvesky were thunderstruck. They told investigators they could not believe that Bob, Christine's husband of nearly two years, would allow his wife to work in such a place. But that was just the beginning.

The discovery that Christine was a prostitute was the first of many surprises this case held for her family, the investigators, and me.

Christine's body was discovered in the late morning of Saturday, April 6, 1996, in a Scranton, Pennsylvania, warehouse district parking lot. She had been positioned on her back at the rear of the facility, between an FBZ Company tractor-trailer and a red Dumpster. Her head was turned left and faced the trash container; her feet pointed toward the rear of the truck.

She was naked except for her gold hoop earrings and the gold wristwatch on her left arm. Both arms were placed at her sides, palms down, and her legs were slightly parted. Her auburn hair had been carefully fanned out over the pitted asphalt.

Whoever had killed Christine had done so in a burst of fury.

At the autopsy, Dr. Gary Ross, a forensic pathologist, noted multiple assault marks around the victim's neck. Her face had suffered a severe battering as well. Her left eye was black and blue, and her cheeks were swollen. She had suffered numerous abrasions and contusions on her body.

Dr. Ross listed the cause of death as asphyxia due to manual and ligature strangulation. However, he found no apparent defensive wounds. Christine was having her menstrual period, but her tampon was undisturbed. She had several superficial tears around her anus, but lab tests revealed no trace of seminal fluid anywhere.

So far, there was little to go on.

The investigation quickly led detectives to the place where Christine worked. The Reflex Center was a four-room enterprise on State Street in the little town of Clark Summit, about five miles from the parking lot where Burgerhof's killer had deposited her body. Within twenty-four hours of her murder, coworkers and clients were telling police what they could about Christine and her chosen profession.

The employees said that a basic massage at the Reflex Center cost fifty dollars. For another forty dollars the girls took off their tops and would masturbate the customer. For an additional sixty dollars they would take off all their clothes and allow the client to fondle them.

Christine was among the more popular of the Reflex Center's regular workers, and records showed that in the month prior to her murder, she had serviced thirty-six customers. She also made house calls and sometimes worked in nearby Wilkes-Barre, where her customers knew her as Crystal. The work was lucrative. Christine made approximately one hundred thousand dollars in the two years she worked at the Reflex Center.

Ron,* one of her steady customers, never learned her last name, but described her as "shy, timid, not a slut." He said he became friends with Christine, and sometimes she would come by his house for their sessions. Ron said she had rebuffed his attempts at kindling a romance between them, and that they never engaged in intercourse. As far as investigators could determine, Christine restricted full sexual contact to just two of her paying companions, and neither was a suspect in her homicide.

Susan, a coworker, said Christine didn't smoke or drink, that she was a very cautious and evasive person, and was sometimes difficult to get along with. Susan said Christine played "head games" and described her as being "paranoid." Another of Christine's coworkers reported that Christine was jealous of her and was intentionally trying to get her fat by leaving cookies and chocolates lying around the Reflex Center.

According to Susan, Christine claimed she was being stalked in the weeks just prior to her murder. Someone was leaving flowers for her at the shop, at her home, and on her Jeep Grand Wagoneer, she said. Since Christine brought some of the flowers into the shop and displayed them there, Susan suspected the story was one of Christine's odd fabrications. Christine became angry when Susan told her this.

On Friday, April 5, the night of her murder, the victim was working alone at the Reflex Center. She was reported to be wearing a purple, short-sleeved sweatshirt and blue jeans over black fishnet tights. She received at least one identified client, who told police that Christine was alive and well when he left her at 11:45 P.M.

Christine's husband said that he awoke at 4:45 A.M. and discovered that his wife had not returned home. She customarily got in around midnight unless she was with a client, such as Ron, who sometimes took her out for a meal after work. At eight, Bob Burgerhof drove to the Reflex Center, where he found Christine's empty Jeep parked in the covered area behind the building. The door to the paneled massage parlor was open, and Burgerhof could see that the bathroom light was on.

Approximately three hours later, he called the owner of the Reflex Center and told her about Christine's absence and the fact that the door to the business was open. The owner suggested that he notify the police, which he did.

What the police found at the Reflex Center was interesting and also contradictory. There was no sign of a forced entry or struggle, yet the business safe had been forcibly and clumsily pried from a shelf in the closet—screwdrivers and a hammer had been used—and sat upside down on the massage table. Portions of the wood shelving were still attached to the bottom of the safe. Someone appeared to have used coat hangers and the screwdrivers to extract client records from the safe. These slips, along with a Caller ID terminal and all known cash, were missing from the scene.

One of the witnesses detectives sought out in the first few days of their investigation was Catherine Biasotto, the victim's former college roommate. Biasotto told investigators that she'd met Christine Negvesky in the spring of 1991, when they both were junior class pledges at College Misericordia, a small coed Catholic liberal arts school in Dallas, Pennsylvania, not far from Scranton.

Biasotto, during a tearful interview, said that Christine was a distant person who distrusted most people. She didn't have many friends, male or female; and Biasotto said she believed the only steady male in Christine's life was Bob Burgerhof, whom she married in 1994. Cathy Biasotto had been the maid of honor at the wedding.

Biasotto remembered that her roommate received occasional visits from "an old man with gray hair," as she described him. Christine told Cathy that he was her former boss "at some mental health place in Wilkes-Barre." Biasotto recalled, "The guy liked Christine, and I used to ask her why he would come to visit her when she was getting married in July. Christine would say that she felt sorry for him because he was going through a bad divorce." Biasotto said the man's visits made her uncomfortable, and she used to leave the room whenever he showed up. When the Burgerhofs were married in July 1994, this special male friend of Christine's gave them an expensive wedding present.

In the midst of her interview, Biasotto suddenly volunteered that most of what she had heard about Christine's murder and its aftermath had come from Christopher DiStefano. She described the twenty-seven-year-old DiStefano as a friend both to herself and to Christine, whom he had once dated. According to Biasotto, who at the time of the murder was living in Virginia, DiStefano told her that the killer knew Christine and had been stalking her for the past few weeks.

The police already were familiar with the name. DiStefano had been actively shadowing the murder case. He was first questioned at Clarks Summit Police Headquarters on the night of April 6. Case records showed that the next morning, Sunday, DiStefano drove his white 1990 Geo Storm past the parking lot where Christine's body had been discovered. Patrolman Michael Carachilo, on duty at the crime scene, waved him over and asked DiStefano his business.

The intense, dark-haired young man answered that he knew the victim and that he felt he should see the site where she had been found. Carachilo said that wouldn't be possible and asked for identification. DiStefano produced a laminated private investigator's license. When the officer asked to see his driver's license, DiStefano obliged. Carachilo recorded his name, and then the young man slowly drove his Geo through the parking lot, stopped, turned around, and left.

Investigators grew increasingly interested in DiStefano. They interviewed Ryan Ofcharsky, his roommate at East Stroudsburg University of Pennsylvania, about sixty miles from Scranton, where Christine's onetime boyfriend was taking education classes in order to earn a teaching certificate.

According to Ofcharsky, DiStefano was an introvert who was either unable or unwilling to carry on a conversation. "I got sick of listening to myself speak," Ofcharsky told them. "He just absorbed everything and never really gave me any feedback."

On Monday following the murder, Ofcharsky discovered that DiStefano had decorated his walls with more than twenty-five photographs of himself and a girl in various poses. Both were dressed in formal attire.

"This was a bit strange," said the roommate. "But since he was a bit strange himself, I just figured he'd gotten back with his old girlfriend and needed me to know."

As it turned out, the photos were of Christopher and Christine, taken at his 1990 college senior dance. Killers often construct "memorials" to their victims and DiStefano actually asked Ofcharsky, "Did you see my memorial? That was the girl who got killed." He told Ofcharsky of his encounter with Officer Carachilo and said he knew that he was a suspect in the homicide.

Usually there are a large number of potential suspects when a prostitute is murdered—all her customers to begin with. But almost from the beginning of the Burgerhof case, Christopher DiStefano made himself a prime suspect by deliberately attracting attention in several ways. Injecting himself into the investigation was just one of them.

When I was called in as a prosecution consultant two years later, I learned that DiStefano's notable preoffense and postoffense behaviors further implicated him. Sexually deviant criminals usually display some, but not all, of the behaviors that profilers look for in particular types of crimes. But DiStefano came as close as any subject I have ever seen to having all of the behaviors that we look for. His actions and abnormal interests rang so many bells that he seemed to have come straight out of a profiler's textbook.

He was very intelligent, deeply troubled, and, as we'll

see, a classic narcissist. Estimates of his IQ ranged as high as 170. He attended Scranton Preparatory School, where DiStefano graduated in 1986 in the top fifth of his class. His younger brother, Mike, a Clarks Summit police officer at the time of the Burgerhof murder, reported that Chris had trouble communicating with people, and that he had been harassed and bullied in high school.

Mike DiStefano also reported that Chris kept a detailed daily diary. This, as I would discover, was an extraordinary document.

At the University of Scranton, where he majored in electrical engineering, DiStefano's grade point average was 3.48. At Penn State, where he earned a masters in physics, he was a 3.38 student.

According to Mike, Chris spent a lot of time on the Internet, where he researched police-related subjects and established cyber friendships.

One of these was with a young woman in Pittsburgh named Stephanie. In 1994, DiStefano moved to Pittsburgh in order to be close to her. The relationship didn't work out. He called home in tears. Chris suffered panic attacks and other emotional problems. A Pittsburgh psychiatrist said he suffered from depression and placed him on Paxil, an antidepressant medication.

On April 9, 1996, four days after Christine Burgerhof's murder, he visited the dead woman's mother. He wrote Cathy Biasotto an E-mail about the visit, saying, "How cold it would have been of me not to call/visit and show support and sympathy! My mom really pissed me off earlier when I told her that I was going to visit the Negveskys and she said that wasn't a good idea since I may be a suspect and all and it wouldn't look good."

On the tenth, he E-mailed Biasotto once again. "I was at Chris's mom's house . . . for about four hours last night," he wrote. "I think they liked my visit."

Donna Negvesky would testify at trial that her daughter's former boyfriend seemed "calm" and "calculating" to her during his extended visit. DiStefano handed her a sympathy card but made no move to embrace the stricken woman. "There was no compassion, no sympathy," Christine's mother told the court.

Early Wednesday afternoon, April 10, Pennsylvania State Police trooper Joseph G. Pacifico telephoned DiStefano at his ESU dormitory.

Pacifico asked if DiStefano would drive over to the state police facility in Dunmore, near Scranton, that evening for an interview. The suspect agreed to do so and arrived for his appointment at 7:08 P.M., according to Pacifico's notes. Appearing polite and cooperative, DiStefano even brought along an album full of photographs of himself and the victim.

When Pacifico asked for some background on their relationship, DiStefano offered to write it all out in chronological order, an obsessive-compulsive trait. His meticulous record keeping accounted for his wonderful ability to recount his relationship in meticulous step-by-step fashion.

Christine Negvesky attended public high school, then enrolled at Keystone Junior College before transferring to Misericordia, where she earned an undergraduate degree in psychology in 1993. DiStefano told Trooper Pacifico that he had met her in early 1988 (he was then nineteen and she was sixteen, at a roller-skating rink in the Scranton suburb of Taylor, where Negvesky lived with her family. As he told the story, Christine was the first to pursue a relationship. After skating a "couples only" skate or two, they left separately and she called him the next day.

Trooper Pacifico later wrote in his report, "Over the next couple months, the relationship got more serious and they would do one activity during the week and one during the weekend (going to a movie, roller skating, playing pool, dancing or concerts)."

By summertime, said DiStefano, he and Christine were

dating three times a week. It was a "good, fun summer," he wrote on the legal pad Trooper Pacifico provided him. It proved to be the high point of his relationship with Christine.

Even at its most intense, the romance was hardly torrid. Christine, whom DiStefano described as being "frigid," permitted a little kissing and some through-the-clothing petting, but that was all. Christopher claimed he was not disappointed and said he believed that sexual intercourse should be confined to the marriage bed and should only be engaged in for the purpose of procreation.

DiStefano recounted that he and Christine quarreled over some unspecified issue in September 1988, and their relationship never fully recovered. They drifted apart and she saw other boys. Then the affair heated up for a while in mid-1989. Christine, he noted with interest, had learned how to French kiss. "But the relationship was never quite the same," DiStefano wrote.

When DiStefano took Christine to his senior dance in May 1990, "Christine was very cold. The romance was clearly over." A week later Christine returned all the dance photographs to DiStefano. These were the same pictures with which he would construct his dormitory room "memorial" to her after her death six years later.

According to his written time line, he and Christine saw one another intermittently from 1990 to 1996. DiStefano noted that Christine called when she needed him for something, often to help with her schoolwork at Misericordia. Consequently, he befriended her roommate, Cathy Biasotto, and even attended Christine's wedding to Bob Burgerhof. Stefanie, the girl from Pittsburgh, was his date for the occasion.

Chris claimed he last saw Christine around Christmas of 1995. His last contact with her, he said, was the Sunday before her murder, when they spoke on the telephone about bruises Christine had suffered in a recent auto accident.

*   *   *

DiStefano finished the time line around 8:45 P.M., accepted the offer of a Coke from Pacifico, and then posed a couple of his own questions. He wanted to know if an FBI profile of Christine's killer was being done and whether the police had developed any forensic evidence. Pacifico later wrote, "I told him the profile had been started and that I couldn't discuss physical evidence."

The trooper asked DiStefano how he believed the crime had been committed. The suspect responded with his "speculation" that the killer was a customer who had an appointment with Christine that night. "The guy had touched Christine in her private areas," DiStefano surmised, "but . . . she wouldn't touch him back."

The killer then left, DiStefano went on, only to return at closing time to ask Christine for a date. She let him into the Reflex Center but declined his repeated requests to go out with him.

"DISTEFANO," Pacifico wrote, "speculated that the guy asked Christine more forcefully if she would go out with him and she rejected him and the guy's love and passion turned to rage. He speculated the guy shoved Christine and she fell to the floor and that she might have hit her head or back on the safe. He speculated Christine was unconscious on the floor and the guy knelt next to her and tried to revive her. He speculated the guy would have panicked and not known what to do." DiStefano speculated that the killer thought one possibility would be the hospital, but "then thought if he brought her body to the hospital they would then think he murdered her." Finally, he decided "to hide the body in a respectable manner and then hide himself."

The Scranton parking lot caught his attention. "DISTEFANO speculated the guy found the Dumpster, but wouldn't throw Victim into the Dumpster out of respect for the Victim. He said he couldn't just throw her on the ground or into the garbage because he loved her and he wanted to show her respect. He said he speculated the guy layed (sic) out Victim on the ground and ran his fingers through her hair and moved the hair away from her face. DISTEFANO then smiled and quickly said he speculated the guy then drove away and found a bar to have a beer to calm his nerves."

After providing Pacifico with an account of his movements on the day of Christine Burgerhof's murder, DiStefano said he worked his security guard job that night and was home at 12:15 A.M.—DiStefano signed a waiver to allow officers to search his car. They would later obtain search warrants for his ESU dorm room as well as his bedroom at home.

He repeated his third-person reconstruction to a second investigator, Det. Walter "Pete" Carlson of the Lackawanna County District Attorney's Office. Pete Carlson, like Pacifico, listened attentively to DiStefano, then compared notes with the trooper. Together, the two decided to confront their suspect a bit more directly.

"Det. CARLSON and I told DISTEFANO that 'the guy' in his scenario was him," Pacifico wrote. "He denied the guy was him and then asked if we had any physical evidence or tire tracks. We advised him that we had physical evidence and that lab tests were being conducted but did not discuss specifics."

According to Pacifico's notes, DiStefano was particularly interested in knowing whether DNA evidence might show "if someone had performed CPR with artificial respiration on a person, and he was advised it would show. He was advised we had obtained swabs from Victim's mouth at her autopsy."

This news apparently jolted their suspect. At 3:50 A.M., "DISTEFANO said he would tell us what happened," Pacifico wrote. The suspect requested a third party be present besides Detective Carlson and Trooper Pacifico, so State Trooper James G. Gilgallon was brought to the interview room as well.

No audio or video record was made of the interview.

Instead, Pacifico took notes as they spoke, and later DiStefano wrote out and signed a confession in long hand. He initialed each page as well. At the trial the defendant's lawyers would argue that his questioners failed to read their client all of his Miranda rights, nor did they have him sign a written waiver of his right to have an attorney present.

DiStefano told the lawmen that he occasionally dropped by the Reflex Center to visit Christine but stressed that he was not a paying customer. He wrote that on the night of the murder, he went by just after midnight. Christine let him in through the back door. He asked her to go out with him to a Mr. Donut. "She said no. She had to go home. I asked her again, not understanding why she would refuse such a simple request. She said no again."

An argument erupted. "It had been a long day for me, and I shouted back frustrations. She returned the outburst, pointing her finger. I stepped forward, pushed her hand out of the way. She pushed me back and that's when I lost control. I put my hands on her throat, and she put her hands on my throat. We struggled. She fell to the floor on her back still clutching each other. When she let go of my throat, I let go of hers and she was asleep.

"I shook her shoulders. I touched her face, but there was still no response. I bent closer and looked, listened, and felt for her breath. There was none. I blew into her mouth and gave her artificial respiration. She didn't respond."

According to DiStefano, after trying unsuccessfully to revive Christine, he decided to head for his family's house. He said he got home about 1:30 A.M., went to bed for a half hour, then got up and returned to the scene of the crime. At this time he put Christine in his car, stripped her body of clothing, and then drove off in search of "a respectable place to lay it."

He told the officers he finally "dropped off the body [at] the first place available"—the Scranton parking lot. He remembered brushing back Christine's long hair; it was at its most sensual when she wore it straight, DiStefano said. "I lay her out, knelt beside her, expressed remorse and fare-wells, and left," he recounted.

The next morning, DiStefano continued, he bagged Christine's clothing, put it in the rear of his Geo, then later transferred it to his dorm room. When the investigators later went to search his dorm room and didn't find the clothing, DiStefano laughed and said he had intentionally put gaps in his account. This apparently was one of them.

Under questioning, DiStefano specifically denied using a ligature, which contradicted the autopsy report. He also claimed he knew nothing about the missing money, Caller ID box, and receipts.

In the investigators' opinion, DiStefano had left no doubt about his guilt in the homicide. He was placed under arrest at 6:07 A.M. However, any hopes local authorities had of an iron-clad case vanished later that morning when the ac-cused summoned Trooper Pacifico to the first-floor holding cell where he awaited arraignment and transfer to the Lak-awanna County Jail.

"DISTEFANO asked me if his written statement was enough to convict him," Pacifico wrote of their five-minute meeting. "I told DISTEFANO that we not only had his written statement, but also lab tests, witnesses and other evidence. He told me he didn't do it and that he didn't know where Victim's clothes were. DISTEFANO said there were holes in his statement. I told him we knew that [but] that he told us things only the killer would know. He told me that wasn't what he meant, that he had left holes in his statement in-tentionally and that he knew of one already. He said the lab tests wouldn't show anything. I asked DISTEFANO what hole he left in his statement and he said he wanted to re-main silent so I left the room."

As it turned out, Chris DiStefano was right about the lab tests. At the trial, prosecutors would have no forensic evidence that proved DiStefano killed Christine Burgerhof or any eyewitnesses or compelling circumstantial evidence against him. They had only the disputed confession and a critical disputed fact within it.

The prosecution contended that only Christine's killer could have known (as DiStefano did) that her hair had been carefully arranged and how it was done. Defense attorneys argued that the hair arrangement had not been kept a strict secret, and that DiStefano could have learned about it before the eleven-hour interview in which he confessed the crime and provided specifics about how he had committed it.

Other than the confession and his interesting behavior after the crime, the only other window on the defendant's mind and actions was an extraordinary collection of material recovered in the searches of his rooms and car. Investigators found letters, nude bondage photos of a former girlfriend (plus a multimonth calendar of her menstrual cycles), a pair of handcuffs, homosexual erotica, padlocks, medical texts on aberrant sexual behavior, various kinds of adhesive tape (both new and used), lengths of ropes, gas masks, articles and drawings dealing with bondage (including a clipped Prince Valiant comic that depicted a man and woman with their wrists bound behind their backs), and even an Internet inquiry he had made asking for gagging techniques that reduce sound but also allow the "victim" to breathe. They also recovered a copy of Pauline Reage's 1965 novel, *The Story of O,* which chronicles the complete sexual submission of a young woman named O, a successful fashion photographer, to Rene, her sadistic lover.

DiStefano's letters, written mostly to women, were often explicit. "I hate sex," he wrote one girlfriend in 1985. "I hate to get hot. You CANNOT tell me that I like sex. You can't change me." Yet just weeks later, he wrote another girl, "I want to love you and fuck you. I really want to go to bed with you and slide my banana up your tight . . . I'll be on top of you and you'll be trapped, helpless, underneath, unable to escape."

At DiStefano's ESU dorm room, searchers might not have found Christine Burgerhof's clothing, but they did recover abundant evidence of an obsessive attachment to her. From the walls above his bed they seized twenty-four color photos of Chris and Christine together (including the "memorial" of 1990 dance photos), and twelve more from his desk. Between the sheets of his bed was another, oversize photocopied picture of her. Several enlarged photos of the victim's face also were seized from DiStefano's Geo.

Perhaps the most amazing artifact the authorities seized was a mammoth secret journal, 2,450 pages long, found in his bedroom at home. DiStefano had begun the journal in December 1984, when he was fifteen. Written in a tiny, cramped script, the journal was a detailed daily record of his life. No fact was too insignificant for inclusion. For example, he made sure to mention on December 21, 1984, that he showered at 6:45 that morning. DiStefano kept lists, such as the dates of every prom he had ever attended and all the times he had gone skating. He even preserved his writing instruments, bundling them and labeling each group with the dates he used them to write in the journal. Parallel with such tame, if peculiar, day-to-day notations, DiStefano maintained an equally meticulous record of his sexual and fantasy life.

In the entry for May 28, 1988, he wrote of dreaming that he'd tied himself up in front of the house, late at night, and was masturbating. Someone discovers him and beats him up. He runs. Kids chase him. The nightmare ends when he awakes in the morning.

On another date he wrote, "Dream I molested girl—around 1/7 plus or minus five days."

He made note of each time he masturbated (sometimes using the code letters NOT), as well as each time he donned a rubber gas mask, which he referred to as GM in the journal, gagged ("gged"), used duct tape (DT), or engaged in some form of sensory deprivation (SD).

Typical entries of his journal are as follows:

NOT OCT. 26—EARLY—GM TAPED—TOOK FOREVER!
NOT DEC. 10—LATE—GGED, NEW GM TAPED—COM-
FORTABLE.
LEAVE 6:20. TOO CROWDED FOR GM. EARPLUGS.
STOP IN WASHINGTON. $28 HOTEL.
NOT SD. EARPLUGS/GM/BLINDFOLD. SLEEP
BRIEFLY.
NO HOME TODAY. TAYLOR'S HOTEL. $25. *NOT* OUT-
STRETCHED ACROSS BED.
GAGGED/GM. GM KEPT KNOCKING INTO BED FRAME.
SLEPT IN CLOTHES.

Bondage was a recurrent theme. On one page he listed twelve different ways to tie a person's hands; three ways to bind feet; four knots that require two people to tie; six ways to gag someone; and five ways to suffocate them. Under "Things to do to someone who's tied up," he included the following measures: suffocation, kisses, tickling, blindfolding, gagging ("hold a one-way conversation"), gently slapping or touching face, unbuttoning her shirt, unzipping her pants, unhooking her bra, mussing her hair, mussing her clothes, writing on her, feeding her candy, and teasing her with food.

DiStefano also obsessively recorded personal bests of all sorts, including his highest bowling score, 185, and "Most girls I've gone out with at one time: 4."

He documented his interest in masochism, too.

LONGEST WITH FEET TIED TOGETHER IN BED WITH
LEATHER BELT: 8 HOURS
LONGEST TIME WITH TAPE OVER MOUTH: 1 HOUR, 30
MINUTES
LONGEST TIME WITH HANDS TIED ABOVE HEAD: 1
HOUR, MARCH 7, 1992
LONGEST TIME WITH GAS MASK ON: 2 HOURS. AUG.
12, 1994.

When Lackawanna County's first assistant district attorney Andy Jarbola first contacted me about the DiStefano prosecution, he asked that I analyze all available materials and address three separate issues: the defendant's sexually deviant behaviors, his behavior after the murder, and whether I believed the crime scene at the Reflex Center had been staged.

I recommended that the analysis be submitted in three separate reports, one for each of the subject areas. My reasoning was that if the judge disallowed any one of the analyses, it wouldn't taint the remaining two. During cross-examination at a pretrial hearing, DiStefano's attorney questioned me on this very point, and I responded, "Of course!" I believe that even the judge smiled at that point. The defense attorney moved on to another area of cross-examination.

DiStefano later waived a jury, so Judge Carlon M. O'Malley would preside at trial *and* render the verdict.

O'Malley was on the bench in Courtroom 2 of the Lackawanna County Courthouse on November 10, 1998, as Andy Jarbola led me through my hearing testimony.

Addressing the issue of motive, I began by testifying that I believed Christine Burgerhof's murder was a sexual crime, motivated by anger. I explained that if robbery or burglary was the killer's original intention, he would not have needed to murder Christine Burgerhof.

Anticipating the defense attorney's cross-examination, I then noted that even if he killed the victim to prevent her from identifying him, there was no need to transport her body, which greatly increased his risk of capture. If he had meant only to kill the victim, he need not have removed her body at all. If all he meant to accomplish was to delay the body's discovery, it certainly was unnecessary to remove her clothing. Finally, if he removed her clothing to reduce his chances of being identified through fiber or hair analysis, then positioning of the body was unnecessary.

When a killer transports the victim's body from the crime scene, I explained, he takes control not only of where (or if) the remains will be found but also how soon and in what condition. Christine Burgerhof's nudity "certainly is consistent with a sexual crime," I said.

Also, I pointed out her body's placement in the parking lot. Because of the locations of the tractor trailer and the Dumpster, Burgerhof's killer had to carry her a short distance to where she was found. He hadn't just left her. But why?

The answer is ritual. Sexual killers often do things that aren't necessary to the commission of their crimes. When this occurs, one possible explanation is that the commission of the crime is insufficient to achieve the offender's goal of psychosexual gratification.

He may have to add his own special touch. A dead Christine Burgerhof lying naked on her back with her hair arrayed around her, her arms and hands and legs arranged as they were, might not mean anything to others, but it meant a great deal to her killer.

Jarbola then asked me why I thought anger was the motivation for the murder. I testified that a number of factors had led me to that conclusion.

First, Christine Burgerhof was beaten before she was murdered. Dr. Ross, the pathologist, had determined that she had been struck at least twelve times in the face and head. "That in itself suggests anger," I said.

Second, Dr. Ross said the victim had been strangled manually from the front. "That requires personal contact," I said. "Frontal manual strangulation is commonly associated with personalized anger."

Number three, Dr. Ross also noted ligature strangulation, possibly with a pulley rope from an exercise machine at the Reflex Center. That meant Burgerhof was physically assaulted in at least three ways. Moreover, she would have been incapacitated following the manual strangulation. As I saw it, use of the ligature meant he wanted to ensure she was dead. That's an indication of anger.

Finally, I pointed out the positioning of her body. She was left nude, face up, her genital area exposed, on an open asphalt surface next to a Dumpster in a refuse-littered industrial district parking lot. Contrary to what DiStefano had "speculated" about the killer's feelings of love and respect, "that suggested to me there was no concern for her dignity. He just put her out there among all of this refuse . . . grossly exposed, if you will. That again suggests hostility to me."

Jarbola asked why, in my opinion, there was so little physical evidence at the Reflex Center. I answered that the killer either was in firm emotional control of himself as he committed the crime, or he regained his composure afterward, possibly leaving and then returning to sanitize the crime scene.

Consistent with this, I added, was his decision to strip the victim. "By taking the victim's clothing," I testified, "you remove the possibility of the police being able to process it for hairs, for fibers, for materials that may have rubbed off the offender and onto the victim's clothing."

The killer also could have wanted Burgerhof's clothing as a trophy.

I said that he appeared organized and probably was not under the influence of liquor or drugs that night. From the care he took he seemed to be of above average intelligence. He might have been experienced at this type of crime. If not, I said he might have given it a great deal of thought prior to committing the crime. By way of comparison, I mentioned Robert LeRoy Anderson's murders in South Dakota, where I had recently testified.

Next, we turned to the question of staging, which in this context meant arranging the scene and removing evidence. The intention of these actions was to mislead investigators as to why the crime was committed and by whom. A thorough search of the massage parlor revealed no physical or trace evidence of the killer. There were no fingerprints, hairs, or fibers. That is highly unusual and suggests that the responsible person spent time "sanitizing" the scene.

I began my crime-scene analysis with the safe. It had

been clumsily and unprofessionally removed from the closet shelf and placed on the massage table, where it was apparently rifled. Wood shelving was still attached to its bottom, and two screwdrivers and a bent coat hanger lay beside it on the table.

There were two possible explanations. One, some unknown third party stumbled onto the murder scene and seized the opportunity to look for valuables. That seemed unlikely because the sort of person who wanders into an unlocked massage parlor after midnight is also the sort of person likely to leave some trace of himself.

The second possibility, far more likely in my view, was that the killer had tried to stage the crime scene as a robbery gone bad. Remember that money and a Caller ID box were missing. If the hypothetical robber took those items, he certainly would have taken Christine Burgerhof's gold watch and earrings. An office stereo was left untouched as well. An opportunistic thief surely would have taken such items before concerning himself with the Caller ID box or the customer slips. I concluded that the killer took what he did "because possibly there's something associated with him there, or fingerprints on the money, or possibly his number on the Caller ID."

My third report dealt with Christopher DeStefano's sexual deviancy. It was based upon my analysis of the evidence in the case and particularly the material seized from his rooms and car. In the end I recommended that Andy Jarbola not submit this lengthy document. I believed that Judge O'Malley would disallow it as being too prejudicial to the defendant. As with our decision to submit the other two papers separately, I didn't want to take the risk of tainting all of what I had to say by the likely rejection of one part.

The analysis does provide insights into Christopher DiStefano's deviant behaviors and is presented here for the readers' edification.

SEXUAL BONDAGE

This is distinct from binding for the purpose of restraining someone's movements. Sexual bondage involves the psychosexual arousal from the binding and control over another person (sadism) and/or arousal from being bound and controlled by another (masochism). Sexual bondage is identified by unnecessary bindings (i.e., restraints on the thighs, calfs, forearms, upper arms) and/or symmetrical bindings and/or binding the victim in a variety of positions (i.e., wrists to ankles, ankles to neck, suspended by wrists, suspended by ankles, spread-eagled).

Throughout his journal and other writings, DiStefano returned again and again to the theme of sensory deprivation (e.g., hoods, gags) and motor bondage (tying of limbs) both of others and himself. I also noted in my report that handcuffs and adhesive tape (new and used) had been recovered in the searches as well as lengths of rope. Such items are commonly found in the possession of bondage practitioners.

On January 11, 1995, DeSteffano wrote detailed instructions explaining how to fashion leather wrist and ankle restraints. The heading was "Something to Make: Wrist/ankle cuffs." The same day he also described how to make a "Locking hood." That Christmas, he wrote a girlfriend: "I really thought that was great that you let me do that to your mouth for 2 hours . . . I promise that I'll never hurt you and I'll un[tie] you whenever you want . . . I can't wait to— [tie] you to a b——[bed]. I'll go crazy!! You'll turn me on so far you won't turn me off."

MASOCHISM

The masochist is sexually aroused by his own suffering and/or humiliation. As with the sadist, he may only fantasize, act out his urges on himself, or he may seek a partner. Male masochists often are fetishists and may also be sadomasochists.

DiStefano's writings, which show his interest in masochism, include extensive notes on ways to be tied up, his interest in the Internet news group <alt.sex.bondage>, and a particular passage from his posting to the group: ". . . allows only a small amount of air in. It allows me to stay awake, but rather panicked when bound and feeling that I just can't inhale enough."

FETISHISM

DiStefano appears to have been sexually attached to at least one inanimate object, his gas mask, an item that is surprisingly common among fetishists. Men frequently masturbate while holding, rubbing, smelling, or looking at their fetish object. In his correspondence to <alt.sex.bondage> DiStefano wrote: "Gas masks enhance feelings of helplessness in B&D scenes" and "they can be impossible to remove if your hands are tied."

According to his notes, DiStefano frequently wore his gas mask for two hours or more, most often while masturbating. His attraction to the masks was shown again with a photograph he clipped from the Scranton *Times•Tribune,* which depicted Japanese soldiers wearing gas masks.

DANGEROUS AUTOEROTICISM

One form is sexual asphyxiation, the mechanical reduction of oxygen flow to the brain (hypoxia), which can create a sense of euphoria and is sexually stimulating to some people. Practitioners may act out fantasies with elements of torture, abuse, execution, helplessness, and sexual arousal through risk taking. Three deviant behaviors commonly observed among these people are masochism, fetishism, and sexual bondage.

Recovered among Christopher DiStefano's possessions during the searches were a gas mask with taped air filter, a rubber foam mask for the nose and mouth, and an envelope marked "special stuff," which contained photographs and printed material on bondage and asphyxiation.

One 5 × 8 color photograph depicted handcuffs, a noose, scissors, pliers, duct tape, a hacksaw, a wrench, a kitchen knife, rubber bands, and some tacks. In another, a hangman's noose was suspended from a ceiling with a sign affixed to the wall behind it with the word JUMP printed on it. A third photo depicted an unidentified young woman at this same scene. A fourth showed a little stuffed puppy, trussed in silver cord and blindfolded, with PUPPY'S DEAD! printed beneath it in red. The messages DiStefano sent to the <alt.sex.bondage> news group also were consistent with dangerous autoerotic practices, as was his design of the "Locking hood."

SEXUAL SADISM

DiStefano's photo collection definitely included some sexually sadistic elements, as did many of his writings about bindings, gags, and suffocation. Strong sadistic overtones were also clear in the nude pictures of his ex-girlfriend in bondage.

His letters were sometimes graphically abusive. He wrote one girl: "The only thing that bothers me is when you stand on a street corner and spread your legs. . . . You act like a slut." A month later, he wrote the same girl: "If you don't believe me I'll rape you! You do believe me? Well, I'll rape you anyway! RAPE!!"

He also clipped and saved a letter published in Ann Landers's newspaper column in which a woman wrote of being robbed by two youths who bound her hands, feet, and mouth during their crime.

*   *   *

The most extraordinary feature of this decidedly unusual case was the variety of postoffense behaviors DiStefano evinced. It truly seemed that he had immersed himself in the literature of sexual murder and then patterned his actions on what he had read. Put another way, it was as if he'd written a checklist of behaviors that we look for, and then went down the list, marking off the items as he accomplished them.

One point of my oral testimony at the preliminary hearing was to explain these postoffense behaviors and then let Judge O'Malley draw his own conclusions.

I began with a well-known fact of crime detection: *Killers often return to the scene of their crimes.* We know from the police report that Christopher DiStefano went to the disposal site and requested access to the precise location where the victim's body was found. Also, in his confession, he said he did so.

Quoting from Bob Ressler, Ann Burgess, and John Douglas's study of killers in the book *Sexual Homicide: Patterns and Motives,* I told the court that in 32 of the 118 murders the authors surveyed, the killers said they had returned to the scenes of their crimes.

I listed several possible reasons for this behavior:

1. The subject may have been mentally impaired, drunk, or high at the time of the killing and returns to see if he actually committed the crime. In such cases he rarely removes the body.

2. The offender may return to sanitize the site, i.e., clean up any possible physical or trace evidence and/or move the body if he hasn't already done so.

3. He may return to be near the victim and to relive the crime.

4. He may be curious to see if the murder has been
   discovered and whether the police are involved yet.

5. He may return to determine the progress of the investigation.

6. He may return to dispose of additional victims he has
   killed.

I told the court that included among the sexual killers
known to have returned to the scenes of their crimes were
Ted Bundy, Arthur Shawcross, David Sutcliff (the York-
shire Ripper), and David Berkowicz, New York's Son of
Sam.

Next, I noted that *killers often try to insert themselves
into the police investigations* of their homicides, as Christopher DiStefano did. Again testifying from Bob, Ann, and
John's data, I told the court that in 24 of their 118 cases,
the killer had intentionally become involved in the investigations.

For some killers involving themselves helps to sustain
the excitement generated by the crime. This is most often
true of narcissistic offenders. It's thrilling for them to be
close to the action. They can see that their crime has pro-
voked attention. They also may glean useful information
unavailable to them in any other way. Famous killers who
have involved themselves in the investigations of their
crimes include Bundy, as well as Wayne Williams, the Atlanta child killer, and Edmund Emil Kemper III, the California giant who murdered his grandparents and his mother,
along with seven hitchhikers.

More rare are sexual killers *who provide police with
third-person accounts of their crimes* or "speculations" as
DiStefano did. These offenders are motivated by a hunger
for the attention such "cooperation" nets them. They can
relive their crimes more or less openly. And it is a means
for such killers to tease investigators with guilty knowledge
without actually confessing to anything. In this regard, the

third-person account can be seen as a form of bragging—more narcissism.

"The piece of literature that's most famous in this case is *The Only Living Witness,*" I told the court, "by Stephen G. Michaud and Hugh Aynesworth. They induced Ted Bundy to discuss himself—or his 'entity,' as Bundy called it—over hundreds of hours of conversation on death row."

Besides Bundy, criminals who have given third-person accounts of their crimes include Gerard John Schaefer, the rogue sheriff's deputy in Florida, and Arthur Goode, a homicidal pedophile from Maryland. Interestingly, all three ended up at the Florida State Prison in Starke, where they met each other and all three eventually died in prison.

Bundy and Goode were executed in the electric chair. Schaefer was murdered by other inmates.

Next I considered *the collection of photographs of victims* and the taking of "trophies." These behaviors are fairly common among sexual criminals. Items they may keep range from clothing (especially lingerie) to jewelry, driver's licenses, and even body parts. Any of the victim's possessions serves the killer as evidence of a successfully completed crime.

The photographs or other items might also be used to help the killer relive his crime. If displayed publicly, photos of the victim can bring such offenders the attention they desire or reinforce their assumed identity of a sensitive and caring individual.

Mike DeBardeleben, the sexual sadist discussed in earlier chapters, kept extensive photographic records of his victims. Other photo and trophy keepers include John Wayne Gacy, Robert Leroy Anderson in South Dakota, and Harvey Glatman, Los Angeles's Lonely Hearts Killer of the 1950s.

Scrapbooks and collections of news accounts of their crimes may also serve as trophies, and press attention serves to validate the sexual criminal's narcissistic belief that he is shaping events around him. It is another way of secretly basking in attention. The news accounts can also serve as erotica, helping the killer relive the crimes.

Finally, I discussed the fact that, though uncommon, *killers may contact the victim's family,* as DiStefano did with the Negveskys. This gesture combines some of the motives for injecting themselves into the investigation (thrills and information gathering) with the attention seeking common to most of these postoffense behaviors.

Arthur Goode wrote letters to two of his victims' parents. Mike DeBardeleben made harassing phone calls to at least one intended victim. Thomas Dillon, a serial killer in Ohio, communicated by letter with one victim's mother, and his continued letters were the evidence that ultimately led to his capture.

Christopher DiStefano reportedly intended to testify at his trial but ultimately did not. After his confession in April 1996, he has offered no further public explanation for his actions.

A jail informant did come forward and said that DiStefano had confessed to him. But a more reliable source was Cathy Biasotto. In September 1997, she visited DiStefano at the Lackawanna County Jail. She later discussed her visit with PSP investigators and Asst. DA Eugene Talerico, who would help prosecute the case. Biasotto told the group that she had visited DiStefano in search of the truth.

"Christopher and I were really good friends," she explained, "and I couldn't comprehend that he was the murderer. In my heart he seemed like an extremely generous person . . . I also went to see what he was like—was he crazy?"

"Did you ask him if he killed Christine Burgerhof?" she was asked.

"Yes. I asked him why he did it," Cathy replied.

"Do you remember the exact words that you used?"

"Yes."

"What were they?"

"Why did you kill her?"

"What was his response?"

"He said I should know why. He asked me, 'Do you know what she did?' I said, 'Yes. I just found out she was a prostitute.' Then he said, 'I had to do it . . . She was not a very nice girl.' "

"What was his demeanor?"

"A smirk on his face. Like he was justified . . . Christine deserved to be killed for doing what she was doing."

"Did he talk about the case at all?"

"Yes."

"What did he say?"

"The evidence was really weak. And [that] he was going to get out soon . . . Through his mannerisms, he also gave me the impression he was very proud of his accomplishment."

"What accomplishment was that?"

"That he murdered Christine and he destroyed the evidence, which showed that he got one up over the police."

"What mannerisms?"

"Cold and calculating stare. The smirk on his face. Not once did he ever flinch. Even when I started crying, he still had this cold and calculating stare."

Christopher DiStefano went to trial in February 2000. Judge O'Malley found him guilty of third-degree murder and sentenced him to fifteen to forty years in state prison. O'Malley's verdict is on appeal.

EPILOGUE

The cases in this book are drawn from the extreme end of the crime spectrum. They are as strange as they are violent, but unfortunately they are not rare. Will the type of criminal behavior characterized in the preceding chapters become more common as even more brutal and bizarre crimes are committed in the future?

The short answer is yes. In my opinion aberrant crime is accelerating today, both in frequency and depravity. This has been the case for decades, and it will continue to be the case.

My pessimism is based on more than twenty-five years of experience with sexual offenders such as those discussed in this book, the first of which was Harvey Glatman, the "Lonely Hearts Killer." I became aware of Glatman's case while in training as a military police officer. At *that* time, Glatman was a unique offender. His case involved sexual sadism, fetishism, sexual bondage, dangerous autoeroticism, trophy taking, masochism, and finally serial murder—a term that had not even been coined yet.

I was confounded by Glatman's behavior. For example, he was one of the first offenders known to photograph his victims, but no one seemed to know why he did so. I couldn't make any sense of it, nor could I find much of anything that had been written for law enforcement about his deviant impulses or practices.

Since that time I have seen hundreds of cases that rival or exceed Glatman's for deviance and violence. Why are there more such criminals today than a decade ago?

In my view a major reason for the increase has been a gradual relaxation of what was once a fairly strict behavioral code in this country. Experience has taught me that criminal behavior tends to reflect what society at large considers normal or acceptable. Ease the restrictions for society at large, and you will see those on the fringe immediately pushing at the new boundaries.

For example, four decades ago a complaint of rape implied that the victim had been vaginally assaulted. Rarely was the victim forced to perform oral sex on her attacker. Today a rape frequently involves anal sex, fellatio, and foreign object penetration. It is not a coincidence that such behaviors are also now more common in the movies and in popular music where *it is treated in a favorable light or at least not condemned.*

Body piercing is another example of the easing of societal restrictions. Today it's a fashion (or culture) statement. Not long ago, body piercing was considered to be sexually deviant, masochistic—*perverse.* Likewise, to physically injure another person for sexual excitement was once a crime. Today attorneys in court refer to it as "rough sex." In the past tying another person up for sexual arousal was considered aberrant. Today bondage is called "sex play."

Objects and instruments put to sexual use have been elevated from "foreign objects" to "toys." Violent pornography in almost any format is easily accessible to consumers of all ages and is frequently called "art."

Our society has grown used to behavior that was once frowned upon and discouraged, and those with criminal intent have taken notice.

A second reason for the increase in bizarre and violent

sexual crime is technological. We can now capture in color and sound those acts that could once only be imagined. How does this change behavior? The knowledge that one is "performing" for a microphone or camera tends to intensify the action. Sexual offenders are no different in that respect. In my experience the most heinous and outrageous sexual crimes tend to be committed in the presence of recording devices.

I remember telling my classes many years ago that the "new" microcassette tape recorders and Polaroid cameras would find a ready market among deviant criminals and that, sooner or later, police would begin to find such recorded evidence of offender's sexual fantasies and crimes. I was right. The advent of computers, video cameras, and the Internet have only intensified this trend.

Physical mobility is a third reason for the rise and spread of aberrant crime, particularly serial rape and murder. The ability to quickly travel long distances provides the criminal with a distinct advantage in avoiding detection, and the fact that we are now thoroughly accustomed to dealing with strangers in our lives gives these offenders an added cloak of anonymity. As we discussed in earlier chapters, the physically violent and ritualistic sexual offender invariably loves to drive.

Finally, there appears to be much more anger directed toward women today than in the past. This anger is expressed in books, movies, television shows, and rap music. I don't pretend to know why such anger exists; perhaps it's a backlash to the long overdue arrival of women as equals in the workplace and elsewhere. Whatever the reason, our society has found it necessary to pass legislation to address these issues, making it easier for women to bring criminal complaints or sue in civil court for sexual offenses. Inevitably, there will be some men who resent this new level of empowerment and feel they can only assert their masculinity via sexual assault.

Unquestionably other forces are at work as well. Whatever the reasons may be, the examples presented in this book make a strong case that we are confronted with a more sophisticated, violent, and aberrant sexual offender than at any time in the past.

INDEX